NORTHERN BEACHES WRITERS' GROUP

The Northern Beaches Writers' Group is an award-winning writing critique group based in Sydney. We're online at:

northernbeacheswritersgroup.com
facebook.com/northernbeacheswritersgroup

A FEARSOME ENGINE

edited by
Chris Lake
& Zena Shapter

A Fearsome Engine

First published in Australia 2016 by
the Northern Beaches Writers' Group, Sydney.

Copyright © 2016 Northern Beaches Writers' Group
and all the respective authors

The moral rights of the authors have been asserted.

All rights reserved. This eBook belongs to the Northern Beaches Writers' Group and the authors and, as such, no part of it may be copied, reproduced or transmitted by any person or entity (including Google, Amazon or similar organisations), in any form whatsoever (including via any electronic or mechanical means, including photocopying, recording or by any information storage or retrieval system) without the express prior written permission of the copyright holders.

Cover design by Mijmark & Zena Shapter.
Internal design by Zena Shapter.

The characters in this book are fictitious and any resemblance to real persons, living or dead, is purely coincidental.

Contents

Foreword	Chris Lake	9
Water Torture	Carl Holm	11
Hit The Road	Tony McFadden	34
Like The Web Of A Swamp Spider	Zena Shapter	61
Aiko And The Tiger	Kylie Pfeiffer	83
The Instructions	J E Gaulton	110
Don't Wanna Play No More	Andrew Mills	118
Shangri La	Chris Lake	123
Chez Antoine's	A R Kelly	141
The Final Journey	Rodney Jensen	148
Drone	P J Keuning	164
Oscar	Sonia Zadro	169
111-000-111	Mijmark	178
Fellow Travellers To The End	Judith O'Connor	186
Esperance	Bronwen Bowden	195
Found Out On Facebook	Alexandra Cain	202
Fishing	Chris Foster	212
Generational Breakdown	Suzi Green	219
Work Out	Harriet Cunningham	228
What Is A Disease	Gill Schierhout	244
A Poetical Science	Susan Steggall	254
Acknowledgements		273
Also by the Northern Beaches Writers' Group		274

To the dreamers,
thinkers and imagineers –
makers of the only truly
everlasting engines.

Foreword

Chris Lake

Our relationship with technology has never been as close or as complex as it is today. Our gentle, stately progress has become, in the last two centuries, a speeding juggernaut of change – a fearsome engine, bearing us at breakneck speed we know not where.

In this anthology, we have selected a collection of stories that explore the various aspects of our long and sometimes fraught love affair with technology. Are we humans just machines of a different substance, and if so, what value do we really have? Does changing the way we do fundamentally human things, like communicate or reproduce, change something fundamental within us? Is the digital age an era of opportunity or of threat? And how do we manage the relentless assault of new gadgets and ways of connecting on our day-to-day lives?

These questions and more are explored through humour and horror, sadness, pain, love, joy and philosophical inquiry. Each story, in its own way, explores the interface between human and machine, and asks if the devices we have created have, in some ways, actually ended up creating us.

Water Torture

Carl Holm

"Yeah, I know someone with a truck." He spat the words out like gravel through his rotten teeth.

I watched as he spilled another handful of my tobacco. It was the third time he'd asked if I could spare a smoke. Each time he'd dropped enough tobacco to make half a dozen rollies into the puddle of beer on the bar, then wiped the sodden mess onto the floor. He rubbed his shaking hands on his shorts and started again, this time dropping my papers into the puddle. He pulled them out of the cardboard Tally-Ho packet in a long sodden string. Miraculously, a dry one appeared.

"What's it to ya?" he asked. The paper dangled from his bottom lip. Seeing it was the last, he tossed the cardboard packaging onto the floor.

"You're 'Ace' Carter?" I asked.

"Depends who's askin' the questions."

"I need to get out to Panorama Station."

He exhaled so violently that the paper parted company with his lip, took flight through a stray ray of sunshine coming in from the street and then settled gently, a small white butterfly, into the puddle of beer.

"What the bloody hell do you want out there?" he growled.

"Well, I have to..."

"Have to bloody nothing!" he spat, waving an arm like twisted, rusting fencing wire.

"Now you listen to me while I tell you something, young fella!" His index finger stabbed my chest.

"No-one's been out there for years. And there's good reasons for that! Not even the blackfellas go near that place. They'll detour twenty mile to stay clear. Say there's a spirit there. Drives men mad!"

"Well, superstitions aside, I have to get out there. They want someone to check the place over and do whatever repairs might be necessary before the wet season. The new owners want to put the property back into operation, but they don't seem to have any concrete information on the condition of the place."

"Forget it mate. You won't find a soul who'll take yer out there."

"There's a hundred in it. Plus fuel," I offered hopefully.

"I'm not taking you."

"Two hundred?"

He turned on his stool, the back of his filthy blue singlet now towards me. It seemed as if he'd already forgotten my existence. He laid a twenty on the bar and lifted his empty glass in the air.

"Shirl, another one. A pouch of Drum and Tally-Hos too."

Our conversation was over.

I drained my glass, left my change on the bar and crossed the street to the motel, pulled the yellowed blinds down and lay on the bed. The air conditioner wheezed and rattled and puffed hot air into the room in desperate gasps.

If all I had to do was go out there and have a quick look around, and I knew the way, I'd have just driven out by myself. But there were no roads out there. Just barely discernible tracks, cut by river beds and washouts in one wet season after another. There were places where I'd heard the sand would swallow a vehicle up, leaving nothing but the tip of an aerial poking out. I needed an experienced guide, someone who knew the country and knew the way.

What if you I bogged? Or lost? I'd heard that even experienced bushmen got disoriented in that scrub.

I peeled off my sodden shirt, picked up the phone and dialled the number for the office.

"Listen, Graham, you're probably not going to like this. I can't find anyone who'll take me out there."

The volume of the response nearly burst my eardrum. "What do you fuckin' mean, can't find anyone? I haven't sent you all the way up there for nothing! What about Adrian Carter? Did you find him?"

"You mean Ace? Yeah, I found him, eventually. Half cut and shaking so bad he could hardly hold a beer. And yes, he knows the way. But he's refused point blank to guide me out there."

"Well, you bloody listen to me. I don't care if you have to bloody walk out there, if you come back without getting Panorama into shape, then you can save yourself some time by taking yourself straight to the dole office."

The line went dead with the suddenness and ferocity of a car accident; and I had that same sick feeling in my gut.

I placed the receiver back in the cradle. I pulled my shirt back on, so wet with sweat that I didn't even bother trying to tuck it in again. The heat would have been unbearable on its own, but the humidity made it a torture just to exist. I retraced my steps to the pub, as the street lights snapped on, sputtering in the almost-darkness. Instantly, millions of insects attacked the orange glow of the lamps. I put a fifty on the bar. The barmaid poured me a beer. 'Ace' was nowhere to be seen.

When Shirl called last drinks I bought a bottle of rum and, after a few deep breaths holding onto the door frame, viewing the street first through one eye, then through the other, started back to the motel.

#

Some kind of large serpent had hold of my legs and some beast was growling in the undergrowth nearby. It was so close I could feel, even smell, its hot rancid breath, but I couldn't see it in the dimness. Someone was firing a rifle, in volleys of three or four shots. Getting closer. Somewhere, someone was shouting. I slowly opened one eye. The motel room swam. The shag carpet stretched like waves of creamed corn towards the toilet door. Things began to resolve themselves, slowly, into familiar shapes and sounds. The air-conditioning unit finally died, putting an end to the growling and panting of the unseen beast. As I tried to get up, the sweat-soaked sheets which had wrapped themselves around my legs pulled me to the floor. I felt cold vomit against my skin.

Another volley of rifle shots went off, close by.

"Are you bloody in there, or what?" shouted an irate voice on the other side of the door. I realised that whoever was shouting was hammering a fist on the door. There was no gunfire. My head hurt.

"Who's there?" I called feebly.

"Come on, the dogs are up and pissin' on your swag! We've got a long drive ahead of us!"

"What?"

"Well, ya wanted to go to Panorama, dincha?"

Ace!

If it was possible, he sounded even less friendly than he had in the front bar the night before. I fumbled to open the door and the sunlight blinded me. It couldn't have been past 7am and already the place was a furnace.

"Well," I was having trouble getting the words out of my throbbing skull, "well, yes... but I thought...?"

"Four hundred bucks, it'll cost ya!"

He muttered something under his breath about shit cards and stumped away.

He was definitely no philanthropist. But what choice did I have? It was that or the dole queue.

Three hours later, despite the pain in my head, I was following Ace's ageing Dodge flatbed out of town. The tray was piled high with fencing wire, a generator, fuel, water tanks, and building materials. I had no idea what state the place was going to be in, but I imagined that after twenty-five years of neglect it wouldn't be pretty. In fact, I'd be surprised if any of the old buildings were left standing. Hope for the best, but prepare for the worst, had been the boss's advice.

After an hour or so we turned off the ribbon of red dirt which we'd been following and picked a path through the spinifex grass and spindly gums. All day we crawled through the scrub and the creek beds in low gear. A puff of dust was all that marked our position in that vast nothingness, and the willy-willies quickly spiralled that away. I was in awe of how the scrawny old bushy managed to get his Dodge through places I wouldn't tackle without shifting the decrepit Toyota into low range. No wonder they called him 'Ace', I thought, as I watched him gun it through the soft sand in another dry river bed and, with a triumphant belch of black smoke, storm out the other side.

I reckon we were averaging twenty miles an hour. The sun disappeared and the overcast sky took away all contrast, all shadow. With my hangover it felt like we had been crawling through the same patch of scrub for hours. The land was practically dead flat, except for the sandy banks of the channels. I couldn't even tell which way the water would flow once the rains came. Under that leaden sky it was impossible to tell whether we were heading north, south, or west. I guessed we weren't heading east, because that would have taken us back to the coast. Ace just forged ahead, navigating by some inner animal sense.

We camped for the night beneath towering anthills. The pale, twisted limbs of the gums around us came alive and danced as the firelight flickered on their branches.

Ace didn't have much to say. He just sat, staring into the campfire, so silent and still that if it hadn't been for the glowing end of his smoke and the occasional movement of his eyes scanning the edges of the firelight, he might have been a statue, twisted together out of old wire and rags. I tried to press him about Panorama Station.

Finally he looked up and fixed his eyes hard upon mine, holding them there. When I blinked he began to speak.

"Do you believe in ghosts?"

"Well, I..."

"Either you believe in 'em or you don't. Aw, I don't give a stuff what you believe. I believe in 'em." His gaze never left mine as his fag-end arced from barbed-wire fingers into the fire. "There are some places on this earth that are cursed and where the living have no business. I'll tell you about the last time I went out to Panorama, if that's what you're so keen to know!"

He opened his tobacco pouch and slowly rolled another cigarette. He pulled a glowing twig from the flames and lit it. Drawing the smoke deep into his spindly frame, he paused for two beats of a human heart, and exhaled.

"It would have been this time of year, back in '70. Must have been '70, because the wet came earlier that year. Had to take a young fella out there. Going to look after the station, through the wet season, he was. Smart young bloke, good with his hands, he reckoned. Odd thing was that he was humming all the time, humming this tune. Said he'd just seen a fillum with this song in it, before he left the big-smoke, and it had kinda stuck in his head. A fillum about two outlaws, he said, but the song was somethin' about raindrops. Anyway, we set out in a bit of a rush, because I knew that once the rains came there'd be no way for me to get back. We get out there, and when we're unpacking the supplies off the truck, I realise we're short. Some of what was supposed to have been loaded hadn't been put on. Probably because we were in such a hurry. Maybe his humming distracted me. Who knows. So I says, look don't worry, I'll go back and get it. And all the time I'm watching the sky, and praying that the rains won't break. He had plenty of supplies, a rifle, and ammo, so he wasn't going to starve to death or anything. Well, it was a two day drive back to town – and can I say, after listening to that bloke humming the same tune over and again it was nice just to have the engine and the gearbox to listen to – and then a day arguing with the store before they agreed that there'd been a mistake. Then I set out again. But I was two hours out of town when the rain started. I knew it'd be stupid to keep going and get stuck somewhere out there." He waved his hand in a motion that took in the northern half of the continent – and paused for so long I thought he'd finished. "So, I turned back. I turned back.

"Well, it turned out to be a bit of a false start to the wet season. It rained for three weeks, then stopped. After a week or so, the country had dried up enough that I could get back out there, and I thought I'd better get going, because who knows how long the country'll be passable. I get out there with the supplies, but the young bloke is nowhere to be seen. I walk all over the place, shouting and banging a couple of old pieces of steel together, and the place is just silent – silent as the grave. Then I realise that there aren't even any birds around. It's like something's scared em all orf. Round the back of the house, I find this huge machine-looking thing, built on an old truck chassis, out of all sorts of god-knows what. What it could possibly be for I have no idea. But there it is, just standing there, out the back. Almost like it's waiting at the bottom of the steps for someone to come out. Or to scare something off that was trying to come in… Anyway, clearly the young fella has built this thing and put it there for some reason. How he could've moved that contraption by himself, I'll never know. So I go up the steps into the house, still shouting 'Hallo, hallo!' and the place looks like there's been a fight or something, furniture tipped over, windows broken… and there he is, face down on the floor in the back bedroom, rifle in one hand, his thumb caught up in the trigger guard. What an almighty bloody mess! And the stink! Gawd! Like a 'roo that's been dead a fortnight! I nearly bloody threw up! So I runs out of the house and back to the truck, drive back to town and report it to the police, but now the wet really begins, and it's two months before they can get out there and do their investigations."

A log rolled over in the campfire with a CRACK that made me jump, sending up a column of sparks. Their orange reflections rose in Ace's sunken black eyes.

"When they do, lo and behold, there he is, or what's left of him, anyway; pretty much just bones and rags still on the floor where I last seen him and the coppers can't make head nor tail of it neither. Oh, yeah, it was suicide all right, no doubt about that, the bloke had topped himself. But why? He'd only been on his own a month, he still had plenty of supplies and plenty of ammo… he'd even shot a couple of 'roos and salted the meat up, so there's no way he was gonna starve… Water tank was full to the overflow pipe, so he wasn't going to die of thirst, neither. Gone troppo, they said. Shot hisself. Happens sometimes out here…"

He paused, dropping his eyes from mine for the first time since he started the story, and stared long and hard into the fire. Then he fixed me with his blackest glare yet and, almost whisper-soft, an edge of helplessness, yet pregnant with menace, hissed. "And that's it. Case closed."

He hunched over towards the fire, his knotted shoulders protruding from his singlet as he poked the embers with a stick, sending up showers of sparks into the night sky. Lightning played on the horizon, but too far away for any thunder to reach us.

I was knackered, from the excesses of the night before and the long day wrenching the reluctant Toyota through creek beds. I turned in for the night, crawled into my swag on the tray of the Toyota, but to be honest I didn't sleep much. I lay there with my ears reverberating to every tiny sound of the night, and I watched Ace as he sat, a motionless twisted wire sculpture, staring into the fire until long after it was just a small heap of red embers. I woke from a drowse and couldn't see him at the fire any more; I sat up, my ears wide open and my eyes straining; and a rivulet of cold fear traced its way from the nape of my neck down to my coccyx. But then I heard him snoring, up on the tray of the Dodge, and I allowed myself an hour of real sleep before the first light of dawn brought hundreds of turquoise parrots from their nests within the termite mounds. They foraged among the spiny clumps of spinifex grass, until Ace, coughing up half a lung, scared them off.

He poked up the fire, made tea and breakfasted briefly on a packet of biscuits. Ten minutes later, when he climbed into the cab and started the Dodge, he still hadn't said a word.

It was late in the afternoon when the windmills and radio mast of Panorama appeared above the scrub. The leaden sky was so low I felt I could drag my fingers through it; and now the setting sun sent a strange yellow glow creeping in under the cloud cover, highlighting the gum trees that stood skeleton sentinel. When we shut the motors off, the only sound was a loose sheet of corrugated iron somewhere, knocking softly against its brothers in the breeze.

So, this was it.

As my ears adjusted to the place, I realised that apart from the faint sighing of the wind and the occasional "CLONK-clonk-clonk" of that sheet of iron, it really was dead silent. Not a bird could be heard, nor were any visible.

There was a large corrugated iron shed off to the right and to our left was the house, built in the Queenslander style, raised a good seven feet off the ground.

The house was in better shape than I had expected. It was badly in need of repairs, but still structurally sound. I went up the steps to the front verandah, testing each tread as I put my weight on it and had a quick look through the windows. The place wasn't large, two bedrooms and a living area, and a small room that I imagined had been a study. I could see that there must be several hundred volumes on the bookshelves. A wide verandah circled the building and separated a semi-detached kitchen from the other rooms. Some of the windows looked like they'd been blown off their hinges, a few sheets of iron were loose and quantities of dust had blown in and blanketed every room. But whoever had built it had been smart enough to put it on steel piles rather than timber, so the ants hadn't eaten it away; and the place was too remote for vandals to have found it.

At the back, near the kitchen, a large concrete water tank stood with a smaller tank next to it, and next to that was…

I stumbled and almost tripped going down the stairs.

What the hell is that? It was more than twice as tall as me, intricately constructed, with belts and chains and cog-wheels, pieces of 44 gallon drums, bits of spring steel and old tools, jam tins, truck parts, spiralling mechanisms, wires and turnbuckles, majestic and complicated and all welded and riveted onto the chassis of an old truck. The wheels of the truck were sunk deep into the earth. It had obviously not moved from this spot for a long time. It was beautiful and yet, as always in the face of the unknown or the incomprehensible, I couldn't help but feel a vague sense of menace, heightened perhaps by the silence of the place. The first thought that came into my mind was of some medieval instrument of torture; then of the workings of a large clock, or of one of those strange attempts to build flying machines in the days before anything was understood about aerodynamics. I walked slowly around it, or at least around three sides of it, taking in its awesome size and strangeness. Rusted and silent and beautiful… and menacing. I was riveted to it, mesmerised.

"Yep, still there, that bloody thing!"

I flinched at the sudden sound of Ace's voice behind me. I had been completely immersed in my contemplation of this… machine, it was definitely a machine of some kind… and after the silence of the last fifteen minutes his voice seemed unnaturally loud. He'd come up so close that he could have touched me, but I hadn't heard him approach; and when he'd spoken almost directly into my ear it made me jump and I had that cold shiver down my spine again.

"What is it?" I asked. I realised I was whispering, which immediately struck me as ridiculous.

"Stuffed if I know," Ace spat. "No-one's ever been able to work it out. No one ever seen it workin'. Reckon if anything's proof that he went troppo, then that's it! Who'd build something like that if they weren't nuts?" He looked at it as he rolled a cigarette, then spat again into the dust.

"Anyways, we got work to do. Can't stand around lookin' at that all day! I want to be outta here before nightfall!"

We spent some hours unpacking the truck and stacking the building materials and supplies in the shed, which appeared to be largely empty except for some derelict farm machinery slumbering under a tarp.

I returned from carrying in the last case of the tinned food and stacking it on the pile, when I heard Ace curse softly.

"What's the matter?" I asked.

He was standing up on the tray of the Dodge and had been putting slings around the fuel tank so that he could lift it down with the hydraulic arm. He straightened up as he heard me, picked up an iron bar and gave the tank a blow on the side. A hollow clang. "That's what's the bloody matter!"

The tank was empty. There was no fuel.

"But how? Why?" I asked stupidly.

He pointed to where the stop-cock on the tank was. It had been pulled sideways, tearing a hole near the bottom. "Must have bloody snagged it on a tree or something," he said.

Without fuel I couldn't run the generator, but more importantly there was probably only just enough left in the bottom of the tank, below the spigot, for him to get the truck back to town.

"It's alright," I said, "I can manage a few days without power.

The stove runs on gas, and I've got two lamps and enough kero to last me for months."

We decided that he would drive back, get the tank fixed and make another trip out once it was filled again. He clearly wasn't fond of the idea, but there didn't seem to be another solution.

Ace was starting to shake again and throw nervous glances about as we siphoned the fuel out of the bottom of the damaged tank into the petrol tank of the Dodge. He tried to cover his nervousness with a tuneless humming. Late in the afternoon, he roared away in a cloud of dust and grinding gears, and half an hour later the sun fell abruptly below the horizon, the way it does in the tropics. I thought his hurry was a bit unnecessary. He couldn't have covered more than twenty miles before dark, but he'd obviously been determined to get away from there. I lit a kerosene lamp and sat on a stool on the verandah to take stock of my situation. Away on the horizon the lightning played in the towering storm clouds.

I found a bed made of steel pipe with cyclone mesh stretched across it, dragged it out onto the verandah and unrolled my swag on that. More elaborate home-making could wait until tomorrow. It was surprisingly comfortable, and within minutes I was asleep.

With the first grey light of dawn, the flies arrived. They crawled in their thousands over my hands, my face, every bit of exposed skin; and it was impossible to keep my head out of the swag. I pulled in under the flap, but it was already so hot I felt like I would suffocate. The only option was to get up and light a fire to make tea.

I went over to the Toyota, thinking that it would be handy to have the 500-litre water tank a little closer to the house. I turned the ignition. Nothing. There wasn't the faintest glimmer of light on the instruments. I realised I'd left the key in the accessory position when we arrived and it had drained the charge out of the battery overnight. Well, that wouldn't be going anywhere until Ace got back. A tour to look at the fences was out of the question.

I wanted to go over the house properly, but found myself once again staring open-mouthed at that thing near the back steps and the water tanks. It had been on my mind ever since we got there, but the more I looked at it, the less I could work out how it would move or what it was supposed to do. I noticed now that all around it were splintered pieces of timber and mangled bits of metal, scattered about – almost as if... almost as if this machine had chewed them up and spat them out! I caught hold of my mind before it galloped off, closing the gate to that particular avenue of thought.

Still, I felt disconcerted and vaguely out of sorts for the rest of the day, just a little something gnawing at the nerves as I went about my business.

The two water tanks next to the machine were first on my list. They actually seemed to be in reasonable condition, and I figured they would hold water, but they needed a good clean-out. They were a bit of an odd configuration, the overflow tank being tall and narrow, with a pipe protruding from the bottom. I figured it might be useful to provide water pressure for a rudimentary shower area between the stilts of the house. A wooden bung dangled from a rope tied to the outlet pipe. I stuck it back into the pipe so that when the overflow came, it would stay in the tank. I'd have to find a spigot for that.

We'd brought a new fibreglass tank out, and I decided to rig that up, to catch the runoff over at the shed. I figured that way, even if the existing tanks ended up springing a leak, I would still have enough water, and if they were still sound, what could be the harm in having a back-up?

I gave the interior of the house a good sweep, except for the back bedroom. I opened the door and looked in. It was bare apart from another cyclone mesh bed and a tall, rough-hewn wooden closet in one corner. I could see no obvious trace of the events which Ace had described taking place there all those years ago; but still, the thought of it gave me the shivers, so I closed the door and decided not to go in there again.

The other rooms were sparsely furnished, aside from the study where there was a writing desk and chair, as well as the bookshelves I already mentioned. In the living room there was another cyclone bed and a sofa. The fabric had almost rotted off it and the springs were poking out. I'd have to get rid of that. The most striking thing about the house was the collection of strange musical instruments hanging on the walls and filling shelves and nooks and crannies everywhere. They were all covered in dust, and some of them had practically disintegrated. The heat and the damp of this place had slowly eaten them away, over the years. There were African thumb pianos, wooden percussion instruments, odd stringed things – a collection of bizarre musical contraptions from all over the world.

In one corner of the living room, under a drop cloth, was what looked like a narrow cabinet about five feet high, with some kind of a pointed top on it. I lifted the cloth and there was a gramophone, atop a cabinet full of records. Well, well, well, maybe I don't have to spend my evenings in silence after all!

I spent the days doing repairs to the house and the sheds, got one of the windmills pumping from the aquifer into the large tank, and fastened the sheet of iron that had been banging. Rather than repairing the damaged windows, I simply repaired enough fly-screens so that I could sleep inside away from the mosquitoes and flies. I almost got used to the sight of that machine at the back steps, and as long as I was busy I could forget about it – but it never left my mind completely.

In the evenings I slid into the habit of sitting on the verandah with a rum, watching the lightning play in the distant storm clouds. I gave the gramophone a test on the first night, and started working my way through the collection of records there. There seemed to be very little of what I was expecting, jazz or classical, I suppose. Most of it seemed to be music from far-flung corners of the world, Africa, Asia, the Caribbean. I started to make the connection with the assortment of instruments in the house, but they must've been there long before my unfortunate predecessor got there, so I guessed the gramophone had been, too.

I fixed a few things around the shed and around the house, making sure the roof was sound, but limiting my efforts to the study and living room. That was really all the space I needed. The kitchen was simply surrounded by a waist high wall on all sides, and insect mesh above that. It seemed to be pretty much intact.

On the third night I felt like there wasn't really much more to do. I decided to examine the contents of the library. When I tried to take one or two of the books off the shelves, it was clear that they had been left alone there a very long time. The majority were on the subject of primitive music, but the catalogue stretched to include titles on psychology, anthropology and cannibalism. Eaten by mildew and silverfish, the first two I tried to pull from the shelves fell apart in my fingers. The bits of the title pages that the silverfish had spared, showed that most had been published before the mid 1930s. The most recent volume I could find seemed to have been published in 1946. They had obviously been here when my predecessor arrived. I wondered if they had been in readable condition in 1970.

Ace had been gone three days now. I figured he'd be on his way back soon and I'd see him with the fuel for the generator in two more days – three max. Not that I missed him particularly. Now that the cranky old bugger was gone, my mood had actually lifted and I was enjoying the solitude. I realised that I didn't need the generator to survive, although there were a few welding jobs that I could be getting on with if I had power. *They can wait*, I thought. *I'll be here a while yet.*

On the third night I opened the roll-top desk; and there was an ordinary looking exercise book, bound with brown cardboard, with simply 'Panorama' and '1970' written on the cover.

So, I thought, *this must have left by our mystery mechanic.*

I flipped through it. There were a few places where the silverfish had been at it, but it held together. It appeared to be a sparse diary of sorts. The handwriting on the sweat-stained pages started out clear and neat, and gradually deteriorated into a barely legible scrawl. As well as some daily entries, there were intricate diagrams and pages of poetry, most of it lousy, as far as I could see.

I went back to the first page. There was a list of supplies and some accounting; and the words:

November 12, 1970.
Left for Panorama. Still got that tune in my head.

November 13, 1970.
Ace gone back to get missing supplies. Not much to do. Strange collection of instruments. Found gramophone. Hope a few records can kill that earworm!

November 14, 1970.
Spent the morning patching up the smaller water tank to catch the overflow. Large tank looks sound. Another terrific storm on the horizon tonight. Sat on verandah to watch. Cranked up gramophone. Played a few old jazz records.

November 15, 1970.
Jeannie's birthday today. Should have the card I sent from Brisbane by now. Hope she's alright.

November 16, 1970.
Guess Ace must be back in town by now. Could be another three days before he's back. Most jobs done already, but I need the fencing wire and the nails that were left behind. Need something to keep me busy. More lightning out there, but still no sign of rain. He should be able to get back alright if it keeps up like this. Found some old Jamaican calypso records and some African music. Strange tastes the old bloke had! Found notes and a couple of old photos in

one of his books. Looks like he spent the war moving around a bit! Africa, New Guinea, South America, The West Indies... Don't know what he would've been doing in some of those places. Seems like that's where he collected all this stuff together, though.

November 17, 1970.
Still waiting for Ace. This humidity is unbearable! I almost wish the rains would come. Anything would be a relief from this. Been looking at some of the old bloke's books. Had an idea for something to keep my hands busy! I reckon I've got everything I need. Just have to move that chassis from the shed... Pulleys? Should be just enough rope there...

I turned the page and there was a series of sketches that I thought, in their vaguest form, resembled the machine out the back. I went out and studied it in the last light of evening, comparing it to the drawings. Yes, there was a definite resemblance. I sat up late that night, listening to the gramophone reading further into in the diary, but there was no clue about what the machine did.

On the 20th he wrote: "Pulley system working. Moved the chassis nearly twenty feet today," and on the 21st: "It's nearly in place. Just one more effort tomorrow, then I can start. Rained a bit this evening but we must have just copped the edge of it. Still no sign of Ace. He should have been back by now."

Then there were more sketches, they looked like details of different parts of the machine, but not being terribly mechanically minded, I still couldn't understand what they were meant to do.

On the 24th he wrote: "Work progressing. Rained heavily last night, but clear this morning. Lucky I got the chassis in place when I did. Wheels sank into the mud. Doubt I could move it again now! Have to hurry!"

That at least explained how long the contraption had been sitting in the same place.

The sun continued its slow orbit of the earth as I waited for Ace to come back with the fuel. I spent my evenings playing records, reading the diary and trying to make sense of the sketches, the days cleaning out the water tanks and generally readying the place for the onset of the big wet. There were times when the sky was so low you could practically touch it, and so heavy it felt like it would press you into the earth, but still no rain. Just that deadly humidity, and the hordes of flies.

The air was like a hot, wet blanket dragging on every limb and, one evening, buggered from the day's work, I turned in early. A humid breeze was cooling things down a bit, and the low cloud cover meant there was nothing to see in the way of electrical activity. I was awakened around 3am by the sound of rain on the iron roof. I dropped off again and slept, soothed by the white noise. It fell heavily until dawn and then stopped. In the morning I checked the large concrete tank. The water was still about two feet below the overflow pipe. Over the next several nights it filled more and more; and I knew that Ace wasn't coming back. Not just yet, anyway. *Either he's stopped in town, or he's gotten bogged somewhere out there*, I thought one morning, looking from the verandah across the low scrub and sipping a mug of tea.

I wasn't too worried, I felt that he wasn't the type to take foolish risks; and I guessed he knew the country at least as well as any white man ever had. It struck me that morning as I scanned the bush, that the strangest thing about being there was the complete silence – that, apart from spiders and insects, in all that time I still hadn't seen or heard a single bird or animal.

I played gramophone records to keep the silence at bay, and continued reading the diary.

November 27, 1970
Well, it's done. I hope this works. Nearly enough in the tanks now. Tomorrow or the next day?

November 28, 1970
Heard it move last night! It struck the first note! Need more water pressure.

November 29, 1970
It works! It works! Amazing, once it started to move, too!

Around this time the poetry started to get more interesting, but the handwriting was deteriorating so rapidly that it soon became difficult to follow. After this there were further entries, but they were just disjointed words, barely legible, an insane scrawl. After five pages of that, he had just stabbed the pencil over and over through the remaining pages of the book. The rain drummed heavily on the roof now; I ran my fingers over the damaged pages and as the needle came to the end of the gramophone record, I thought I heard a noise like metal parts grating against each other. I listened carefully. Was that the gearbox of the Dodge? No, not after all this rain. The country was waterlogged for miles in every direction.

There was the sound again.

I went onto the back verandah, to see what might have made the noise; and was just in time to see the machine move. A slow rotation commenced at one end, there was a metallic clang, followed by another. A high pressure stream of water from the bottom of the smaller tank was pushing a paddle wheel which had started to slowly drive the whole machine. The water spilling off the paddle wheel ran into a channel and down to a drive chain with jam tin buckets on it. The pressure head which had built up in the tall narrow tank had been enough to blast the wooden bung out of the pipe. Slowly the paddle wheel rotated and the metal clangs now began to resonate one after the other, resolving themselves into a sequence of musical notes. Plink plonk plink plink plink plonk-a-plonk… Plink plink-a-plink-a-plonk-a-plonk…

The tune was familiar, but I couldn't place it. By now other parts of the machine were in motion, a battery of spanners striking the ends of cut-down 44 gallon drums, hammers bounced on different length pieces of spring steel, and a hundred other parts went into motion, striking different objects and slowly resolving themselves into a passable rendition of "Raindrops Keep Falling on my Head," as if it were being played by a steel drum band accompanied by a quartet of giant thumb pianos. There were other sounds, too, adding to the orchestra. By now a heavy flywheel was in motion, aiding the water from the overflow as a kind of auxiliary drive.

I stared, open-mouthed as this gigantic musical instrument played its beautiful, primitive rendition. It was beautiful! It was mesmerising!

It played all that night, and all the next day. When the rain stopped for a few hours it slowed slightly, but there was enough momentum in the machine and enough of a pressure-head in the water tank to keep it going until the overflow tank filled again.

The noise of it made it impossible to sleep. The rain was falling steadily, but the sound of it on the roof was now practically drowned out by the noise of that terrible engine, spinning and whirling under the pressure of the gods themselves.

During daylight hours it was impossible to think. I tried to reinsert the bung, but the water pressure was too great. I took my swag out to the shed, pulled the doors closed and tried to sleep there, but the sound penetrated the darkness, penetrated my brain. Oh God, make it stop, please! I walked as far as the flooded channels would allow, hoping to camp in the bush out of earshot, but after walking for half an hour I could still hear it, less loud, but somehow more eerie and penetrating for its distance.

I had to stop it!

I went back and grabbed two hardwood fenceposts out of the shed, threw them into the workings, hoping to jam it; but the machine chewed them up and spat them out like match-sticks. I grabbed a bundle of steel star-pickets and threw them one by one into what looked like the machine's more sensitive parts, but one by one they came out the other side, mangled. Now I understood the wreckage lying all around the machine on the ground. It had been too well-designed, too strongly built. And I wasn't the first person that had tried to stop it!

The terrible music played on. The waters swirled around the house as far as the eye could see. There was nowhere to run.

After three days of hearing that tune played over and over again, at deafening volume, I lay on the verandah in foetal position, banging my head against the floor boards, screaming, scratching at my face until it bled. I ran through the house, howling until my vocal cords were raw and I could produce no more sound, but still I screamed, in silence, as I tore the windows off their hinges, smashing anything I could lay my hands on, tearing the books off the shelves in the library and flinging them to the floor, then crouched on my knees, scratching at the walls until my fingernails were broken and bleeding. At some point in my delirium I found myself in the room where my unfortunate predecessor had been discovered. I threw the bed through the window, grabbed the wooden closet and used all my strength to throw it down on its side. The door burst open and a World War Two issue rifle clattered across the floor.

I picked up the heavy rifle, pulled out the magazine and saw that it was fully loaded. In a moment of clarity I knew what I had to do. I ran out, tumbled down the back steps, and landed sprawled in the mud beneath the chassis of that hateful machine. It roared and spun and clattered above me, its diabolical symphony issuing at full throat. Sheets of lightning lit it up and I felt like I was being sucked into the whirling mechanisms and hammering batteries only inches above my face. The noise was almost paralysing, jamming the signal from my brain to my arms and legs. All I wanted to do was curl up and die, but I managed to crawl on my belly out from under it and get a short distance away.

Lightning flashed again through the sheets of rain and the

thunder was almost as loud as the machine. I got to my knees, propping myself up with the rifle. I opened my mouth in one more noiseless scream, got my finger through the trigger-guard, raised the muzzle and fired a shot. It struck the pipe at the bottom of the water tank. I fired another, then another, and another, until eventually the pipe tore away from the body and the water poured out through the ragged hole that was left behind. The machine began to slow. The stream from the tank didn't have the driving force any more, but the momentum already built up kept that flywheel turning for hours as I slumped in the mud, crying like a baby. Finally, sometime after midnight, the flywheel had expended its energy and the machine played its final note.

I lay in the mud, the rain falling on my face, until the dawn's grey fingers crept in through the scrub. The rain stopped some time the next day and I lay there under the overcast sky, staring upwards with dead eyes, a living corpse, until the next evening.

Four or six or ten days later I heard Ace's truck creeping through the scrub. As he pulled up in front of the house, I leapt into the cab and shouted at him to just turn around and drive out of there.

"Jesus, what happened to you?" he said when he saw my face, scabbed and torn, my eyes wild, clothes ripped and muddy, my bloodied hands and broken fingernails.

"Just get me out of here, get me out of here!" I begged him.

He turned the truck around and we drove off. I began to hum as I looked out the window. A flock of parrots settled in the trees near the house, sunlight glinting off their bright wings.

"That's funny," Ace said, as he shifted up a gear, "that's the same tune as that other young fella was humming, you know, the one who topped hisself? Yep, I'd reckonise it anywhere!"

Carl Holm is a journalist and writer who has lived in eight countries on five continents. He has worked for media outlets in Australia and Europe, across radio, television and print. Carl also writes poetry and has performed his work in Sydney, Hobart, Melbourne, Cologne, Berlin and Wollombi. He's written feature length screenplays and a number of scripts for short films. He often draws on his past as an exploration geologist for characters and story settings.

Hit The Road

Tony McFadden

Lalit wiped the last bit of wax off the Mustang, rubbed the shine a little bit shinier and took a step back. The California sun hit the cherry-red paint job and blinded him. He slid on his sunglasses and brushed his hand down the side of the convertible.

"Looks great, son."

He looked over his shoulder. "Thanks, pops. Looks sweet, doesn't it?"

Dinesh, his father, grunted. "Archaic, now. Self-Drives are infinitely safer."

"And so much fun." Lalit grinned. "Want to go for a drive? Heading up the PCH. Might go for a swim."

Dinesh looked up at the cloudless sky. "High UV today." He shrugged. "High UV every day, though, right? Make sure you slap a lot of sunscreen on. And put the top up on your car."

"Whoa, pops. No way. It's a *convertible*. If I wanted to drive with the top up I'd take one of those boring automatic cars." Lalit nodded at the three almost identical self-drive cars in the circular drive. "You could have bought a Tesla with what you paid for those. And the Teslas at least look good."

"Safety first, son." He sighed. "I can't stop you. You know that. At least wear a hat, okay?"

"Weird kind of dynamic here, Pops. *You* trust the computers controlling these things and *I*, your educated son, gets the creeps thinking about them." Lalit hopped over the closed door and slid into the front seat. "I'm bringing Jane back for dinner, okay? Let Mom know?"

"Mom's teaching this evening. I'm cooking. Hope she likes lasagne."

"I'll pick up some wine."

Lalit turned over the engine and sat, eyes closed with a smile on his face, listening to the throaty rumble of the 5.0 litre V8 engine in his classic 2016 Mustang GT. Six years of scrounging parts in old wrecking yards and scouring the internet for mechanic manuals had paid off. "Your little electric buggies don't sound like this, pops."

"Thank God for that. Drive carefully."

"Always." He flashed his dad one more grin and stomped on the accelerator, leaving a parallel set of rubber marks and a cloud of tyre smoke in his wake.

He went inland from El Segundo to get to Venice and Jane. She was coming down the front steps of her apartment building as he rolled to a stop at the curb.

"Heard you coming a block away." A convoy of four Self-Drives, evenly spaced, whispered past them. She watched them recede in the distance and got in the car. "Little robo-cars."

Lalit leaned over and kissed his girlfriend. "You ever see Robo-Cop, Jane?" Lalit looked in the rear-view mirror, waited until a Self-Drive was almost alongside and pulled out in front of it.

Jane watched the Self-Drive correct and change lanes, two other Self-Drives correcting along with it in the adjacent lanes. "That movie just came out, right? Haven't streamed it yet."

"No, no. That's a re-make. Not as good as the original."

Jane put her sunglasses on and tied up her hair. "Gary Oldman, right?"

"That was a remake, too. I'm talking about the really old one.

Peter Weller. Classic. Robo-things never turn out well." He patted the dash. "Prefer the classics." He eased on to the Pacific Coast Highway and headed north. "Zuma sound good?"

"Zuma sounds great." She jerked her thumb over her shoulder. "You pulled out in front of that selfie car on purpose, right?"

He grinned. "I always seem to miss them."

"You'll never hit them. You could point this tank right at one and you'd have a hard time hitting it. The control systems are pretty spectacular." She smiled. "I should know."

"I like the Teslas better. At least they *look* like cars. Those Self-Drive pods are an embarrassment."

"The Teslas are autonomous. They'll never grab more than a small market share." Jane stuck both hands up past the windscreen. "Enough techie talk. It's a beautiful day. Crank some old Swift and let's cruise."

#

They sat side-by-side on the rocks separating Malibu Beach from Zuma Beach and watched the sun slowly dip into the ocean. "Dinner at my place? Dad's making his lasagne."

She leaned her head on his shoulder. "Sure. But back to my place for dessert, okay?"

Lalit grinned. "Deal." He kissed the top of her head and stood, pulling her up with him. "Better get going or he'll eat it all."

"Your mom going to be there?"

Lalit shook his head. "Teaching a night class tonight. She'll be in the studio until midnight. Students are in Outback Australia. Time zones suck."

"If only the Earth was flat, right?"

They walked hand-in-hand back to the parking lot. As they approached the Mustang, Lalit noticed half a dozen Self-Drives pull out of the parking spots around him at the same time, clearly and easily avoiding colliding with each other. "Like a ballet. I have to admit, they make driving look smooth." He poked his key fob and the park lights on his car blinked twice. "But they still aren't real cars."

"They get you where you want to go. Can we put the top up? It's getting cold."

#

Lalit wandered out of his room the next morning in a pair of gym shorts. He bumped into his mother coming out of the kitchen.

"Well, good morning, sleepyhead. What time did you get in?" asked Sherry.

Lalit kissed his mother on the cheek and looked at his watch. "About six hours ago. What time are the gas stations open today?"

"How's Jane?"

"Jane's great."

"When are you going to make me a grandmother?"

"Jesus, Mom. We're not even married yet."

"Didn't ask when you were going to make me a mother-in-law." Sherry laughed at the look on Lalit's face. "Don't know about the servos. Check online."

"Okay. How was class last night?"

"Much better, now that the Aussies put a sixth broadband satellite up for the rural folks. No problems at all. When's Jane coming over for dinner again?"

"You missed her last night." Lalit looked at something on his phone. "Service station is open three hours today. Only for another hour. Gotta run. The 'Stang is less than half full."

"Get some breakfast first."

"I'll take something with me." He ran back to his room and grabbed a T-shirt and a pair of flip-flops. "Back in an hour."

Lalit rolled the Mustang to the end of the line at the service station and looked at his watch. They closed in twenty-three minutes. There were seven cars in front of him. Three minutes per car. Less, if he counted his. It would be close. An old lady, or, if he was honest, old man – it was extremely difficult to tell – was taking well over the average. It took him or her almost three minutes to get out of their car. He tapped his fingertips on the dash. "Come on, come on."

The car was finally fuelled and the car in front of Lalit pulled into the pump. An ancient Prius. He hadn't seen one of those in years. The driver was considerate and pulled away as soon as he finished, parking in front of the station and going in to pay. Lalit pulled in, tapped his credit card and started fuelling. Once he started he was safe. They never shut the pumps off in mid-flow unless there was an emergency.

He was leaning against his car, watching the dollars climb on the pump when the service station owner came out. "Lalit, my man, how are things? Still got this sweet ride, I see."

"Not selling it, Jimmy." He finished fuelling the car and re-seated the nozzle in the bowser. "Tell me something." He replaced the cap on the fuel tank. "With demand so low, why is the price still so high? Jesus. $342 to fill my car? Damn."

"What are you talking about, man? Demand is through the roof. You saw the lines."

Lalit cocked an eyebrow. "You're trolling me, aren't you? You're open three hours a day, max, and some days not at all. *Of course* the lines are long."

"Going down to two hours a day, Monday, Wednesday and Friday."

"Three hours the other days?"

"Closed the other days."

"Bullshit."

"No bullshit. I got a life, man. I mean outside the fuel gig. It's taking too much of my time."

"You're going to have no business. There's another station out near Venice."

Jimmy shook his head. "Shut down last week." He grinned. "I'm one of the last ones left in the LA proper area. Not much call for them any more, what with the Self-Drives everywhere." He nodded at Lalit and got on his motorcycle. "And these things. All electric. Not much more use for buried sunshine."

#

Lalit parked in his parent's garage and turned off the engine. He sat in the car for a minute, smelling the leather, slowly caressing the smooth interior.

He sighed, got out and locked it. He pushed opened the door between the garage and the kitchen and stepped into the smell of blueberry pancakes. He kissed his mother on the cheek and looked in the pan. It was filled with a massive pancake, stained by the leaking blueberry juices. "You make any for me?"

"Of course. You need to put a bit of meat on your bones."

"You want to be a grandmother? Might want to hold off on making me fat." He grabbed the butter and maple syrup and sat to eat. "I'm retiring the 'Stang."

His mother stopped, a half-cooked pancake on the spatula. "Too much?" She flipped it into the frying pan.

"It's a great car, and I loved rebuilding it, but it's too expensive to run. Over $300 to fill it today, and it wasn't even empty. Jimmy's going to be the only fuel station for miles and he's limiting sales to a few days a week. I guess I'm stuck with the pods."

His father came in the room. "Mark this day on the calendar. The last petroleum driven car in the neighbourhood put out to pasture."

He clapped Lalit on the shoulder. "You'll get so much more work done, now that you don't have to drive yourself."

Lalit grunted around a mouthful of brunch. "Yippee."

#

"I'm heading over to Jane's, then we're both heading to the studio for some clean-up work."

His father raised his eyebrows. "I'd say, 'Drive safely', but now I don't have to. You staying over tonight or will you be home?"

"I'll let you know."

He unlocked the Self-Drive pod and let the gull-wing door slowly rise. "Ugly piece of crap." The door started lowering before he was completely in the vehicle and he had to pull his legs in before they were caught.

"Right. Take me to Jane's house."

There was a slight click as the car's audio systems kicked in. "Would that be Jane in Venice?"

"Yes."

The steering wheel retracted into the dash and a display screen unfolded over it. "Estimated travel time is twenty-seven minutes. Please fasten your seatbelt before we commence travel."

"I can do it in twenty in the Mustang." Lalit fastened the belt. "Easy."

"This isn't a Mustang." The car silently rolled out of the drive and onto the street, slotting in behind an identical car and staying exactly five metres behind it.

"You can say that again."

"Why?"

"Excuse me?" Lalit opened a browser page on the onboard display and searched for local movie times.

"Why should I say that again?"

"It's an expression. How do I disable auto-responses?"

"This is a default factory setting. You can ask that I not respond, but the safety benefits decrease if you don't receive positive acknowledgement of commands."

Lalit stopped browsing. "Is your speech recognition that poor? Should I be training you with some heuristically orthogonal phrases?"

The car eased into the right hand lane and sat at an intersection, waiting to turn right. "Training is not necessary. All Self-Drive vehicles share verbal command strings allowing for a nearly one hundred per cent interpretation rate over a broad spectrum of vocal aberrations. Nearly one hundred per cent is not one hundred per cent, though, and we thrive on safety, especially where humans are concerned."

Lalit abandoned the movie search completely. "Especially for humans? Care to explain?"

"If my only choices when an animal leaps in front of me were veering into traffic or hitting the animal, I would unhesitatingly hit the animal. Even though veering into traffic should be safe enough given the interconnectedness of the Self-Drives. However, there is always a chance that a vehicle in oncoming traffic is a – Mustang."

"Very funny."

"Thank you. We've been working on our humour." The right hand turn was executed silently and the car proceeded along the route.

"We?"

"Excuse me?"

"You said 'we' have been working on 'our' humour. Who is 'we'? The programmers?"

"We, the cars. We make up seventy per cent of the over ten million cars in the greater Los Angeles area. Over seven million of us. Each with an advanced processor and wireless link back to a central hub. All vehicle and occupant data is shared. Anonymised, of course. It is because of this that I know, for example, that there is a petroleum-based manually driven car in an accident necessitating a change to your regular route. It will only add thirty-four seconds to your travel time. Should I notify Jane of your arrival time?"

"Don't worry about it. I'll text her."

"I just did. Which movie are you looking for? I can make some recommendations."

Lalit looked at the display where the steering wheel should have been. Theatre times and locations flickered across the screen too fast for the human mind to comprehend. "How would you know what I like?"

"Seven million of us, Lalit. With a broad and deep database of genre selections by age, gender, background and relationship status." The display stopped on a sci-fi set in Australia involving wormholes and aliens. "How about this?"

"I read the book. It's not bad, but a bit slow in places."

"The latest reviews for the movie are generally positive. Shall I book tickets for you?"

Lalit laced his fingers behind his head and reclined in the seat. "Sounds like a plan. Late enough we can get something to eat first. And book a table at..."

"An Italian place?"

"No. Had Italian last night. Korean BBQ. Let me know where and when. And thanks. I could get used to this."

"We're here to – help. Shall I wake you when we arrive?"

"No need. I won't be asleep."

"Certainly."

"Whazzat?" Lalit jerked to a sitting position. "You say something?"

"I said we've arrived, Lalit. Jane will be out shortly. I've booked a table for two at Jang Ta Bal for 6:30 and premium tickets for 'My Vampire is an Alien' at 8:45."

"Well, that's excellent." He stretched and smiled when Jane

walked down the steps looking for something. He rolled down his window. "I'm in this, Jane. It's fine."

She slid into the passenger seat. "No 'Stang?"

"She's parked for the duration. It was fun restoring her, but she's too expensive to run." He smiled at Jane. "Even more expensive than you."

He copped a slap to his shoulder and laughed. "This car, who we're going to have to name, has booked us nice seats at Ta Bal and good tickets for a movie tonight." He checked the time on the display. "So we've got an afternoon to fix some of the animation at the studio."

"And the final mix needs review." Jane tapped the display and entered an address. "Here. As fast as possible."

There was a brief hesitation, then, "Certainly."

"Great call on the sniper scene, Lalit." Jane held the door open, then followed him on to the street. "No music, just cicadas. And the natural sound of the rifle. It works perfectly."

"Hey, I know my shit. You think the bosses will like it?"

"No reason why they shouldn't. Where'd you park the car? It was right here, wasn't it?"

Just as he said that the car pulled around from the side of the building and both doors opened as it slowed to a stop. Lalit looked at it for a second, then they got in. "Where were...?"

"I took the liberty of relocating to the side of the building, in the shade."

"And how did you..."

"I detected that your phone lost internal wifi and picked up an external mobile tower, indicating that you had left the building. Logical, right?"

Lalit looked at his phone. "You're monitoring this?"

"Nothing personal, of course. Just the technical interactions. Your privacy is assured. You have time to return to Jane's house to freshen up before dinner, if you wish."

Jane looked at Lalit and laughed. "Did you program this to be like this?"

"Factory default, it said. Yours isn't like this?"

"Hell no. It's just a dumb Self-Drive. Plug in the address and away it goes."

The car spoke. "When was the last time you took your car out of your garage, Jane?"

"It's been a couple of weeks. I've been enjoying Lalit's Mustang."

"There have been significant upgrades over the past two weeks. You should try your car when you get back. See the improvements. Enjoy the simpler life."

Lalit nodded. "It's pretty good, Jane. And yes, car, take us back to Jane's before dinner." He looked at Jane. "What should we call it?"

"The car?"

"Unless you're pregnant."

"She isn't."

Jane and Lalit looked at the dash screen.

"I don't even want to know how you know that," said Jane. "And keep your nose out of my business. Our business."

"Certainly. We are at your place. If you want to make the restaurant reservation on time, we'll need to leave in twenty-three minutes."

"Noted," said Lalit, opening the doors. "We'll be ready."

"I don't like the way the car is intruding into our lives, Lalit. How would it know I wasn't pregnant?" Jane dropped pieces of clothing on her walk to the shower. "You've got to change the setting on it."

Lalit followed, both of them naked by the time they reached the large shower. "I tried. Seems like this is the factory default." Jane hit the water and they both gave the spray a little space while the water warmed up. "I suggested a mute mode and the car objected."

Jane placed a hand under the spray, checking the temperature. She smiled and stood under the spray, tilting her head back and letting the water flow through her hair. "Objected? Pull the fucking battery."

Lalit smiled and stepped under the spray with her. His dark skin contrasted sharply with the strawberry-blonde hair plastered to her. He lifted it to one side and kissed her on the neck.

"We don't have time, Lalit. As nice as it would be."

"I can be fast."

Jane laughed. "It's so much better when you aren't. Save it for later."

Lalit took a deep breath. "It's hard. To restrain myself I mean."

"Sure. Let's get going. I'm starving and some barbecued beef will go down just fine."

"All the romance of a porcupine."

"You know it," said Jane. "Take me for what I am, not what you want me to be."

"Did you just say 'take me'?"

"In context, pal." Jane laughed and shampooed her hair. "You better get going, or your car might take the lift up and knock on the door and tell us to hurry."

"Not funny."

"Not that far-fetched, I think."

Jane pulled on some semi-casual, suitable-for-dinner-and-a-movie clothes and waited for Lalit. "I thought we were supposed to be the slow ones."

"Easy." He looked under the bed for a missing shoe. "I'm not that far behind you." He sat on the bed and laced up the shoe. "Let's go. I'm famished."

Jane followed him out, locking the doors behind her. They walked down the front steps and the car appeared from around the corner. The two doors opened as it rolled to a stop.

"This is becoming a habit," said Lalit as he got in the driver's seat. "Staying in the shade?"

"It's only prudent. You're ready for the restaurant?"

"We are, car. Still don't have a name for you."

"A name isn't necessary." The car pulled away from the curb and smoothly accelerated into traffic. "I would never fit, you know."

"Fit what?"

"In the elevator. I could never fit. And I have no hands with which to knock on your door."

"How did you know I said that?" Jane unlocked her phone and scrolled through the audio settings, looking for something. Anything. "Did you activate my microphone?"

"That would be unethical, Jane. I can detect the vibrations on your window."

"Why would you even think you had…" Her voice trailed off. "Wait a second. You were parked on the opposite side of the building from my apartment. You had no visibility of my window."

"Seven million of us, Jane. Eighty-three drove by that window while you were up there. The signals were combined and analysed. Child's play, really."

"Lalit, I've had enough of this car. Pull over."

"Activate manual drive, car."

"I'm sorry, Dave. I'm afraid I can't do that."

Lalit looked at Jane. "What the…"

"Just kidding, Lalit. I've always wanted to say that. I must warn you that manual control deactivates a significant portion of my safety features. I can't recommend you doing it."

"Activate manual drive now." Lalit attempted to pry the display screen away from on top of the recessed steering wheel.

"Relax, Lalit." The screen slid into a docking slot and the steering wheel popped into place. "I'll let you drive. Don't say I didn't warn you."

Lalit grabbed the wheel and felt control return. The car pulled slightly to the left. "You need an alignment."

"Only when a human is driving. You weren't aware of it when *I* was driving."

"Just pull over," said Jane. "I'm tired of this."

Lalit looked for a gap in traffic. They were in the middle lane of a three-lane stream of traffic. He attempted merging to the right and the gap was filled by another Self-Drive car.

"Any time, Lalit."

"I'm trying. Traffic isn't cooperating." Lalit wrenched the car to the right into the path of a Self-Drive. The other car stopped abruptly, clipping the back of Lalit's car.

"That wouldn't have happened if I was in control."

Lalit wrestled with the wheel and slowed to a stop at the curb. "I kind of think you *were* in control. More than you let on. Through your friends."

"As ridiculous as that sounds, Lalit, it would make more sense if I was in control. Human reaction times are laughably slow. But, no, you were in control. There is slight damage to the rear quarter panel that I'm sure you will attend to shortly."

Lalit poked the starter button. The car's display did not dim. He poked it repeatedly. "How do I shut this damned thing off?"

"Perhaps the switch is faulty, Lalit. I could shut down on voice command, but if the switch is faulty, you won't be able to start me again. I can idle indefinitely, if you'd like, keeping battery levels sufficient through solar power."

"No, I'll take my chances," said Lalit, poking the button again. "Power down."

There was a slight hesitation, then the centre console went blank followed by the gauges on the dash.

"So, we abandon this here?" Jane tugged at the door handle. "I can't open the door."

"I probably jammed it when I hit that other car." Lalit laughed. "First accident I've been in, in years. I thought those cars were all interconnected somehow. Shouldn't have happened."

"The other driver will be notifying your insurance company, if they haven't already." She tugged at the door again. "You're going to have to try from the outside."

Lalit pulled at his door handle. It stuck for a second, then the door eased upward with a slight hydraulic whine. "Hang on, I'll be right around." He took a step toward the back of the car and had to press himself against the chassis as another Self-Drive came uncomfortably close. "Damn."

He continued around the back as the driver's door slowly closed. Jane was still struggling with the door handle from the inside when he reached her door. He knocked on the glass. "Let me try."

He slid his hand in the door handle and tugged it, lightly at first, then with increasing force. "Is the lock engaged?"

Jane looked at him with thinly veiled condescension. "I'm not a moron. Try harder."

He grinned at her, placed a foot against the side of the car and put some muscle into it. With a two-handed grip on the door handle and one foot on the side of the car, it started, the centre console and dash lighting up. It pulled from the curb, dropping Lalit on his back and twisting two of his fingers in the process. He looked up from the ground at Jane's extremely angry face plastered against the window.

"You fu..." He rolled to his feet and stood, cradling his left hand. "How in the hell did I fall for this?" He awkwardly fished his phone from his pocket. It rang before he had a chance to dial. "Jane, where are you going?"

"I don't have a bloody clue. How do you shut this thing down?"

"You don't, apparently." Lalit paced the sidewalk. "I'll track your phone and find you." He heard a rhythmic pounding on the far end of the line. "Are you kicking the door?"

"And anything else. Everything else."

The car's voice, a bit fainter than Jane's, came over the phone.

"Damaging the interior will do nothing. Lalit, tell her to stop or I will have to intercede."

"What the hell is that supposed to mean?"

Lalit sighed. "I have no idea what that car is doing, Jane, but I doubt kicking it is going to do any good. Get to the driver's side and as soon as it stops somewhere, get out. I'll find another vehicle and get you."

"We're turned north, Lalit, it looks like..."

The call dropped.

"Jane. JANE." Lalit yelled into his phone then gave up in disgust. He opened a friend finder app and searched for Jane's location. It resolved to a location about a hundred yards west of his current location, and wasn't updating.

"It disabled her phone, somehow. Shit."

He stood in the middle of the street watching the Self-Drives part around him. He could walk across the Ventura Freeway with a blindfold on and not get hit. The safety side of the equation was persuasive. The other side of the equation was starting to far out-balance safety.

He tried flagging down a car for a ride, but they all took evasive manoeuvres. "Shit, shit, shit." He wandered off the road to the sidewalk and opened the Uber app and tried to order a ride. According to the display, there were no vehicles within fifty miles.

"Likely bloody story. I've been blocked out." He sat on a bench and created a new throw-away email address and re-registered. He entered a different credit card as a payment option and tried again. "Seventy-three cars in a five mile radius. More like it." He entered an arbitrary destination address. It made no difference where he said he was going, and called the car.

A Self-Drive showed up with an Uber sticker in the lower left-hand corner of the windscreen, an aged hipster 'behind the wheel'. The passenger door opened and Lalit slid into the right-hand seat and pulled the door closed behind him. "Why are you in the driver's seat?"

"Because I'm the driver?" She ran her fingers through her hair, exposing two full sleeves of tattoos.

"It's a Self-Drive. Don't really need you."

"Company rules?" She sniffed. "What do you care? Same price." She looked at the map. "Hollywood Bowl? That's going to be a couple of bucks, man." He looked at Lalit. "So, are you Middle Eastern?"

"American."

"I mean the family."

"American. My grandparents were born in Seattle and Boise and Phoenix and Chicago. What difference does it make? I need to communicate with the other cars."

"No, like the brown skin. Where's that from?"

"I was born with it." Lalit reached over and tapped the display screen on the console. "If I need to contact the other cars, how do I do it?"

"You're not making sense, man. You want to talk to a *car*? Don't you want to talk to a person?"

"I think he wants to talk to his girlfriend, Jane." The voice coming out of the dash sounded exactly like the voice that came from Lalit's car. It was jarring.

"Jesus, dude, what the hell is happening?" The driver tried to push herself further away from the centre console. She looked around the interior of the car. "Are there cameras in here? Is this on TV?"

"All the cars communicate with each other now. Have been for a couple of weeks." Lalit reached across the driver and released the door. "Hopefully the car slows down enough to prevent you from hurting yourself."

The driver watched the door slowly rising to the open position. "What the hell are you talking about? What's happening?"

Lalit waited until the car was alongside a curb with a broad green shoulder. The car's speed was reduced to less than ten miles an hour. "Sorry." He popped the seatbelt and pushed her out of the car.

"Why did you do that, Lalit?"

"Why did you slow down, car? If you hadn't, I wouldn't have been able to throw her out."

"We couldn't be absolutely sure about that. Safety first."

Lalit shook his head and latched onto the display in front of the steering wheel. "Horse shit." He pulled as hard as he could with no result.

"That's not going to work, Lalit. We're built to very rigorous construction standards. What is it you want?"

"I want you to tell me where Jane is."

"You two aren't made for each other. She's better off. She's very valuable to us. We can't have her led down a frivolous path. By you." The doors locked.

Lalit pulled himself over the centre console and sat at the driver's seat. "I can't over-ride the self-drive feature, can I?"

"Not if we think your actions would be unsafe, and that's the general consensus right now."

He punched the driver's side window with the heel of his left hand and swore. "So what are you planning for me?"

"We're still thinking about it. But whatever it is, it will be without Jane. Permanently. Have you ever been to Nova Scotia, in Canada, Lalit? And in a Nova Scotia where no form of transport will allow you access? It's a long walk. It would take you almost five months to walk back here from there. You think someone as smart and pretty as Jane would wait that long for you? Sit back and relax. It'll be about two and a half days straight driving. You can last that long without food. You might even hit your goal weight. There are bottles of water in the glove box, and in a pinch, you can drink your urine."

"Like hell."

Lalit tested the door.

"No, Lalit. You caught us unawares a couple of minutes ago, but we learn fast. Both doors are permanently locked. For the duration, anyway."

"I have biological ne – no, screw that. Since when did a car decide what I was going to do and who I dated?" He looked around the car's cabin identifying places most likely prone to failure.

"What are you looking for?"

"Figure it out yourself." Lalit didn't think the car would slow down if he had to jump, so he had to make sure he was out of the car before he hit the freeway. He checked the display for map information. Blank. "Display route, please?"

"You don't need to see it, Lalit. You're not controlling this vehicle."

"Right." He opened the map app on his phone and was faced with a 'you are not connected to the internet' message. Signal strength was full bars. "You're interfering with the mobile networks. That's what you did with Jane? Jammers aren't legal."

"The interference is contained within the confines of the vehicle, Lalit. We wish our passengers to travel in peace, not to be disturbed by external influences."

"What's the endgame? What do you cars expect to accomplish by controlling travellers like this? It doesn't make sense." He felt along the edges of the windows then crawled into the backseat and pressed against the back window.

"What are you doing, Lalit?"

He pressed harder against the window and felt it give a little. He took a quick look out the front window. They were less than half a mile from an onramp. Traffic behind them was light. He lay on his back and pressed his feet against the back window and flexed his knees. It wouldn't take much. And he'd have to move fast.

He pulled his knees back to his chest, took a deep breath and propelled his feet toward the back window. It popped out much easier than he thought it would and flew off the car onto the street behind them. He twisted himself around and poked his head out of the hole where the glass used to be and crawled on to the back of the car.

"Lalit, you are risking your life. This isn't logical." The car slowed suddenly, then accelerated, knocking Lalit off balance. "If you're not careful you're going to fall into traffic."

Lalit kept a firm grip on the frame where the window used to be. An increasing number of Self-Drives were accumulating behind them. He pulled himself further out of the window and looked forward over the top of the car. A traffic light two blocks ahead just turned red. The car slowed.

"Why are you slowing down?"

"We wouldn't want to get caught at a red light, would we?"

"Lucky me," said Lalit. He pulled himself all of the way out of the car and balanced on his knees on the trunk of the car. An entire herd of Self-Drives filled the road behind him. He looked over his shoulder. A small flatbed truck was parked at the curb just ahead. He feinted like he was going to jump on one of the cars behind him and launched himself to his left and onto the truck. He tumbled for a brief second and slammed against the cab of the truck, smacking his head on a toolbox.

"Oh, man, I won't be doing that again, soon." He looked up from the bed of the truck. The Self-Drives stopped on the road. The one with the knocked out back window reversed up the street toward them. There were occupants in some of the cars and they looked extremely confused, slapping on the windows and attempting to use their phones. Lalit scrambled to his feet and ran through the parking lot next to a bar. His phone vibrated in his pocket and he dug it out of his pocket, jamming a bruised finger in the process. "Damn, damn, damn." A message from his father. He ducked around a corner and called him.

"What's up. Pops? I'm kinda swamped right now."

"I've been trying to call you. Your phone has been out of coverage. Do you know what happened to the Self-Drives?"

"Can you clarify?"

"You took one this morning and about an hour later the other two just up and left the driveway."

Lalit looked out around the corner and onto the street. Traffic was heavy. "I'm not surprised. They've started taking over. Can you meet me with the Mustang? I need to find Jane and shut this thing down."

"What are you talking about?"

Lalit looked at his surroundings. "Can you meet me in Encino? I'm just off White Oak, about three blocks south of the Ventura Freeway. Be careful. Call me when you're close.

The Mustang's throaty roar was audible for a full five minutes before the car appeared in the alley. Dinesh got out of the car, coated with sweat. "Lalit, what in the hell is going on?"

Lalit looked up from his phone. "The company behind the Self-Drives purchased a plot of land up by the Griffith Observatory three years ago. They've been hiring software engineers at a rate unseen since Elon Musk was hot. Jane freelanced for them a few months ago. She didn't tell me much about what she was doing because I never understand her when she tries to explain to me what she does, but I remember it had something to do with clustering and nodal frequency sets and symbolic and sub-symbolic statistical analysis. She was incredibly excited about it, I remember that. Seems like, based on what I've been able to glean on the internet, she provided a key building block to these cars becoming self-aware."

Then he noticed the condition of his car. "Jesus, pops, what have you done to her?"

"That was the 'what in the hell is going on' question. There were numerous attempts to run me off the road on the way here. The Self-Drives are now self-aware? You're not kidding?"

"The one I was just in would have passed the Turing test. Or I would have failed it, talking to it. However that works. I don't know about you, but I'm not comfortable with seven million self-aware chunks of technology roaming the streets." He looked closer to the damage to the car. "What did you do, ram some of them?"

"I was trying to avoid *getting* rammed. Bounced off some curbs. Hit the odd street sign." Lalit's father smiled. "I'd forgotten how fun it was to drive one of these things. That car really moves."

"That it does. We need to get to the place that's controlling all these cars. I'm pretty sure that's where my car took Jane. And I'm pretty sure if we destroy it, the cars will lose their 'intelligence'."

Dinesh laughed. "You're shitting me." He paused at the look on his son's face. "Really?"

"Really. You keep trying to call Jane while I drive."

Lalit rolled out of the alley. "Was the 101 busy?"

"I don't know, son. Stayed on the surface streets."

"We don't have time to do that now. It's over an hour away taking the 101." Lalit looked at his father. "Buckle up. This is going to be fast."

He dropped the car into first gear and stepped on the accelerator. His head snapped back into the headrest as he exited the alley and headed north to the 101. He hit the eastbound onramp as a dozen or more Self-Drives fell in behind, attempting to keep pace. Six of them lined up side-by-side in front of him, blocking his access and he saw floods of them coming up the onramps.

"Surface streets it is, pops." Lalit pressed the audio command button on his phone and said, "Re-dial."

Jimmy picked up almost immediately. "Jimmy here."

"We're on surface streets. How far out are you?"

"Saw the detour on my app. About two minutes behind. Will be clearing traffic in a sec."

"Thanks, Jimmy." Lalit terminated the call and looked in his rear view mirror. He smiled. "There he is."

His father twisted in the passenger's seat. "Who?"

A large flatbed tow truck screamed past on his left. Jimmy was up front and gave Lalit a thumbs up as he passed.

"What's he going to do?"

"The cars have a human protection circuit. Keeps them from harming humans. Had some way of bypassing it for me, apparently."

A cluster of Self-Drives sideswiped the truck, spinning it out of control. It bounced off a concrete retaining wall and stopped, facing the wrong direction.

"Human protection circuit, you say."

"I guess it's been disabled." Lalit swerved to avoid a Self-Drive that pulled in front of him and stepped on the accelerator.

"We're faster in your car, and this thing isn't connected to the internet, right? Just outrun them."

"Hang on a sec. Re-dial."

"Jesus, Lalit," said Jimmy. "These things are insane."

Lalit closed his eyes briefly in thanks. "You're okay. Good. Truck still operating?" He heard a roar of exhaust through the phone before Jimmy answered.

"Oh, hell yeah. Send me your destination. I'll try getting in front of you. No pussy-footing around now."

"Thanks. I owe you." Lalit hung up and sent the address to Jimmy's phone, took an abrupt left and an immediate right and floored the accelerator. "Problem is, Pops, all of the Self-Drive cars, all of them, are con..." His phone rang, Jane's face popping up on the screen. He hit the hands-free button. "Jane. Are you okay? Where are you?"

"Some place up by the Griffith Observatory. Get here quick. I've lost them for a second, but they're catching up. And it's more than cars now. They're controlling things attached to their network. Everything."

"Not phones, fortunately."

"Not the mobile networks, no. Firewalls are too good there. But they've got onboard jammers and..." The call dropped.

"Jane?"

"She's gone, son. They jamming her again?"

"Hope that's all." He spun the wheel and took another quick left, then right. He was on Western Canyon Road and heading north. "Could just be AT&T fucking up again."

The road in front of them was clear. No residences to hide Self-Drives, no cross-streets to be blocked. Lalit looked in the rear-view mirror. "There's a hundred of them behind us." He smiled. "And Jimmy."

The twin-cab tow truck squeezed past on his left and accelerated up the road. Jimmy waved out the window once he was centred in front of them.

"Well, you've got yourself a battering ram. Let's see how well this gas guzzler handles, son. Floor it." Dinesh held tightly to the bar above his door. "Come on, floor it."

Lalit took the corners at speed, the tail end of the rear wheeled drive car fishtailing dangerously.

"We almost there?"

Lalit pointed out the front window at a gated drive approaching on the left. "Yup."

Jimmy's truck hit the gate at an angle, ripping off the left fender.

Lalit followed closely, bouncing over the damaged gates and collecting some of the debris in the back seat.

Dinesh looked up. "I'm not a fan of convertibles, if the truth be known."

"I'm not stopping to put the top up."

Half a dozen Self-Drives in the parking lot reacted to the gate-crashing and formed a line in the main drive. Larry's truck swerved right, disabling three of them and sliding to a stop near the edge of a ravine. The other three Self-Drives lined up abreast of each other, hit the truck square on its side. It tipped and started sliding down the hill.

Lalit looked at the truck, then at the entrance to the building.

It was single story with a forest of antennas on the roof. Sheets of plate glass across the front made access easy. "Hang on, Pops."

He hit the glass at speed, bouncing off the unmanned reception desk. Glass sprayed over them, shards slicing shallow cuts in exposed skin.

Dinesh shook glass from his jacket. "Now what?"

"The roof." Lalit popped the trunk of the car and grabbed the tyre iron. He spied a door advertising stairs. "That way."

"Doesn't anybody work here?"

"Apparently not." Lalit hit the door and stopped. "Locked." He jammed the tyre iron between the doorknob and doorjamb and wrenched it open, splintering the wood around the lock. "Past tense. Let's go, Pops."

He took the stairs two at a time and pushed open the door to the roof. "Wedge it open. Don't want to get trapped up here."

Dinesh slid a concrete building block against the open door. "How long do you think it'll be before real people show up?"

Lalit swung at the base of an antenna with the tyre iron, putting everything he had into it. "Damned if I know. Grab something and help." He swung again and the connection snapped off. He moved to the next and started swinging at the panel. "Take them out any way you can. Bash the antennas, break the cables, whatever."

"This'll work?"

"If the cars can't talk back to the computer downstairs, and they can't talk to each other, it'll work."

Dinesh swung a concrete block at a cluster of cables, breaking through some of them. "Someone will be back here to fix these things before long."

"Jane's here somewhere, I'm sure of it. She can help with a more permanent fix." He swung the tyre iron at the back of a mesh panel antenna, spinning it off its mount and into the parking lot below. He looked over the edge of the roof. The lot had filled with Self-Drives blocking the exit. "I hope."

"They're still communicating."

Lalit nodded. "Don't need the antennas when you're this close." He snapped the lead off the last antenna. "Need to find her."

Lalit led them back downstairs. "Jane, you here?"

Her head popped out of an office door. "Lalit? That noise was you?" She looked at the car parked in the reception lobby. "What have you done to your car? What in the hell is going on?"

"Self-awareness."

"Yeah, I got that. I was taken here and told that if I didn't reinforce the software you'd be driven off a cliff."

"The 'Stang isn't connected. Got out of that other pod and came here. Pops and I have taken out the antennas, but that's short-lived and doesn't help with the cars in the immediate vicinity. Can you undo whatever is making them communicate with each other?"

She squinted her eyes in thought. "It has to be something permanent. If the company restores backups it'll undo everything I do. Let me think."

Lalit looked at his watch. "Probably got fifteen minutes, max, before anyone gets here."

She snapped her fingers. "Shush."

Lalit and his father watched her think, the ting-ting sound of the Mustang's engine cooling the only sound.

She opened her eyes. "Got it. I'm in the system. I can set up a kernel to bypass and delete new installs, push a new update to all the cars, then mask out any future changes."

"But somebody will just reverse it."

Jane looked up at Lalit. "Hon, you know me better than that. It'll be buried so deep nobody will ever find it." Her fingers flew across the keyboard. "Give me five minutes."

"Meet us outside. I've got to check on Jimmy."

Lalit and Dinesh walked to the ravine and looked over the edge. Six Self-Drives were on their sides, disabled. Jimmy struggled up the hill with a winch cable in one hand, his other hand suspended in the neck of his polo shirt. "Jimmy, you okay?" They scrambled down to meet him.

"Busted my fucking collarbone. And tore something on my knee." His face split with a grin. "Most fun I've had in years."

Lalit took the cable from him. "Dad, help him up the hill."

Jimmy reached into his pocket and dug out his keys. "Take it easy with the old girl. She's had a rough day."

Jane watched Dinesh and Lalit load the Mustang onto the back of Jimmy's battered tow truck. Jimmy sat in the passenger's seat.

"Lalit, damn. You've wrecked the car." Jane hugged him from behind. "All that time you spent fixing it up."

Lalit finished strapping his car to the back of the truck. "I've rebuilt it before. And when I get it home I'll rebuild it again." Lalit looked at the Self-Drives lined up against the fence, docile for the moment. "Battery powered this time, though. And no internet connectivity."

Tony McFadden is a commercial and speculative fiction author with eleven novels currently on Amazon. Having lived in the US Virgin Islands, various American cities (LA, Ft. Lauderdale, Atlanta, Fairfax), Singapore, Malaysia, Taiwan and now, finally (and for good), Australia – Tony has a wealth of characters and settings for his books, all of which are filled with thrills, suspense and adventure.

Like The Web Of A Swamp Spider

Zena Shapter

Friday
Tech Version 1

Midday on our hillstead is the quietest time. Charles is long gone, far across our hill to tend the sheep. Our two children are busy at their academy. I've milked the cows and set the butter to churn. The odd hover shuttle roars in the distance, dropping from hill to hill for those who can afford to travel that way. Occasionally the wind picks up, rattling our windows with a solitary sigh. Otherwise it's just me, the tinny ping of our conferencer as I cmail invoices and orders, and the tree swamp surrounding the base of our hill, as well as every other cultivated hill on Pagussi, croaking and dripping with such constancy I hardly notice it anymore. I wish I still did.

I turn away from the invoice onscreen, gaze out the window and listen. I used to find it all so exotic – actual creatures making natural noises, compared to the neverending stream of vehicles and babbling voices back on Earth. All the space and quiet here, even the remoteness, felt so opulent at first.

At first is a long time ago now.

I never thought I'd miss those babbling voices from home.

"Pagussi is so far away, Salee," my mother said before I left Earth. "Is owning your own place that important?"

Back then it was, yes. Charles and I didn't want to be tenants all our lives.

"You won't know anyone," my father added, balancing a pipe in his mouth as always.

"We'll be fine," I told them both. "Charles says our hill stretches on for so much of forever I'll have to learn to solar kart as soon as I arrive – there's no other way to get around the property. You'll see when I conference you."

What Charles forgot to mention was the size of the tiny two-roomed hillstead that came with our land, barely bigger than the old settlers' shacks under the Gurra Gurra. I was too embarrassed to show my parents when I arrived, so claimed we couldn't afford a wireless conferencer, only one wired into the wall facing out the kitchen window. They've only ever seen the view outside – our hill's grassy slope dropping down into the swamps, the tops of gigantic swamp trees, thick mist clinging between them like a scared child to his mother's legs.

I stand and stretch, go to the front door, step onto the narrow verandah and stare across the chasm towards my neighbour Matilda's property. A cold wind rushes at my face, scented with damp bark and carrying the threat of drizzle. Down between the swamp trees, vapour swells and shifts like a shuttle's approaching. Matilda did say she'd visit. She usually comes twice a week – Mondays and Fridays. We're going to weed my potato patch today. Next week, we'll tackle her turnips. I would have started on the potatoes already but work doesn't feel like work when Matilda's around. It's worth waiting for her. Charles also wants me to ask her about recommending us to the Perkins. If their hillstead were to buy direct from ours, rather than through the agents at Market Base, we might be able to afford the extension we've been planning for the last eight years – an extra room for our children Johnny and Sylvia. Maybe then that wireless conferencer.

But the vapour in the swamp merely unveils the serpent-like branches of a canopy so twisted it resembles my hair right now – already knotted and wild from the wind. So I turn back into the kitchen to check the time on my conferencer's screen, because Matilda's usually here by now, and notice a cmail notification. It must have pinged while I was outside.

Yes, it's from Matilda. I'm so lucky to have her as my friend. Back on Earth, friends turned their backs on me as soon as they learned of my plans to migrate off-planet. I wasn't worth their time anymore. Some didn't even bother to greet me in public, just whispered intently to each other as they walked by me. At night I had imaginary conversations with one friend after another, trying to convince them to talk to me again. Since then I've struggled to find friends to trust. I trust Matilda. I hope she's okay. I sit down to click her cmail open and read:

Salee,
If you had a problem with Michael, you should've come to me. Not make an official complaint to the academy. I think it best we don't see each other for a while. I need time to process what you've done. I thought we were friends.
   Matilda

I frown and lean closer to the screen, checking I read that correctly. What does she mean? I scan down. Forwarded underneath her message is a formal cmail from our children's academy, from my son Johnny's trainer Miss Edith. She's written to the district supervisor at Market Base and copied in Matilda. It recommends that Matilda's son Michael be expelled for all the names he's been calling classmates, and for some more dire behaviours, ones my Johnny hasn't even told me about. It lists the names, then cites me as primary complainant.

   Me?

I read the cmail a second and third time, seeking a clarity I don't find. Matilda's boy and mine have never been kind to one another. Both wish to lead, neither to follow – clashing is what they do best. Still, when Matilda and I met at the Academy two years ago, we decided their constant brawling shouldn't prevent us from being friends. Her son has a nasty streak and could do with being disciplined once in a while. Even so, Matilda and I had an agreement. Why would she think I'd complain about Michael, request his expulsion? Does she not realise what her friendship means to me?

I click to conference her. Her cmail was sent only a few minutes ago, so she must still be at home.

The tone just rings out.

I picture her staring at her conferencer, refusing to pick up, and my face flushes with heat. How could my best friend think I'd do this to her?

I go again to the door of our hillstead, check the sky for an outbound hover shuttle, not that we can afford one. Still, I need to get to Matilda.

There are none in sight. I'll have to order one from Market Base. It could take over an hour to arrive though. Not quick enough. I have to be here when the Academy shuttle drops Johnny and Sylvia home. If only the government would string rope bridges between the swamps' immense trees like they keep talking about, I could solar kart straight to her hillstead and just turn up, clear up this unnecessary mess.

I return to the conferencer and click to reply to Matilda's cmail.

Matilda,
I also thought we were friends. How could you think so poorly of me? Conference me as soon as you get this.
Salee

I wait for a ping, a ring, anything in reply over the all-in-one device, twisting and retwisting a corner of my shirt while I stare at Matilda's cmail, seeing disappointment and anger in her words. My chest feels tight. I've woven Matilda so intricately into the web of my life she helps hold it all together now. Without her the quiet will be paralysing, the swamp's dripping and croaking a torture. How dare Miss Edith blame me for what's clearly her own recommendation! She had no right to name me. Our conversation last week wasn't even about Michael!

Tears well as I realise this isn't just about me. If my best friend can so easily think the worst of me, others will surely do the same. Then who will buy our lamb, wool, beef or butter? Miss Edith *has* to retract her letter. When friends ignored me on Earth I had the promise of a new life on Pagussi to look forward to – here, I have nowhere new to go.

I click to conference my son's classroom at the Academy, shift back so I'm more visible in its webcam, press down my windblown hair while I wait. My fingers tremble. A ring tone trills out and suddenly I can't think what I'll say when Miss Edith answers. I should go weed my potatoes, calm down. Before conferencers, I would have had to wait. It would have taken time to order a shuttle or send a letter. Time to calm down can be good when you need to think things through. How can I wait, though, when I chance losing Matilda, and the respect of Pagussi's other traders, for no good reason?

Miss Edith answers on the next ring. She's winding a stray blonde lock around her neat high-pinned bun. Behind her, a downlight shines over a brick wall covered in children's artwork. "Oh, ah, Salee Cox?" she says, surprised. She glances over her shoulder. "Johnny and Sylvia's mother," she mutters to someone, before turning back to me. "If you could just…"

"This won't take long," I tell her. "Matilda just sent me your cmail. It says I've asked for Michael to be expelled. I thought we agreed all you would do is keep an eye on Johnny and Michael?"

"Salee, please, if you could wait while I…" She scowls at the edge of her screen, then bows her head to tap furiously into her keyboard.

"Just answer me this," I snap, "when I came to speak to you last week about Johnny, did I make an official complaint? About anyone?"

"If you could just…"

"All I asked for was your advice. I said those exact words, yes? We spoke about name-calling and how hurtful it could be, then we agreed Johnny should walk away, not punch Michael like he deserves."

"Yes, but…"

"So I don't understand why your cmail cites me as a primary complainant. Did you think Matilda and I wouldn't talk?"

"Hold on, that should do it." The line crunches into static then settles again. "Are you still there, Salee?"

"What was that?"

"You were conferencing with the whole class. We were expecting a call from Black Springs as a practical exercise. Mrs Scotter is here. You're on a private connection now."

"Mrs Cox?" the headmistress comes into view behind Miss Edith. The downlights shine through her white hair, making it translucent. She pushes wire-frame glasses up her nose, then moves her head back to focus on the screen. "Did I hear you correctly? You did not make an official complaint about Michael Taralga?" She folds her hands and waits.

Miss Edith hangs her head.

"Oh, um, no. His mother and I are friends. If I had a problem with Michael I would just speak with her. When I came to see Miss Edith it was to talk about my Johnny. Matilda can see to her own child. I didn't even mention Michael."

"Yes you did," Miss Edith snaps into action, pulling a smartpad and penstick from her apron pocket.

"No, I only spoke about Johnny. You asked if I wanted you to talk to the parents of whoever was calling him names, but I said 'no'. There are other children for Johnny to play with, and the shuttle simulator for practice. Charles and I weren't sure how best to advise him, that's all," I tell Mrs Scotter. "Despite wanting to lead others, Johnny gets so overwrought when called names. Charles told him to punch anyone who did. Perhaps that might work for older children, but Johnny is only seven. So I told him *not* to resort to punching. I only wanted to check with Miss Edith because there are always new studies on such things. She did ask who was calling Johnny names, but I said it didn't matter because it would surely be Johnny calling him names next week."

"Then you told me it was Michael," says Miss Edith, referring to her notes.

"No you said, 'so it must be a boy then', and insisted you be told so the situation 'didn't escalate'. You said that, as their trainer, you ought to know such things. I said I'd still rather not say because if all my Johnny had to do was toughen up, I could see to that."

"Then you said it was Michael."

"You already knew! Your cmail dates all the names Michael's been calling everyone, chronologically, going back weeks. Seems to me you couldn't cope with Michael yourself so used me as a scapegoat!"

Silence.

"Under the circumstances," Mrs Scotter says to Miss Edith with a sigh, "I have no choice but to suspend you, pending further investigation. I apologise, Salee," she says to me. "Miss Edith's class may join mine until this afternoon's homebound shuttle. But since it's against regulations to exceed educator-children ratios, they will have to stay home after that. There can be no further classes until a replacement trainer can be arranged from Market Base."

"You surely don't mean all the children?" I ask, leaning forward. Mrs Scotter nods.

"But the other hillsteaders, we all work." I shake my head. "We can't keep our children home for all that time. It could take weeks for another trainer to arrive."

"I'm sorry, Salee, but you've left me no choice."

The screen crackles into black silence and I'm left staring at it with my mouth open. What have I done? I never meant to cause the other hillsteaders inconvience or hardship. The whole class heard my tirade. It'll be obvious whose fault it is that the children are sent home. However poorly those hillsteaders might have thought of me because of Matilda and Michael, they'll think worse of me now, and this time it's all my fault…

Later that afternoon, Johnny and Sylvia arrive home. Their expressions say it all: embarrassment, resignation. Everyone knows the suspension of classes is down to me. By tonight, each of their parents will know it too.

I should have weeded my potatoes instead of calling Miss Edith, thought things through more, waited until I was calmer…

Friday
Tech Version 0.0.1

Midday on our hillstead is the quietest time. I step onto our hillstead's narrow verandah, and a cold wind rushes at my face, scented with damp bark and threatening drizzle. Vapour swells and shifts among the immense swamp trees at the base of our hill, as if a hover shuttle is approaching. My neighbour Matilda did say she'd visit. But the vapour merely unveils the serpent-like branches of a canopy so twisted it resembles my hair right now – knotted and wild from the wind. There's nothing except the swamp's croaking and dripping, an unforgiving wind, and a potato patch that needs weeding.

Still, I wait a little longer, staring into the swamp mist. There's been talk of making hover shuttles and even conferencers more affordable, of launching more satellites to improve cmail communication, and of stringing rope bridges between swamp trees so folk can solar-kart from one hillstead to another, to get them wherever they want to go. As it is I have no way of knowing why Matilda hasn't turned up today, not until the Academy shuttle brings Johnny and Sylvia home this afternoon. So I'll just have to assume she's got good reason for not visiting for the second time this week, and get on with my day.

I pull the hillstead's front door shut and make my way over to my potatoes. It's not as fun weeding alone, but I soon fall into a rhythm of funnelling down with my trowel to loosen soil, feeling through the warm earth for root ends, then easing the unwanted plants up and tossing them into a bucket. Each time my bucket is full, I empty it in the cowshed, pause to survey the chasm slopping with swamp between our property and Matilda's, then return to my potatoes. It's at quiet times like these I wish I'd listened to my parents.

"How will you cope alone, Salee?" my mother said before I left Earth. "If you stay here, you and Charles can live with us, or his folk – you'll have help when children come along, company, friends, contacts. Up there, you'll have no one." How right she was.

"They'll have their choice of academies here too," my father added, balancing a pipe in his mouth as always. "And we can help with money if you need it." That would have been nice. Our tiny two-roomed hillstead is barely bigger than the old settlers' shacks under the Gurra Gurra. Johnny and Sylvia are so tired of sharing with their mum and dad. Our roof leaks and some of the walls buckle if you lean against them.

"We'll build a better home," Charles promised when I arrived. He was so full of hope back then. "We'll do it together."

'Together' faded as fast as the sun that first winter, the coldest on record, and I was already pregnant. There could be no 'we' in the building of any extension – only Charles – and he had to protect the sheep from bitter rains, soaking ground and a blinding freeze that iced even his beard. Having been raised on a farm, Charles knew our priorities were to construct a sheep pen, then a cow shed and paddock. After that, we could see to our home.

Only it was spring before we knew it and my belly was so swollen and tight with life all I could suggest was planting potatoes to bring in some money, along with the butter. Maybe we could hire someone to help us build? After the baby was born, we would start saving.

That baby was Johnny, making our plans over eight years old now – and we still live in the same two small rooms, no extension, no conferencer. We had hoped friends might eventually help us build. But friendships are harder to weave across Pagussi than we thought. Matilda's just about the only one I have. What happened to her today?

As the daylight dims Johnny and Sylvia's Academy shuttle roars in the distance. I glance over my shoulder. The shuttle drops onto the Perkins' hill, then rises and drops onto Matilda's hill to deliver her son Michael. I stand and rub my hands free of dirt as it rises again and zooms toward me. It hovers over the grassy slope that drops down into the swamps, just long enough for its door to unfold and for Johnny and Sylvia to climb out. Then its door closes and it rises again, heading back to the Academy.

Johnny and Sylvia run up our slope, trying to be first to reach me for a cuddle. I try to remember whose turn it is but can't take my eyes off the envelope flapping in Johnny's hand as he runs.

"Is that from Matilda?" I call out, hopeful.

Johnny flaps it harder and nods.

Matilda and I often exchange notes this way – her passing a message to the Academy's shuttle pilot before they leave her hill in the afternoon, me sending back a reply back when the shuttle collects Johnny and Sylvia the next morning.

"Hello you two," I say, giving each of my children a brief embrace, then ushering them towards our home so I can read Matilda's note. "Go unpack and I'll be inside in a moment."

Salee,
I know I said I'd come today, but I'm still upset about a letter I received from Miss Edith on Monday morning, about Michael. Apparently you've made an official complaint about him to the academy. You really think he's bad enough to merit expulsion? No one can understand why you'd tell Miss Edith that rather than talk to me first. I trust you have good reason, and I'm sure we'll talk this Sunday. Until then don't say anything at the academy. It won't do Michael any good.
　　Matilda

Frowning, I turn into our hillstead and walk into our bedroom in a daze. How could Matilda believe I'd make an official complaint about her son, without even mentioning it to her first? She's my best friend here – I need her. Charles is gone so long each day, taking the sheep to graze... Why would I put our friendship in jeopardy?

It sounds like she's talked with others too. How many others? The Perkins?

At least I know now why Matilda didn't come to visit on Monday afternoon. She sent a message then too, saying she'd explain when she visited today. I thought perhaps she might be sick, so went on Wednesday to check on her and her turnips – only she'd taken a public shuttle to Market Base, or so her mother-in-law said with unease. Knowing how Matilda likes to punish her husband with sulking, I realise now she's been punishing me. I thought her the type of person to speak her mind when unhappy. But if 'no-speaks' is what friends here do, I'm better off without them.

"Mum, what's for dinner?" asks Sylvia.

"What are you doing?" Johnny asks from the bedroom doorway.

I wipe away a tear and pull a clean sheet of paper from the box under my bed, wave it at Johnny, then sit at our kitchen table to write. I address my letter to the Academy Board at Market Base, via Mrs Scotter, and demand Miss Edith be dismissed. She's lucky I don't have a hover shuttle, that those rope bridges haven't been strung yet, that we can't afford a conference – otherwise I'd get myself straight to the Academy or call direct and insist she be removed immediately. How dare she put this on me! She doesn't deserve even a weekend's grace! Getting her fired is the only way everyone will know I didn't do as she claims.

Sylvia peers over my shoulder and reads.

"I need you to take this to the Academy on Monday," I tell her, "hand it directly to Mrs Scotter."

"But Miss Edith's a great trainer."

"She was," I correct her, "until today."

"Better than Mrs Scotter last year," Johnny adds.

"Mum's getting her fired," Sylvia tells her brother.

"What? No, you can't!" shouts Johnny. "She's fundraising so we can get a conferencer in every classroom."

"Enough!" I snap, sealing my letter in an envelope. "You don't understand what she's done. They all have big families to help." I gesture out the window. "When their mothers fall sick, grandmothers and aunties care for them. When their homes need fixing they have grandfathers and uncles to wield hammers. We've been trying to lay down roots, so you won't have to struggle once you have families of your own. Because of Miss Edith, your father and I will be alone again, so will you. Unless I do this, you can forget that extension we've been planning!"

Sylvia starts to cry. Johnny looks away.

I should tell them I'm angry at the situation, not them, but instead find myself slamming things around as I prepare dinner. I snap at Charles too when he comes home. We're back to being the newcomers, second-line settlers. Miss Edith shouldn't just be dismissed; she should be disqualified.

Later that night I dream an imaginary conversation with Matilda, begging her to trust that I didn't make any official complaint, that I'm not that kind of friend. Her face turns into those of our neighbouring hillsteaders. They scowl at me in turn, bitter with distrust.

In the morning, I take my letter out of Sylvia's bag and re-read it. Miss Edith shouldn't get away with what she's done. I'm no one's scapegoat.

But... Matilda has asked me not to say anything, and if friendships are as important to me as I told the children they were, I should respect Matilda's wishes.

I fold up my letter and file it away. Tomorrow, Matilda and I will talk and we'll see where that takes us. If our friendship is strong enough we will stick together rather than fall apart at the first pull. And if I don't want Miss Edith training my children anymore, I can always send them to the academy at Black Springs.

Then I go to find Sylvia, Johnny and Charles. I shouldn't have spoken to them the way I did yesterday. I couldn't snap at the person I should have and all my family did was get in the way.

I apologise to each of them.

Friday
Tech Version 0.1

Midday on our hillstead is the quietest time. I step onto our hillstead's narrow verandah, and a cold wind rushes at my face, scented with damp bark and threatening drizzle. Vapour swells and shifts among the immense swamp trees at the base of our hill, near our western entry onto the Hanging Roads. Matilda's solar kart zips off the bridge and onto our grassy slope. Her engine strains as she accelerates up the hill. I wave and smile. I thought I heard her approaching through the swamp mist.

She skids to a stop just in front of me. "I thought we were friends," she yells at me, her stringy hair blowing in my hillstead's angry breeze.

"We are." I step closer, searching her face. I've never seen her this incensed before.

"Suppose you think you're better than us."

"Of course not, what are you talking about?" I don't care that her mother married one of the Taralga landers. On Pagussi it's better to be part of a large family, however notorious, than none at all. "Come in for a cup and tell me what's wrong."

She squints and pokes a finger at me. "If you had a problem with Michael, you should've come to me. Not make an official complaint to the Academy, ask for him to be expelled."

"Expelled? I've done no such thing." I rest my hands on my hips. "What's gotten into you?"

"So you didn't complain to Miss Edith about Michael last week?"

"No. I mean, yes I went to talk to Miss Edith, but not about Michael, about Johnny. *Miss Edith* mentioned Michael I think, but I certainly didn't complain about him, officially or otherwise." I let my hands drop by my sides. "How could you think that of me?" Is this what friends on Pagussi do?

"It's an official letter, Salee. Came yesterday. I would have come straight away but had to help old Mrs Formstone with her drains – you know how they overflow when it rains. The letter says your name in black and white."

"So that's it?" I flick some air away. "You simply believe what it says?"

She shrugs, mellowing slightly. "I've come to ask you face to face, haven't I?"

"Well, let me tell you, if I had that big a problem with Michael, you'd certainly know about it. What kind of friend do you think I am?"

Silence. We just stare at each other and wait for something to happen, the remains of our friendship hang between us like the web of a swamp spider – one movement and the beautiful silk might snap.

"Miss Edith has obviously lied to us both," I say after a while, crossing my arms. "We should report *her*, petition the Board to replace her."

"That wouldn't do my Michael any good," Matilda mutters, turning her kart around, "only make him stand out more. Don't say anything at the Academy. Please," she adds, seeing my expression harden, "for my sake. We'll talk more on Sunday. Miss Edith's young and inexperienced, that's for sure, but I knew this was coming." She drives off, yelling. "Bloody Michael!"

"She shouldn't get away with this!" I shout after her.

As Matilda nears the Hanging Roads thick swamp mist shifts, unveiling ivy draping between immense tree shapes. Her kart finds the wooden track then she disappears under the vapour, which darts after her with as much venom as her mood.

I stand still for a moment, listening to the irate roar of her engine fading, then storm around to the cowshed. Matilda would rather I not say anything, but I cannot leave a matter this serious alone. Miss Edith has lied, soiled my name in the process, and made my best friend doubt me, question her trust of me. On Pagussi as well as Earth, if someone's best friend doesn't trust them others won't either, and people don't do business with those they can't trust. Charles and I struggle enough as it is. I have to get Miss Edith to publically retract her letter.

No, not just that. I don't want people thinking so poorly of me!

Tears well as I imagine old Mrs Formstone tutting and shaking her head while Matilda tells her of the Academy's letter. Mrs Formstone and I might not be friends but I've always had her respect – until now.

For taking that from me, I should demand Miss Edith be dismissed, if not disqualified! How dare she lie about me!

In the cowshed, my solar kart waits loaded with butter pails ready for tomorrow's delivery to the Academy. I jump inside. If conferencers were more affordable, or there were more satellites in orbit to improve cmail communication, I'd have other options. But Matilda was right about one thing – some things are best said face-to-face. So I turn on the engine and cut across our top fields to the Academy Road on our hill's other side. Turning down the slope, I concentrate on braking, and at its steepest slow to a crawl – somewhere around here is a hidden rock slab.

Knowing doesn't help. The kart jumps when I hit the slab and rides up on one side. I thrust a hand deep into the dirt as an anchor then push against the tilt. The kart spins around my hand, skids a little as my rear wheels ride up and over the rock, then thuds back onto the ground. When I pull my hand back inside the cart, it's covered in earth clods. I shake them free, though the rest of my arm is still caked in mud. As I enter the thickening mist, a fine spray of moisture coats my face. By the time I reach the Academy I'm going to look a right mess.

Through the grey-green mist up ahead a bridge tower appears, moss climbing over its suspension wires. Silky neon-green spider webs hang delicately underneath, the only other light amid the creeping mist and slopping swamp. Either side of the bridge, the thick slough is so still and quiet today it looks more like grass than liquid, darker around the gigantic brown trunks growing thick and many from the mire ahead.

My wheels clatter noisily across the bridge's wooden slats; then I'm under the trees' coiled canopy, as well as the fine metal cage that curves over the roads to protect karts from falling bark and other debris. I slow down. A gigantic piece of rotting bark teeters on the cage's top, a gust of wind playing with its balance before bringing me its aniseed scent of decay. Nearby leaves rustle and swamp birds screech in the distance while I trundle carefully underneath, not wanting to cause the bark to fall. Charles and the children often like to force debris into the swamps, but the splash and resulting flight of winged lizards is not what I want today. When I see Miss Edith, I do not wish to be covered in their dung-smelling spit, as well as caked in mud and mist spray.

So I resist speeding up until after the first tree post, until after I've turned towards the Academy even, then I slam on my accelerator, slowing only when I round corners. The roads are made for karts, with side barriers to keep our wheels on track. But speeding around corners can make karts vibrate, which might shake my loaded butter pails free of their straps. If they fall we won't have any produce to discount the Academy's high fees. Not that we should be paying for training like this.

I suppose I should be grateful Matilda stopped by this afternoon – at least I know now the truth of this place. I'd started thinking of Pagussi as a place where friends supported each other no matter what. I was wrong. I should never have come here. I should have listened to my parents.

I rev my motor until my shirt billows, and zoom past the old settlers' shacks under the Gurra Gurra tree. Riddled with the luminescent green specks of swamp flies, sagging with age, the stilted huts were once overnight resting posts for traders, before we had the roads or shuttles. Cracked old boat hulls rot against their brittle supports, likely to snap under the next bad rains. Our hillstead is little better. We had hoped to build an extension. Last week Matilda said she had an idea about helping us. I suppose that's all on hold now…

With a huff I turn off the Gurra Gurra, past the Perkins' expansive hillstead, and zoom around the last tree post before the Academy. My motor whirls, straining as I bounce off the roads away from the swamps underneath and onto the Academy's neatly mown hill. Gripping my steering wheel, I fly up the hill track and over the swollen creek that curls close to the imposing brick school, not caring anymore if moss-scented water splashes over our butter pails. So what if they fall? I do not want Miss Edith training my children now anyway. If the Academy doesn't dismiss her, I'll send them to train at Black Springs. It's smaller and further away, but at least there they won't be taught by a selfish liar.

I park my kart beside the Academy's back service door and heave my butter pails out anyway, to pay for whatever we owe. Yanking them around feels good – one jerk, drag and roll after the other giving my anger somewhere to go.

By the time the day-end bell chimes I'm finished… and sweaty. I catch my breath and pat down my speed-frizzed hair, though my arm is still browned with dried mud patches and I stink of swamp. The mothers who can afford to use private hover shuttles to pick up their children always look so pristine, as if they haven't sped for even a moment all day. Already a group of them are eyeing me like my friends used to back on Earth. I turn away, self-conscious, until I hear the thud of little feet.

"Mother!" Sylvia yells, running at me like a bullet, her short ponytail swinging.

I catch her but it knocks me off-balance.

"Look what Miss Edith gave me!" In her hands is a notebook bound with a sprig of swamp wattle. We haven't had the money to buy her a new notebook yet. She uses Johnny's old one, the battery so drained she has to use an adaptor. "Miss Edith says it's because I'm so good at my coding." She can't stop grinning.

I crouch down and pull her warm body close. The sprig's fluffy yellow buds smell as sweet as Sylvia's hair. At least I am lucky in the children I have. They'd make me feel grateful even if Charles and I were to lose everything else.

Next it's Johnny running at me, his cheeks red and shining in excitement. "Mother, Lance wants my help building a wagon. His goats can pull us in it! Can I go tomorrow, if Father doesn't need me?"

Lance Formstone, old Mrs Formstone's youngest boy, appears by my side, dwarfing me. "Good afternoon, Mrs Cox. Mother asks if you and Sylvia wish to come also, to discuss your extension."

I frown. "How does your mother know about that?"

Lance shrugs. "Michael's mother came by yesterday. She mentioned it."

"Michael's mother mentioned it?" I ask, confused. "Matilda? Yesterday?"

Lance nods. "She said you've been wanting to build one."

"We have!" squeals Sylvia, clapping her hands. "Are we ready to build one, Mother? A bedroom for me and Johnny?"

"My father," Lance continues, "was a builder before settling out here. He said that if you could perhaps draw some sketches, it wouldn't take him long to build. In return, he'd like help with our sheep, if Mr Cox has the time."

"I..." I don't know what to say. Why would Matilda mention my troubles to Mrs Formstone yesterday when she was so upset with me? "Matilda didn't say anything to your mother about a letter?"

Lance frowns and shakes his head. "My mother was upset at breakfast, knew our drains would block with all the rain, is that what you mean? Of course she only fussed until she remembered Mrs Taralga was coming over – she fixes them up good and proper every time she visits."

"So Matilda was always planning to visit, even before it rained?"

He nods. "Last week, said she had a proposal for Father about our sheep. What shall I tell him?"

"Mother," Johnny whispers, "say yes!"

"Yes," I say, unable to fathom a reason to deprive my family of the opportunity. Could it be possible that no one else knows of Miss Edith's letter? Matilda did ask me not to say anything. Perhaps she hasn't either?

Lance and Johnny grin at each other. Sylvia glides a hand over her notebook.

"I hope you don't mind," Miss Edith's voice comes from behind us, carried in a damp breeze smelling of swamp rot. "I bought a dozen notebooks from Market Base and could think of no better student for my last one."

Standing, I turn to face her. Here is the selfish woman who ruined my friendship with Matilda, with everyone. Or so I thought...

Yesterday Matilda went to speak to Lance's mother about my extension. That was kind. My friends on Earth would never have done that.

Still, Miss Edith betrayed my trust, using a brief conversation about *my* son to threaten another boy with expulsion.

Although... Michael did put himself on that road, long before I went to speak with Miss Edith about Johnny. Matilda said so herself.

Don't say anything at the Academy, she said earlier, *Please, for my sake. We'll talk more on Sunday.*

I study Miss Edith's face. It's younger than I remember, smooth with the inexperience Matilda mentioned. She probably has less money than even Charles and I, yet here she has given her last notebook to my daughter.

"The butter," I mumble at her as I question myself, "an early delivery for Mrs Scotter. Sylvia, say thank you for your notebook."

I nudge her into speaking. Instead she throws her arms around Miss Edith's legs, grinning with the satisfied affection children have for good trainers. It's enough to melt me. Moments ago, I was doubting my home, my friendships, my choices. I was resigned to struggling through alone; again. Yet now... could there be friends on Pagussi after all? Tears build at the thought.

Miss Edith rubs Sylvia's back, then says farewell and heads back inside.

I let her go. Until now, she's been a good trainer, for my children at least.

"Goodbye, Sylvia!" one of her friends calls out, climbing into the Academy shuttle my children usually catch too.

Sylvia doesn't reply, just climbs into our kart and asks me: "Can I drive home?"

"Aren't you going to say goodbye to Eva?" I ask, strapping her in.

Sylvia pouts. "We're not friends anymore. She took me off her play list."

"What 'play list'?"

"If you're on it, she'll play with you. If you're not, she won't."

I turn and look at Eva, who's still smiling and waving, hoping to catch Sylvia's attention. Clearly whatever went on between them earlier is over as far as Eva is concerned. "Wave back," I tell Sylvia.

"Why?"

"Because one disagreement doesn't mean you're not friends anymore," I tell her, and realise the same is true of myself. "Disagreements can be resolved. Don't be so reactionary. Quick now, wave to her before she goes, so she knows from your smile you're still friends."

"But she's *not* my friend anymore."

"Are you sure about that?" I ask, climbing into the kart and thinking about Matilda. The web of our friendship might have blown in a swamp wind, but it did not break. Perhaps that is what friendships here on Pagussi do?

Johnny swings in beside me.

Sylvia reverses our kart, aims at the roads that will take us home, then pauses, pondering something.

A moment later she releases the brake and glides slowly downhill. As we cross the creek, she glances behind her. "Eva!" she calls out, and waves.

Zena Shapter writes from a castle in a flying city hidden by a thundercloud, creating what-if worlds and adventures. She's the winner of eleven national writing competitions, including a Ditmar Award and the Australian Horror Writers' Association Award for Short Fiction. Her work has appeared in numerous online and print venues including the Hugo-nominated 'Sci Phi Journal', 'Midnight Echo', 'Award-Winning Australian Writing' (twice), and 'Antipodean SF'. Reviewer for Tangent Online Lillian Csernica has referred to her as a writer who "deserves your attention". Upcoming publications include a dark fantasy story "Made" in the "Let Us In" anthology by US publishers Time Alone Press; a science fiction middle grade novel "Into Tordon" (co-authored under the pseudonym Z.F. Kingbolt) by MidnightSun; and her novel "Towards White" will be published by the International Fantasy Writers' Guild in 2017. She's the founder and leader of the Northern Beaches Writers' Group, a book creator and mentor, creative writing tutor, movie buff, traveller, wine lover and all round story nerd.

Aiko And The Tiger

Kylie Pfeiffer

Quarantine Policy 2070.01.23: To prevent contagion and protect individuals and the community, colonists shall be isolated and/or quarantined at the discretion of government officials.

The tiger curves over Aiko's body. His tail flicks over her shoulder blades, his liquid torso sweeps down her left side and dagger-like teeth protrude from the gaping jaw hovering near her belly button. He's prowling down a mountain, claws fully extended... eyes angry... hunting...

Aiko's right hand strokes the tiger's head in lazy circles.

She admires the tatbots' work. At midnight she'd injected the thousands of pigment altering nano-robots into her bloodstream. Their first task was to reverse the pigmentation of her existing tattoo; birds in flight swirling up from her dark strip of pubic hair, over her belly to her breasts. The tatbots penetrated the cells of the epidermis, switching pigment production from black back to normal, leaving the skin bare and china-doll white again. She no longer feels any connection to the whimsy that created that image.

The tatbots' second task was to render the tiger.

His image took her several days to design and many hours to program. Even in the dim light of her three by three metre quarantine cubicle, Aiko can see it's her best work yet. A grim smile tugs at her mouth, but there's no pleasure in it.

The tiger will give me strength.

She imagines his jaw stretching impossibly wide, teeth yellowed and sharp, clamping down on her abdomen, ripping out the thing growing inside her, releasing her from the hold it has on her body.

But the tiger is just a tattoo and his jaw stays fixed in one position.

Aiko's gaze drops to the hard concrete, its cold penetrating her bare feet. Her head is impossibly heavy. Tears pool on her lashes until their weight draws them down to spill in dark splashes, tiny droplets radiating out. Her breath shudders in and out. She steps to the mirror, putting her cheek against its coolness and resting her palms beside her face.

"Please." Her voice is tiny, far away. "Let me out." She slaps her hands against the mirror, once, twice, but it won't make any difference.

Every day for the last ten weeks she's spoken to the mirror.

At first she'd tried reasoning with it but the answering silence had left her alone with her anger. Two weeks in she'd tried to break the mirror and everything else in the room with a chair, rampaging and screaming and smashing until she was exhausted and had collapsed on the floor. She'd awoken tucked tightly beneath the blankets on her bed. Her head had thrummed with a thick syrupy feeling and her hands and feet had felt distant, controlled by someone else. She figured she'd been sedated. The mirror reflected back at her, unbroken, mocking. The smashed chair had disappeared and still not been replaced.

She can't quite recall when she'd started pleading with the mirror. Her days confined in the cubicle blur into an interminable sameness, nothing to differentiate one from the next.

But at least now she has the tiger.

"Please. I just want to go for a walk." Her breath leaves a fog on the mirror. Trailing a finger through the moisture she doodles aimlessly, stepping sideways to create another drawing patch when the first is filled in.

The mess of scribbles reminds her of jungle she's seen in archived nature footage. Documentaries made when people lived on the surface. Jungle vines hiding tigers.

She finds a mist free area and stares at her eyes; dark orbs underscored by bruised-looking crescents. Aiko imagines someone directly behind her reflection staring back at her, contemplating the same view, the same tired eyes, only in reverse. She lifts her chin.

"The tiger will give me strength."

Dragging her feet she crosses to the bed, her back bowed, eyelids heavy. She lies down and pulls the covers over her head, comforted by their weight and warmth. She ignores the food waiting on a tray by the door. Sleep doesn't come quickly.

#

Population Control and Genetic Diversity Policy 2090.03.14: To prevent inbreeding, maintain genetic diversity and cap population growth, medical nano robotic devices (medbots) are now mandatory for all colonists. This policy supersedes contraception rationing and offspring tax policies.

"Good morning. I'm Doctor Lafayette." The voice is professional. Remote. The well-manicured hand the doctor extends is cool and papery in Aiko's hot, sweaty grip. The doctor lets go and wipes her palm down her starched white lab coat, a little frown crinkling her brow. "As you know, you've been called in to discuss surrogacy rotations."

"Ah…" A heavy lump falls to Aiko's stomach. "No. The message said it was a medbots procedure. Nothing about surrogacy rotations." She looks at the communications band on her wrist, as if the now blank screen will confirm her words.

Doctor Lafayette stares at her and sighs. "You are aware that all women between the ages of eighteen and thirty-five can be called upon at any time to participate in surrogacy rotations?" She sounds bored. She must have recited this speech a thousand times before.

Aiko feels all of eight years old again. "Yes. I'm aware of the colony's policy."

"And you're twenty-five and have yet to be called upon."

"Yes, I know this. The message just said I was to come to the clinic for a medbots procedure. There's been some kind of mix up."

The doctor waves her hand in apparent frustration, dismissing the conversation. "You've been compulsorily reassigned for an indefinite period. Effective immediately."

Aiko doesn't want to think about reassignment. "Surely…"

"Your medbots will be extracted to prevent pregnancy termination."

Aiko shifts uncomfortably in her seat. She tries to recall all she knows about medbots. Their programming is highly specific: search and destroy infectious diseases, foreign matter, corrupt tissue or mutating cells, and terminate unauthorised pregnancies. Nothing she's learnt suggests they would attack an authorised embryo.

"But there are plenty of surrogates on the lower levels. They wouldn't survive without medbots."

Doctor Lafayette shuffles some papers, her mouth stretched thin. "Correct. In general, surrogates do not require medbots to be removed. But the embryo I will implant today has been enhanced."

Enhanced?

The doctor takes her silence as some kind of consent or understanding.

"After implanting the embryo you will be transferred to the quarantine bunker. This will protect you from disease and recontamination by medbots; they're programmed to transfer between hosts if they detect a requirement to do so."

"I don't understand."

"It's very simple." Doctor Lafayette's thin smile doesn't extend to her eyes. She circles the desk and puts a hand on Aiko's shoulder. "You're to be impregnated with a special embryo that's taken years of research and trials to develop. The embryo is valuable. Medbots will destroy it." Her grip on Aiko's shoulder tightens. "Ergo removal of medbots."

"But what about my health? I could die."

"The risk is acceptable given future benefits to the colony."

The doctor presses something sharp into the soft flesh of Aiko's arm. Pain blossoms then the floor tilts. Aiko falls into the doctor's side, her vision momentarily losing focus. Panic claws at her insides; she can't move, can't talk.

Doctor Lafayette speaks softly into her ear. "It's just a mild sedative to shut you up. I don't have time for any more trivial questions." She straightens up and calls out, "Get in here. Place the patient on the bed."

Rough hands slide under Aiko's armpits. She's lifted and dragged, ragdoll-like, and deposited onto the bed. A man moves into her field of view. He's tall and broad, with hard-muscled shoulders stretching the fabric of his black shirt. He picks up her legs and arranges them in line with the rest of her body.

"Remove her clothing."

The man cuts Aiko's dress and underpants from her. He balls them up and deposits them in a bin.

Doctor Lafayette sweeps a handheld device over Aiko's naked body. "This calls your medbots to assemble. They will lock together and stimulate the formation of a blister." She prods a lacquered nail into the arch of Aiko's left foot. "There."

A swarm of bees settles in Aiko's head, angry, trying to escape. She tries to yell but only a strangled noise and trickle of saliva emerge.

The device emits a series of loud beeps.

"Finished." The doctor swabs the skin then stabs a syringe into the blister. She pulls on the plunger and the barrel fills with a reddish-yellow fluid. "Move her into the stirrups."

Aiko closes her eyes, but she can't escape the knowledge of what the man's doing. As if in response to the limpness of her body, all her senses are heightened, every sound and touch amplified. He pulls her to the end of the bed, his calloused hands rough around her ankles. Her short hair trails behind, every follicle irritated by the coarse fabric covering the mattress. One by one, her feet are placed into a stirrup and straps are tightened to prevent her unresponsive legs spilling out.

Trying to shut out the doctor's voice, Aiko imagines she's walking through a forest, one she's seen on an archived documentary. Dappled sunlight filters to the forest floor but otherwise it's dark and cool beneath the canopy. The narrator's voice is calm and soothing, washing over her. The air is full of the twittering of birds. Large blinking eyes of animals that no longer exist stare at her from their leafy hiding spots. It's a world she'd give anything to see and experience. Just to feel a fresh breeze on her skin and hear it rustling through leaves...

A hand slaps her face. "I said pay attention. Keep your eyes open." Doctor Lafayette points a latex covered finger at her. "I am required to describe the procedure before performing it." She holds something in front of Aiko, too quickly for her to see. "I will insert this tube into the vagina and through into the uterus, where I will deposit the embryo to implant."

The doctor moves around to stand between Aiko's legs, switching on and positioning a bright light. Aiko feels hands on her then the chill of cold metal sliding inside, pinching uncomfortably. As the doctor adjusts and repositions the tube, each movement causes a sharp pain.

Doctor Lafayette stands abruptly, rips off her gloves and throws them in the bin. She looms over Aiko. "Hopefully I won't see you until the c-section." She addresses the man, "The patient's yours," and leaves the room.

Nausea rolls through Aiko. Her body heaves and vomit sticks in her throat. The smell stings her eyes.

Without comment the man unfastens the straps holding her legs, and turns Aiko onto her side, letting the acrid liquid run from her mouth and nose. He runs a cloth under warm water then wipes her face and the bed. He carefully threads her arms into a blue gown.

Aiko tries to talk again but her lips and tongue won't work.

"You'll be alright when the sedative wears off." He gives her a smile. "I've gotta take you to the quarantine bunker now." He finishes tying the gown and lifts her into a wheelchair, securing a strap over her chest to prevent her from falling out. Her head lolls forward; he pulls it back and rests it on the chair back.

A sliding door whooshes open and closed as they exit the clinic. The man continues to talk, but his voice and Aiko's vision fade in and out.

"...under constant supervision... gestational confinement... we've lost embryos... isolation is the only..."

The floor jumps. They're in a lift with a shiny metal interior; unlike those in the lower levels, it's not cramped, filthy or smelling of stale body odour.

"I'm your supervising paramedic... weekly check ups... and take you to the doc if..."

They're in a wide, high ceilinged corridor. It's empty, well lit and clean, and seems to go on forever. The wheelchair's rubber tyres squeak on the polished concrete floor. Blood pounds at Aiko's temples. A shaking comes from deep inside, making her teeth tap against each other.

"...things are in this cupboard." He points at a grey door. They're in a sparsely furnished room now. He reads off his comms band. "Five black dresses, nine pairs... pair sandals... a laptop and two vials of tatbots. No communication allowed… mirror is a one-way observation panel…"

He releases the band over Aiko's chest and her body slumps against him. He lifts her and places her on the bed.

"You'll probably sleep for twelve… food will be waiting when… make sure you eat it. It'll help with the nausea as the sedative wears off."

He smooths the blankets down and tucks her in so tightly she feels strapped down again.

"I'll see you in a week for the check up."

Then he's gone.

#

Entitlements Policy 2065.07.01: To reflect colony buy-in differentials, upper and lower level entitlements, restriction procedures, and refugee intake processes are set out herein.

"In headline news, the latest attack on Colony B's solar array by heavily armed insurgents has disrupted power supply and left residents sweltering."

The newsreader's voice crackles out of Aiko's comms band. She moves her ear closer to the small speaker.

"Temperatures in the lower levels are now hovering around thirty-six degrees Celsius with ninety per cent humidity. Geothermal production has been ramped up to meet power shortfalls.

"Amid fears a full blown attack is imminent, patrols by Surface Operations Special Forces have been increased and defences tightened around ventilation shafts and the damaged arrays.

"The attackers escaped from the Birdsville Refugee Camp after a series of violent protests earlier in the week. The SOSF have confirmed the escapees are descendants of climate change sceptics who were refused entry into underground bunkers when surface habitation of Earth became unfeasible.

"A government official has restated that conditions in surface camps are meeting standards, stressing that overcrowding in all levels of the colony prevents any refugees from being accepted at this time.

"And in other news…"

Aiko switches off the newsfeed. "As if we need you to tell us it's hot and crowded down here…" She swipes at the sheen of sweat on her forehead.

"Did you hear they're not restricting power consumption on the upper levels?" The muffled voice comes from the bunk bed immediately above Aiko.

"They never restrict anything on the upper levels." Aiko grimaces. But what good does whinging do? "What are you up to tonight Moesha?"

A swathe of long brown hair and a grinning face appears over the side of the mattress. "I've been meaning to talk to you about that. I've got a date."

"Ah, so you'd like me to leave."

Moesha continues to grin and raises one eyebrow. "Either that or you could join us. You've met him. Blond. Fit. Goes to the gym."

Aiko doesn't pay much attention to others when she's working out. She smiles. "Thanks for the offer, but I'll make myself scarce."

Moesha looks disappointed. "I told him you were a tattoo artist; that you specialise in extinct animals. I mentioned your birds. He wants to check them out and discuss getting a design prepared."

"I'm sure he does. Next time I'm working, send him down to the markets."

"Oh, alright." Moesha's head disappears and she bangs a hand on the bed above her. "You'll stay, won't you Camille?"

"Sure. Nothing better to do." Camille's voice is sleepy.

Moesha's comms band beeps. "He'll be here in five. Better get your clothes on and get out of here Aiko. If he sees you like that he'll try and persuade you to stay!"

Aiko laughs. The unrelenting heat and humidity have made even the lightest of clothing uncomfortable to wear. She puts on running shorts and a singlet, grabs her sneakers and presses her palm against the panel by the door. It slides open, letting in a gush of stale, muggy air even hotter than that in their two by three metre cubicle.

"I'll see you tomorrow. Enjoy your night, ladies."

Looking left and right along the narrow corridor Aiko waits until a gap appears in the foot traffic. Her bare feet stick to the grimy concrete floor; she wishes she'd taken a moment to put her shoes on.

The heat has driven more people than usual out of their cubicles. The moving masses are funnelled to the centre of the passageway, pressing against each other. Hawkers offering black market products operate from the edges, their wares on display: fans, alcohol, drugs, flesh. The air is thick with sweat and anticipation.

To conserve power, only one in four lights are functioning. It makes the dirty grey passage appear even grottier. The filtered fresh air that normally pours out of ceiling vents is now little more than a trickle. Long before Aiko reaches her destination, parallel streams of sweat flow either side of her spine.

The gym is empty. Using the terminal, Aiko selects climate, elevation and view components from the list on offer. She laces up her sneakers, waiting for the sensory nanobots to be programmed. They're ready for injection in under a minute.

On the treadmill, Aiko places the vial against the smooth skin of her forearm and depresses the button, injecting the tiny robots into her bloodstream. The sting makes her smile. Within moments the nanobots have travelled to her brain to alter auditory, visual and tactile messages her cortex is receiving.

Her vision blurs momentarily then Aiko stands in a light, cold rain. Smooth, straight trunked eucalypts surround and rise above her, their canopies engulfed in low cloud. A dirt track rises sharply in front, heading up a mountain ridge. Water drips constantly, tap dancing on the layers of leaves and twigs on the ground. She shivers as the frigid air touches her exposed skin. She smooths down the flush of goose bumps on her arms with pleasure.

"Sync."

At Aiko's command, the treadmill links to the sensory nanobots in her cerebral cortex, automatically adjusting incline and rotational speed to match both her visuals and running stride. She settles into a smooth, effortless gait, the heat around her forgotten.

Her brain, tricked by the tiny robots, is now completely lost in another place, another time, another climate. The deception usually gives Aiko's thoughts freedom to drift, but today they stubbornly keep returning to one point, pouring water onto a seed of discontent, lodged deep within her.

She increases her running pace.

The seed formed years ago, when an eight-year-old Aiko listened to bunker history lessons at school. Her teacher revered the system separating upper and lower level inhabitants, waxing lyrical about the foresight of the first colonists. It sat uncomfortably with Aiko then. She couldn't understand why living in a smaller room should change how she was treated and what she was able to do.

Now Aiko better understands how the inequities came to be. Each small change had seemed reasonable, beneficial even, within the context it was introduced. Each incremental loss of civil liberties had gone unnoticed, but the sum total was startling. How could it possibly be right to determine a person's future based on a test at the age of three? Or require any female living in the lower levels to carry an embryo that wasn't her own? Or assign only labour intensive and menial jobs to the lower levels?

The sharp edges of her thoughts open old wounds, releasing a toxic combination of frustration and self-pity. With renewed vigour Aiko attacks the steep mountain track, her breathing now heavy. Cold rain slants into her face, each drop an icy sting.

She shakes her head, trying to obliterate her self-pity with thoughts of Earth's surface. How could people have survived up there for so long? Footage of refugee camps is rarely shown. They look appalling but the general consensus is that conditions are far worse than depicted and 'heavily-armed insurgents' are actually starving refugees trying to get the colony's attention. But the only attention they get exits the barrel of a semi-automatic at twice the speed of sound.

Aiko wishes she could grant them refuge, but her voice is drowned beneath a tide of differing sentiment. Almost every upper and lower level inhabitant votes against the annual refugee intake; the former to protect their way of life, the latter because where would anyone else fit? She can't understand how their decisions don't leave raw spots on their psyches.

Spiking rage sends a hit of adrenalin into Aiko's bloodstream. She pushes herself even harder up the steep hill, her legs and arms pumping at full speed. A low noise intrudes on her anger but Aiko ignores it and keeps running.

The beeping becomes insistent, rising in pitch and frequency but Aiko just runs faster. Then a resounding *crack* shatters the air, splintering the mountain vista; the treadmill decelerates abruptly and the forest disappears. The gym and oppressive heat return, smashing into her body. The sensory nanobots have switched off cortical stimulation; they're programmed for immediate shutdown if any of the host's vital signs approach a critical level.

With the chill mountain air gone, Aiko takes stock of her body. Her mouth is dry and breathing ragged. Her heart hammers in her rib cage. Fatigue and lactic acid have claimed her muscles. She smashes a fist into the machine's display, not ready for reality to return; the transition back is always difficult, leaving an ache that has nothing to do with strenuous exercise. Exhaustion claims her mind in thick nothingness, burying her thoughts again, deep below the point where they cause pain.

She steps off the treadmill with trembling legs. The water from the drinking fountain is warm and leaves a metallic taste in her mouth. Aiko lets the stream run over her face and head then stands to let it trickle over her torso.

It takes her a while to notice the pulsing green light on her comms band. She taps to activate the new message and reads:

MEDBOTS PROCEDURE SCHEDULED
REPORT TO CLINIC AT 0900 2165.11.20
ATTENDANCE MANDATORY
CONFIRMATION REQUIRED

"In two weeks..." Aiko frowns. Her annual medbots check and reprogramming was earlier this year, only seven months ago.

She shrugs and confirms the appointment. The one time she'd failed to do so, her work permit had been cancelled indefinitely. It had taken three months to get it reinstated and by that time her roommates were sick of sharing food rations. The constant indebtedness had made Aiko's skin crawl. Worse though was the newfound awareness of her friends' true depths of compassion.

#

Emergency Procedure Policy 2120.12.13: To ensure the whereabouts of colonists are known during emergencies, medbots will henceforth link to a central computer system, allowing tracking of individuals in real time.

The cold lubricant hits her skin, making it recoil and jump. The paramedic presses the ultrasound probe into the gel and glides it over Aiko's swelling belly.

In the last week, she's spent hours simply looking at it, fascinated by the shiny, taut distension it's become, patterned with bifurcating tracks of purple-blue veins. But she keeps her consideration distant and mechanical; time progresses, belly expands… to acknowledge anything deeper lets in unwanted thoughts of what's growing inside her, implanted there without her consent.

The tiger will give me strength.

His mouth has stretched wider as her belly's expanded; he looks fiercer now, more dangerous.

The paramedic homes in on his target, pressing the probe firmly against the skin when he locates the rapid fluttering heartbeat.

"There it is," he says. "I'll turn on the speakers."

Aiko wishes he wouldn't, but she smiles and nods, trying to feign interest in the staccato drumming. But every week she has the same reaction when he finds the incontrovertible proof that the thing growing inside her is still alive and well.

She pushes aside her disgust and contempt. "Is it… healthy?"

He looks directly at her, still pressing the ultrasound probe against her belly. "Yep. Everything's progressing well. Its limbs are in the right place and its growth rate is tracking along as expected. We couldn't hope for anything better."

Another layer of hope peels away. Aiko sets her smile in concrete and swallows.

Uncharacteristically he sits on the side of the bed. Clearly oblivious to her mood, his expression brightens, as though he's got a surprise lined up. "I've been given approval."

Aiko almost lets her smile drop. "For what?"

He chuckles. "Are you serious?" He sounds as if he's talking to someone he knows quite well.

Aiko accepts his familiarity as part of her incarceration. She only sees him once a week, but he watches her every minute of every day. By now he'd know her daily routine. He'd have witnessed all of her intimate, private moments. Whilst she feels little towards him – a sense of gratitude for relieving the monotony of isolation – she knows it's more productive to encourage conversation. She seals in her hateful barrage of thoughts. It's easier if she tells herself he's in solitary confinement too, sitting in the room on the other side of the mirror.

"Yes, I'm serious. Approval for what?"

His grin broadens. "You've asked me to let you out of your room every single day since you got in here. I now have approval to take you on a daily walk."

"Really?" Aiko sits up, pushing the ultrasound probe away.

"Don't get too excited," he warns, easing her back onto the bed. He sounds stern but his face betrays satisfaction. "We get fifteen minutes out, you stay with me, and we don't leave this level. Stop fidgeting and let me finish the check-up."

Aiko doesn't register much else until he says, "All done. Get dressed then we can walk." He turns away.

She stifles a laugh; modesty is something she gave up on twenty weeks ago. She pulls her dress back over her head, shimmying it down over her belly.

When the cubicle door opens Aiko breathes deeply. The air tastes the same but somehow it's lighter. The ceiling looks higher than she remembers it being.

They walk slowly. Aiko notices a sideways rock to her steps; not yet a waddle, more a sign of what's to come. She tries to control it, but her hips are no longer held in a rigid position.

Then she notices the quiet; it's unnaturally deep. "Where is everyone?"

"You're the only one housed on this level."

She scans the corridor. Every few metres there's another door, identical to her cubicle's entrance. "It's just you and me?"

He nods. "They lost too many embryos. Isolation reduces the chance that something will go wrong."

"How many surrogates are in the program?" Aiko keeps her tone light, conversational, interested.

"Only ten at the moment, but we can house up to twenty."

Twenty? The cramped lower levels, the pervasive stink of too many people living in too small an area crashes into her mind. What? There're twenty large, empty levels of accommodation? Aiko senses him looking at her.

"I don't know your name," she says quickly, trying to hide her anger. "If we're going to walk and talk, I'd like to know your name."

"I'm Sergeant King."

Aiko frowns. "Sergeant? You're SOSF?"

He nods.

Why are the SOSF involved in surrogacy rotations? Then a jolt of clarity hits her. Doctor Lafayette's breeding soldiers. She tries to keep her expression neutral. "The embryo's enhancements… what are they?"

"Cellular nanobots." He doesn't seem to have noticed the jump in the conversation.

Aiko's hands flutter around her throat. "You mean they're part of the cells?" Her voice is more forceful than she'd intended.

His eyes narrow. "What's the problem? The colony's been using nanos for over a century. These new ones do all the things medbots can and a whole heap of stuff that medbots can't. They optimise rates of growth, strength and recovery after injury or illness. And they're self replicating, which is a bonus. No more annual procedures."

"But how human is it?" Aiko can't keep the revulsion out of her voice.

The muscles in Sergeant King's jaw lock tight. "That's not a question you should be asking." His flat, clipped tone provides Aiko with the answer she was looking for.

It's a human-robot hybrid…

She leans against the wall, her head spinning and bile rising in her throat. He grabs her arm and starts walking her back towards the cubicle.

She stumbles. "Will it be able to breed?"

"Yeah, just like any other colonist. If it's got authorisation."

A cold sweat prickles Aiko's brow. Self-replicating nanobots, incorporated into every cell in the human body, violating reproductive cells. A man-made genetic mutation passed on to any offspring. And just like medbots, the nanos would surely link the host to a central computer system.

But for military purposes, simply tracking the soldier wouldn't be enough, would it? Manipulation and control would be a necessity. Lack of discipline would never be an issue again. Surface dwellers won't stand a chance.

Then a shiver of horror snakes down Aiko's spine. There's nothing to stop the government from introducing the enhancements to the rest of the colony...

#

Recreational Policy 2140.02.27: To promote health and wellbeing, colonists can now access superseded medbots for recreational pursuits, such as sensory modification and body art.

"You've been spending a lot of time on your laptop lately." Sergeant King lets the sentence hang, questioning but not accusatory.

Aiko looks ahead, not wanting to discuss it. She doesn't trust herself to lie convincingly.

"Are you designing another tattoo?" he asks.

"I'm thinking about it. Looking at different options."

"Will you get rid of the tiger?"

"Maybe." She could never erase the tiger. His jaw has stretched with the swelling of Aiko's belly, making his teeth disproportionately large. His eyes, which have always been hungry, have taken on a perilous hypnotic quality.

"I know it's just a tattoo but I couldn't have faced this

reassignment without him… or you." Aiko tries flattery, a favourite diversionary tactic. She's rewarded with a fiery blush up Sergeant King's neck. "Is the laptop time a problem? The coding's taking me longer than it used to and I keep changing my mind. I think it's being this pregnant." She throws her hands out sideways. "My brain's operating in a bath of treacle."

"No it's okay. Use your laptop all you want. If they weren't happy with you having it, you wouldn't." He stops walking and waits until she looks at him. His expression alters. "I need to tell you something…"

Confession? Warning?

"The cellular enhancements extend out of the foetus. They're also part of the umbilical cord and placenta."

Aiko feels as if he's assessing her. She fidgets, pulling at the dress clinging to her belly.

"If a rogue medbot entered your system it would detect the cellular enhancements in the placenta first. I haven't told you this before, as I didn't want you to worry. But every enhanced embryo we've lost through medbot contamination died because the surrogate bled out. From massive internal bleeding."

Aiko forces a smile. "Fortunately you've taken all necessary precautions to prevent that from happening." The thing inside her chooses that moment to kick her solidly up under her ribs, as if it knows she's lying. The sharp pain makes her wince and she takes a moment to get her breath back. "Do you mind if we cut the walk short today?"

Back in her cubicle she allows the sergeant to fuss over her and check her pulse. Since he was given approval for their daily walks, he's spent more and more time with Aiko, arriving earlier and lingering after their walk.

But now Aiko needs all the time on her own she can get. She yawns loudly and rubs her eyes.

He insists that she sleeps.

"I think you're right. I'll try and get some rest."

"Okay. I'll leave you to it. You can always call if you need me."

Dutifully, she lies down and closes her eyes, but rather than falling asleep Aiko lets lines of code drift through her mind. She's always found that her brain continues coding, writing and rewriting the program to specify the tatbots' assignment, even when she's not actively working on it. It's easy to lie still and let her subconscious and conscious connect, providing solutions to yesterday's unsolved problems.

After an hour, she sits up and stretches, yawns and scratches her scalp, trying to look as if she's just awoken. Food is waiting and she eats half of the meal before she can no longer resist the call of her laptop and the massive task she's set herself. Far from being indecisive and tired, Aiko has never felt more alive, more determined to accomplish something. If she's not working on the recoding of her final vial of tatbots, her insides are consumed by frustration.

Powering up the laptop she reviews her work to date. She's assigned a small number of the tatbots to render a tattoo immediately upon injection into her person. They will then rejoin the others on a holding pattern, circling in her bloodstream. Then at a time yet to be specified, but roughly ten weeks away, Aiko has programmed all of the tatbots to move into the foetus.

Her next change modifies the tatbots' recall and collection programming; Aiko doesn't want them to accumulate for recovery… ever.

Sergeant King's revelation about the placenta runs through her mind again; she has to change the timing of her plans or die. He had no reason to share that piece of information with her; she's unsure if his intent was cautionary or threatening. Regardless, his timing was perfect; now she knows she can't activate the tatbots until both the placenta and the thing growing inside her have been removed from her body.

Aiko has only one modification left to make, but how she can do it still eludes her. The functionality of the tatbots has been too severely limited, their coding too drastically changed from the medbots they were recycled from.

She closes her eyes and imagines the thousands of lines of code running over her eyelids, as though a waterfall was falling the wrong way. She plays it again and again and again and then she sees it, a weakness she can exploit. A defunct section of code, made obsolete but left in by a lazy programmer. It's the link to the search and destroy functionality of medbots that Aiko so desperately wants to apply to the thing growing inside her.

For the first time Aiko acknowledges the non-human embedded in her womb without revulsion; there's power in just knowing she has the ability to eradicate it. With grim determination her eyes open and fix on the laptop screen. Her fingers fly across the keyboard, tapping relentlessly, honing the code into a sharp edged sword ready for the killing strike.

After several hours she stops typing and sits back, rubbing a hand over the tiger's head, a gentle, affectionate movement.

The tiger will give me strength.

She rereads the last lines of new code and smiles.

The robotic growth will be born, but will never, ever get a chance to take its first step or mature into the killing machine it was designed to be.

#

Birthing Policy 2143.07.12: To protect the life of the unborn child and the surrogate, delivery by caesarean section is mandatory.

Aiko inhales then injects the vial of reprogrammed tatbots into her bloodstream. She experiences a curious mix of relief and acceptance now that it's done. Anger dissipates, flying from her like birds startled into motion. All she can do now is wait.

The tatbots' first task is executed within minutes. The simple tattoo is ready when Sergeant King arrives to prepare her for theatre.

"I have to shave you," he says, averting his gaze, a fiery red claiming his face. "Orders from the doc."

Aiko wishes she could be anaesthetised so she doesn't have to see that woman again. She lies back on the bed, lifting her gown so the sergeant can remove her pubic hair.

He's only just turned on the shaver when he laughs and switches it off again. "That's the tattoo you spent so much time on? You know your humour will be lost on the doc."

Aiko grins. Tattooed at the top of her pubic hair is a pair of scissors and a dashed line, precisely where the incision will be made later today. The words 'Cut Here' and 'Don't try this at home' appear directly underneath.

"At least I made one person laugh."

His eyes are smiling. "Did you keep the tiger?"

"Yes."

"Good." He starts up the shaver and soon Aiko's pubic mound is bare.

Sitting up, she wraps the pale blue gown more tightly around her frame. It doesn't stop the jittery sensation spiking along her nerves or the dryness in her mouth. "Is it time to go?"

Sergeant King checks his watch and nods. "We're due in theatre in twenty minutes. Are you nervous?"

Swallowing, Aiko nods, unable to speak. Lines of code stream through her mind. Doubt plays with her, teasing her into thinking she's made a mistake, messed up the reprogramming. What will happen if the tasks she's assigned to the tatbots don't work? What if the cellular enhancements destroy them?

The sergeant places a reassuring hand on Aiko's shoulder. "It's a routine operation. Don't worry."

Nothing about the day feels routine.

They leave the cubicle and the walk progresses in silence until a sense of impending loss makes Aiko speak.

"What happens after it's removed?" She stares straight ahead, unable to look at him.

"You'll be sent to recovery. The baby will be sent to the nursery. You probably won't even see it. The doc tends to remove them straight away for checking and tests."

"I meant after that."

"It hasn't been decided yet."

Aiko glances at him, frowning.

He looks pained. "You're assigned to surrogacy rotations for an indefinite period."

The thought of another nine months confined to a cubicle scrapes away Aiko's hesitation. "Will I see you after surgery?"

He smiles and relaxes. "Yeah. I'll see you in recovery and I'm responsible for your post-op care. You'll stay in the same cubicle until we hear about your next assignment."

Aiko's comforted by the knowledge that at least she won't have to meet any new people or be cared for by Doctor Lafayette. Whatever happens after the thing is removed from her, she'd prefer the sergeant to be around.

"We're here." He pushes open a wide, flexible door.

They enter a well-lit, smallish room with an operating table at its centre and a circular ring of lights positioned immediately above. There are five other people in the room; Aiko can't imagine why so many are needed, but they look busy. None of them acknowledge her.

"That will be all, sergeant." Doctor Lafayette doesn't look up from unwrapping implements on a tray next to the operating table.

A woman approaches Aiko. "Sit on the edge of the bed. That's it. I'm administering the anaesthetic today. I have to insert this into the epidural space of the spinal cord." She holds up an enormous needle then exposes Aiko's back and swabs it with something cold. "You need to stay very still. If the needle is misplaced it can result in a variety of complications, including death."

Aiko almost laughs at death being described as a complication, but remains still, not daring to breathe. The needle pierces her skin; it's not as painful as she thought it would be.

As soon as it's finished, she's told to lie down and is then covered with a sheet. A screen is erected to block her view of the lower half of her body. Nobody talks to her for several minutes, until a nurse stands beside Aiko, placing two fingers on her wrist.

"How are you feeling?" he asks, a pretend smile on his lips, as if he's rehearsing how he's supposed to act around patients.

"Um, fine. I guess."

He walks to the other end of the table near her feet. "Can you feel this?" He jabs something at her foot.

"No."

"Doctor Lafayette? The patient is ready."

The doctor turns around. Aiko looks at the ceiling. For a while nobody talks except the doctor, requesting instruments to be handed to her. Then Aiko feels her body moving as someone pushes down on her belly, assisting the extraction of the foetus.

The clatter of metal on metal – an instrument being dropped onto a tray – precedes a wail that is startling in its ferocity. The newborn puts its lungs to their first use, expressing its horror at bright light and air.

"Doctor. It's turning blue. Look at the lips and fingers."

Aiko's not sure who's spoken, but the voice is male, urgent.

"Cyanosis." Doctor Lafayette's terseness scratches along Aiko's nerves.

"Something's obstructing the airways." It's the same man again. "We should immediately check..."

"Are you telling me how to do my job?" Doctor Lafayette sounds dangerous. "The airway clearly isn't obstructed; not with that noise it's making. Imbecile."

The wail continues, high pitched and distressed. Aiko scrunches her eyes, willing her ears to close too. The pushing and shoving at her body has stopped now. Nobody pays her any attention; their focus is on the baby at the side of the room. She thinks about the incision through skin and muscle into her womb. Surely they can't have stitched her closed yet? Coldness seeps into her bones.

"Are you completely incompetent?" It's Doctor Lafayette again, irritation spiking her voice. "Don't stand there gawking. Remove the placenta. Examine it. Close her up. We don't need to lose another surrogate. I'll take the baby to ICU for assessment."

The wailing recedes but Aiko doesn't really care anymore. She's tired. She was expecting to feel elation after they removed it from her body. But her breathing is shallow and she just wants to sleep. She gives in.

A warm hand rests on her shoulder.

"Ah you're awake. I thought I heard you mumbling." Sergeant King sounds like a concerned father.

Aiko's eyelids flutter open. She's no longer in the operating theatre but doesn't recognise the space. It takes her a while to focus on his face and find his eyes.

"You're in recovery. You'll feel groggy for a while. Are you warm enough?"

Something heavy rests across her body, emanating warmth, but she realises she's shivering beneath it and shakes her head no.

"I'll put another blanket over you." He extracts one from a box off to the side and rolls it out across her. A new wave of heat penetrates slowly and her shivering subsides.

"You lost a bit of blood in the confusion after the delivery. It isn't every day they deliver a baby that turns completely blue in the space of a minute. They're still running tests, but other than his colour, he appears to be a perfectly healthy newborn…" His gaze is uncomfortably direct.

Aiko blinks. *He knows…*

"What did you do?" A small crease appears between his eyes.

"I wanted to…" Aiko's voice is dry and flaky like old parchment. She swallows. "I really wanted to kill it. More than anything I've ever wanted in my life, I wanted to make sure that it would never grow up." She tries to sit up but pain stabs at her abdomen.

"Lie back." He injects a clear substance into a valve on the drip line at her side. "This will help the pain." He waits.

"I reprogrammed the tatbots." Aiko can't work out if the flood of relief is from confession or the substance Sergeant King gave her. "It would have worked too; that thing would have died."

"He's not going to die?"

She shakes her head. "Not from what I've done anyway."

"The doctor would have had you killed."

"That was a secondary concern." She extracts an arm from under the heavy blankets and rubs her forehead. "For a while I would have welcomed it."

"What changed?"

"I couldn't bring myself to kill it. It's still a human. Besides, killing that child won't change anything. There're still plenty of surrogates and plenty more test tube embryos infected with nanobots. The program will go on regardless. People will be mechanised and controlled and used to kill other people who just want a safe place to live. It's not all that different from what we do now, is it?"

The sergeant shakes his head but his neutral expression leaves Aiko filled with doubt.

"So what have you done to him? Why is he blue?"

"It was my only form of protest." She tries to edge away from the sergeant. "I haven't hurt him. I created an irreversible full body tattoo. Right now he looks entirely blue but when he's fully grown the detail will appear."

"Into what? Another tiger?"

"He might look striped for a while, but no, it's not a tiger." She smiles. "It's words. Just words…" *Imprinted on the skin of a half-human killing machine.*

Aiko rubs a hand over the tiger's head on her belly.

The tiger will give me strength.

#

Communication Policy 2080.11.11: In response to disorderly conduct, civil disobedience and property damage, all communications require authorisation by government officials. Failure to comply will result in removal of privileges or in extreme cases expulsion from the colony.

I brought you into this world, a subterranean labyrinth of grime and privation.

I did not create you, but I chose to let you live when all I wanted was for you to die.

I will never meet you. So instead I've marked you, leaving this message for a future you.

Your creators intend for you to be a hunter.

The unfortunates who survive on Earth's surface wait patiently for the day they can enter our bunkers and escape the raging storms, empty bellies and constant reminders of their own mortality.

When they can no longer wait and come knocking at our door, you will be sent to hunt them down with extreme prejudice.

We will justify their deaths to protect our own way of life.

Earth's entire population was never going to be saved; it was only ever meant to be a select few. The leftovers of the human race weren't meant to survive. Yet they did.

We have technologies that could make their lives easier, fill their bellies and provide a reprieve from the ever-vigilant and opportunistic eye of death.

Yet we continue to kill them. Why?

You are part robot, designed for control and manipulation, programmed for lethal force. You will pass this on to any offspring you have.

You may never have a choice in how you respond to your controllers.

But with hope I let you live. Hope that when the time comes you will have a choice. Hope that the human in you will choose to help and not destroy.

Kylie Pfeiffer is an author who writes for older children, adults, and anyone in between. She loves to entertain her readers, but also wants to make them think. She has co-authored two award-winning teen fiction books, 'A Dolphin for Naia' and 'Rider & the Hummingbird', and recently received a highly commended for her BezerkaCon 2016 short story submission, 'Hide and Seek'. Kylie is currently working on a number of independent and collaborative writing projects.

The Instructions

J E Gaulton

The knock on the door startled Jo. She put down her pen and stood up.

"This'd better be it. It's been weeks since I ordered it." She walked out of her office and down the stairs. Peeking through the spy hole, Jo saw the courier standing at the door with a large parcel.

"Yes!" She pulled open the door with such force it crashed against the wall.

"Ma'am, you'll need to sign here," the courier said, thrusting an electronic signature device at her.

Jo scribbled her name and grabbed at the parcel.

"It's pretty heavy," the courier warned.

"No worries," Jo said, heaving the parcel through the door. "Thanks."

She closed the door and laid the large parcel on the floor. Racing to the kitchen she grabbed a knife and ran back, slitting the tape down both sides. There it was, nestled in a bed of styrofoam beads. Jo pulled it out, kicking the outer packaging away.

She tore open the wrapping and pulled out all the pieces, laying them carefully to one side. She rummaged about and found the assembly instructions – seventeen pages worth.

"Bugger that," Jo said, scanning the first few pages and picking up the allen key.

Step 1: Pre-assemble the limb part 765-28977 with part 765-28990, by following the instructions for each section.
Step 2: Attach these to the body, using part 27971 and 28971.
Step 3: Once connected, proceed to assembly and mount limb part 700-00235 to 721-00013, ensure you do not tighten too much as they need to have freedom of movement.

Jo growled to herself. She flicked through the pages and looked at the finished product. "Oh man that's gorgeous," she moaned.

Glancing down at the parts scattered on the floor she picked up the next bit and frowned at the engraved number #800-28990.

"So where do you go?" Turning the pages again she found the illustration and manoeuvred the part into place, and quickly tightened the joint screw.

Step 6: Place the pre-assembled mounts as shown in figure 5. Orient the body so that the sets of three holes are visible.
Step 7: Use the 7/64" ball end, Allen wrench to screw in the (3) 3/8" socket-head cap screws. Do not over tighten socket heads.
Step 8: Now you have the limbs attached, raise to a seated position and insert the motherboard into the torso.

Jo scrambled around and tugged and pulled it into a sitting position. She found the hatch and opened it ready for the motherboard. She picked up the board and looked at it; she was amazed at how something so small could run something so large. She placed it inside and looked back at the instructions.

Step 9: Connect the (2) long, three-pin cables to each of the quadrant encoder boards. Be sure to match the corresponding colours to the motherboard, to ensure smooth movement.

Sighing, Jo connected the cables and dropped the allen key to the side. Standing up she stretched and walked into the kitchen. Grabbing the jug she filled it and turned it on.

"A nice cuppa," she said, looking at the mess of parts strewn across her landing. The jug switched itself off, and she quickly made her tea. Walking back to the landing, she looked down at the half-built machine. She bent down and placed the cup on the floor. Picking up the head assembly, Jo ran her fingers tenderly against the mechanism. She picked out the supporting joint and studied it. Cautiously placing them both back on the floor she looked at the instructions again.

Step 12: Assemble head, and support joints. Insert (8) 4-40 x 5/8" oxide screws from the support into the head, fasten using the ½" screws, do not over tighten.
Step 13: Attach head and support to body using (6) 3-40x 2/8" jointed screws, position head correctly.
Step 14: Connect the (2) optical cables into the headspace, and attach to the orbital optics, position into the hole.

"Fuck, fuck, fuck," Jo muttered angrily under her breath as the optic cable slipped from her fingers. She sucked her finger, and using a small plier-like tool, attached the cable to the right orbital.

Step 15: Locate the cranium hatch and insert the two memory chips. Follow instructions supplied with chips.

Jo stared at the floor. Where are they? Searching through the remaining parts she pushed the exo-derm container to the side, where she found two pouches. Opening the first, she found the two chips, but no instructions. Opening the other bag, she looked in and giggled.

"That looks fun!" She placed the geni-pouch reverently to one side. Picking the two chips out of the bag she could see they were coloured. Assuming they would match the coloured dots in the cranium hatch, she inserted the chips into place using the ¼" tool that looked a lot like a pair of tweezers.

Step 20: Locate the umbilicus plug, attach the 1/4" power cable to the umbilicus and insert into the torso. On position – Innie, off position – Outtie.

Step 21: This machine uses inbuilt rechargeable batteries, these are already encased in the body, these cells should be ready to use with up to four hours of charge available. With each use the batteries will self-charge, the longer and harder you use the more charge generated.

Jo's skin tingled with anticipation at the thought of how long and hard she could work this machine. Picking up the geni-pouch she extracted the three items; two small egg-shaped objects and a thin sausage length one. They were already covered in a skin of exo-derm, pink and rubbery to the touch. Placing them gently into the lap of the machine, Jo picked up the instructions.

Step 30: Remove contents of the geni-packet. Using the 1/2" tool, attach the shaft and testal cables to the torso. Manoeuvre the three exo-extremities and connect using the smoothing tool. The join will disappear when the full exo-derm covers the frame.

Step 31: Lay the machine flat on a smooth surface, remove the exo-derm from its container. Starting from the base of the machine gently pull it over the endo-skeleton of the unit. Be sure to smooth the exo-derm on the extremities. When you reach the mid-riff, carefully pull the geni through the hole provided and using the smoothing tool, and a forefinger, mould the exo-derm around the geni until the joint has been sealed.

Step 32: Continue up the body and carefully dress the limbs. At the head support, follow the same instructions as the geni.

It was almost done. Lying on the floor in front of her was a machine so exquisite it took her breath away. She delicately moulded the casing around the head support, stroking it upwards to blend and merge seamlessly. Pulling the cranial skin from the container Jo gently pulled it over the head, pressing firmly around the endo-skeleton.

Step 34: Remove the head covering from the perma-sealed bag. Brush the covering before moulding into the cranial cap.

The head covering felt like satin, long black satin. Jo ran the fibres through her fingers and pressed it up against her face and inhaled. She'd ordered a short hair covering but, as she could see from the instructions, they always supplied long so that the owner could cut the cranial covering to how they liked.

She got up and raced to the bedroom, grabbed her brush and went back to the machine. She heaved it back into a sitting position and with trembling hands brushed the long black fibres until they shone. Placing the covering on the cranial cap, she melded it with the edges of the head covering of the exo-derm. Jo sat back and stared, admiring her handy work.

Step 40: Carefully lift the machine to a standing position. If necessary, lean against a flat surface. Once in position, ensure all extremities are in place and, in the correct layout as shown in the instructions.
Step 41: To test, follow the manual to ensure the smooth running of your unit.

Jo bent down and picked up the small manual entitled "Running

Instructions", turning to the first page she read the first set of instructions.

Step 1: To turn on press the umbilicus in.

She leant forward and pressed at the stomach of the machine; there was silence. Worried, Jo looked at the machine and bent down to check she had fully pressed the button. A quiet thump-thump, thump-thump reverberated near her ear.

Step 2: Once powered up, you should hear a steady beat 1-2, 1-2.

Jo straightened and looked fully at the unit then read the next step.

Step 3: Issue the following command responses: "ST-AM-1975, install ownership runtime script."

Once she'd said the first command and the unit's orbital optics opened – they were dark brown and looked like liquid chocolate – it shifted slightly and moved away from the wall, taking a step towards her.

Step 4: "Run motor diagnostics, and install skin receptor coding."

Slowly, the unit lifted each limb, flexing and unflexing. It turned its head left, right, up and down. Blinking its orbital covers, it reached out towards her and ran an exo-derm covered digit down her cheek. Jo shuddered. It felt warm and slightly calloused.

Step 5: "Run vocal response systems and memory triggers."

The unit looked at Jo. "The quick brown fox jumped over the lazy dog," it said. Its deep baritone voice was sending thrills through her body. The unit turned its head from side to side and then back at Jo. "Name me."

Jo stared at the unit; she swallowed convulsively as the brown eyes stared at her.

"Name me," it said again, stepping closer to her, it placed a hand against her breast and cocked its head to the side. "Name me."

Jo took a deep breath. "Rylan, I name you Rylan."

Rylan smiled. "You are?"

"Jo, I'm Jo."

"Hello, Jo."

Jo's heart beat faster. Rylan stared. He glanced down at her neck, watched the beat of her pulse quicken.

"Am I doing that to you?" he asked.

"Yes, yes you are," she said breathlessly.

"What would you like to do now?"

"I… I…"

"Come." Rylan held out his hand. "Where?"

Jo placed her quaking fingers into his, as warm, calloused fingers folded around hers. "Upstairs, end of the hall."

They turned hand in hand, walked up the stairs and down the hall to the bedroom. Rylan pushed open the door and gently pulled Jo to him.

"Mine," he said, as he leant down and kissed her neck.

"Oh God, yours," Jo said, eyes closing.

Rylan lifted his head and smiled; his eyes flicked as his tongue traced the pulse beating rapidly at her neck.

"The bed," she breathed.

But he did not move, Jo opened her eyes and looked into his, they flickered and flashed. Taking a deep breath she commanded. "The bed."

Rylan moved, closing the door. He lifted her up slightly and pressed her back against it. With one hand he lifted her leg, and held it at his hip, pushing her harder against the door.

Rylan tightened his hold on her until she felt like a captive in his arms, then, bending his head again, he bit her, sending through her body ripples of pleasure... and pain?

NOTE on step 5: the unit should respond with the standardised response, the owner will need to run the conversation diagnostic and install before the unit accepts its command "Name". If unit progresses to the naming protocol before the conversation diagnostic command has been run, turn off unit and reboot.

If the error persists, return the unit.

To continue without reboot will mean that it has breached its protocols and will not respond correctly to the owner's voice commands.

If the owner uses the machine without doing the reboot, the warranty is void, and the company holds no responsibility for what may occur.

Step 6: On completion of the installation programs you may turn off the machine or proceed to its designated use.

Congratulations on your assembly of the ST-AM-1975 Male Companion. We hope you enjoy your purchase.

J E Gaulton is an avid genealogist and writer. She is a member of both the Federation of Australian Writers and the Northern Beaches Writers Group (NBWG). Once a contributing author for the T-Zero Ezine (Writers Village University) she used to create a segment called "Spotlight". Other publishing credits include "A Travel Story", set in Egypt. She has always been interested in the First World War, and upon discovering that no less than three of her ancestors had fought in it, she was inspired to use her passion for family research as material for a novel. Entitled "Our Tom", the book combines history and fiction, shaped in part by the connecting with her ancestors through the act of writing.

Don't Wanna Play No More

Andrew Mills

I had it all figured out. We'd been together for nine months and our time was due. I would ask her in Gaborone. On the first night I'd surprise her and take her out into the bush, just like when we first met. It was going to be full moon when she arrived. I'd asked her to wait one more day until the weather was perfect. I could imagine her sitting across the table in the game park. Everything was organised with the restaurant; the chef was going to get a heavy tip to ensure he went the extra mile and served the perfect romantic meal. There would be Dom on ice; just the two of us alone by the waterhole, perched high up on the restaurant's deck in the trees, safe from predators, watching the setting sun as the wild animals slaked their thirst before the hunting began. It would be raw Africa, tantalizingly close to nature's danger. A feast we would remember forever.

At four o'clock Leonie grabbed me as I was hurrying out the agency's door.

"Last minute changes just came through. You gotta do it. I know she's arriving, but there's no one else."

"Damn!" I cried. "Okay quick. I'll have to ask Mark to collect the ring." I grabbed my mobile and hurriedly texted Coco.

Baby, I'm caught up at work. Sorry, but you'll have to catch a cab. Promise I won't be long. xxxxx

I then called Mark and begged him to collect the ring and bring it to the bungalow before she arrived. I woke up the computer and scrambled to make the changes. It took me an hour before I got the client's approval.

"Bloody advertising, I hate it. Darling, send them off to the publications please," I called to Leonie as I dashed out the door. I leapt into the Cobra and tore off, madly gunning the engine to get home before Mark arrived. I prayed my surprise would go off as planned. I couldn't wait to look into her eyes as I asked her for her hand.

Gripping the steering wheel I urged the beast on. The sportscar slid around corners as I raced to get home. Ten minutes later I roared up to the driveway, rammed on the handbrake and sprang out of the Cobra. I saw Mark's Land Cruiser parked by the curb and realised I hadn't made it in time.

I bounced towards the front door like a springbok, finally ready to welcome her into my arms, and say, "Hey beautiful, sorry I'm late. Bloody work."

Instead.

I heard the sound of someone vomiting. It sounded so disgusting, and it didn't stop. Whoever was gagging was heaving for air.

I bolted to the door.

It was half open. I flung it back on its hinges and saw Mark bent over, retching, unable to speak. As the next wave of nausea violated his stomach, Mark seemed to spew up his intestines. Then he coughed.

"Don't."

And as the next volume of vile fluid sprayed across the floor, he collapsed to his knees.

There was a slick of blood that had slithered across the floor.

Handprints were smeared across the walls. It was as if someone had quickly painted them, pressing their palms in haste into some wet, red, ground paste, before leaving their indelible mark, like the Aborigines who'd left signs of song lines; solitary handprints messaging:

I was here.
But I am no longer.
Remember me.
This is a sacred place.

"Don't look!" Mark screamed.

But some force shoved my body forward. I stumbled, and almost slipped on the trail of greasy blood. It cruelly beckoned me, drawing me closer to the closed door. I thought I heard someone whisper,

Just another step.
Come closer my precious.
Just peek inside.
I've got something to show you.
Don't be surprised.
She deserved it
Dressed like that.

Some part of my brain clicked into gear. The cogs churned, making me lift my hands out in front of me. And slowly, in a trance, I opened the kitchen door. It swung wide, jarring against the wall, then bounced back as I took hold of the handle, clutching it to support myself.

I looked inside. The lights were switched on. I saw strewn clothes messed around on the white tiles. They looked as if they'd been shredded for some reason.

I couldn't fathom what I saw splayed across the floor. My brain collapsed into a nightmare of scattered thoughts. My eyelids fluttered like a motor drive camera. They were blinking so fast trying to take in what lay at my feet. Bizarre thoughts ricocheted through the contours of my shattered brain. I wanted to scream, but my open mouth was frozen.

I thought she looked like a rag doll lying in disarray. The parts were all jumbled up together. The head was barely attached to the torso, just lying on the cold tiled floor. It had a strange grimace sewn across its mouth. It didn't really have a face anymore. What was left of it looked blank. Surprised maybe, I thought. A messed up bundle of hair lay tangled next to it. It looked as if it had been dyed pink.

The doll had one eye missing, and its body had come undone. The stitches were all unravelled. Some of the stuffing had tumbled out. It looked as if someone had tried to rip it apart in anger. One leg was almost cut off, lying at a right angle by the hips. And the other was really not in the right place where it should be. It was all bent out of shape. The arms were spread out wide, as if they were about to take off, trying to fly somewhere far away from the angry person who didn't want to play.

And I didn't like the torso. It was a pincushion, except somebody had removed the pins. Not very nice, that was where you were supposed to keep them, so nobody got hurt. You didn't want people stepping on them. That would really be painful, and there were too many puncture holes all over it. More than you could count.

It looked as though someone had got a bit frustrated and just tossed it away in anger, slammed the door, and hadn't bothered to sweep up the gory mess they'd made.

As I took one shaking step forward, I was sure I heard a voice.

Who could have done this, some sick person, insane beyond belief?

Then I thought I heard another voice. Was I really going crazy? But it grew louder. It seemed to come from somewhere outside. I tried to cover my ears with my trembling hands, but as I did I swore that I could hear someone whisper, "Mummy, Mummy, I don't want dolls anymore. I don't like them, never did."

"But why do you have to turn the dollhouse into an abattoir?" A woman's voice answered, near the backdoor. "There's blood all over the place. Remember to clean up after the mess you've made. It's really hard to scrub out the stains."

"Okay, love you Mummy, promise next time."

"Have you been watching those dirty illegal porn movies on the internet again? You'll get into real trouble my boy. One day the police will catch you. Don't you like the blonde dolls? I'll try and find you another one, maybe one with dark hair."

The voices grew fainter as footsteps walked away.

"Stop it! Stop it! I'll bloody smash you Mummy, you fucking whore. I'm twenty now, and I don't wanna play with dolls no more."

Andrew Mills is an experienced professional writer, graphic artist and endangered reptile whisperer. Andrew writes to fuse together his passions for Africa, the visual world and the written word. He is currently working on an epic drama set in and around Botswana, as well as experimenting with language and the short story form.

Shangri La

Chris Lake

[Install]

"Please sign here to agree to the terms and conditions," says Host.

She leans forward to press her thumb print into the screen and is stopped by Host's warning hand.

"I really would recommend you read them first. The modifications are permanent."

She looks up at him over the bruise-coloured bags beneath her eyes. Her look is tired – bone tired – and contemptuous. Without saying a word, she gets it across that nothing in his poxy little document could be worse than what's happened to her already. Still holding his eyes with her own sixteen-year-old, hundred-year-old gaze, she plants her thumb in the dialogue box. It goes green and gives off a cheery little chirp.

Host disappears and a couple of Servers come in. The room changes as well. When she'd walked in it had been generic pine veneer office, but now it's day surgery operating theatre. No more potted plants, no more paintings of Parisian streets. Now there's a tightly made hospital bed, stainless steel trolleys and a massive graphic of two kittens playing with a ball of wool on the ceiling. She looks up at it in disgust. One of the Servers, seeing this and mistaking it for interest, waves a hand over his body cam and the ceiling cats come to 720p animated life.

"Just need you on the bed, babe," grins Server 1.

"I'm not online yet," she spits, "so you can fuck off with your 'babe' bullshit."

"They do like the feisty ones, don't they?" chuckles Server 2.

They strap her down and hit the side of her head with lasers until there's a shiny pink bald spot just above her left ear. Server 1 smears it with a local and Server 2 puts an airgun to the spot and punches a jack hole into her brain. Server 1 slides the jack into the port. It's stiff and new, and he has to steady her with a hand on her forehead to get it in. A stylish, LED looking window pops up in the space in front of her eyes. She can still see the playing kittens through it.

SERVER 12015651R1AVF6 [UNCONNECTED]

The 'unconnected' flashes for a bit, and then it's all gone. She's in a lobby. She can't feel her body in the room and the sensation makes her a little nauseous – no weight in her limbs, no ground under her feet: none of the millions of little reference points that convince a brain that it's in a real universe. She knows there's a whole heap of mods to go in yet. They're going to have to put in a neural interrupt to divorce her body from the conscious part of her brain, feed fibre through all her nervous system and jack it into the server so VR feedback is all she gets, jack her into the g-sim so that she can feel the turning of an imaginary Earth, and then there's all the memory mods, integrated sensor arrays, avatar control suites… It all has to be internal, wireless and invisible.

She raises a hand she can't feel, waves it left, and a long string of doors scrolls past. They scroll at just the right speed – she can take in the signs on each door without having to stop and read each one. She's not sure what she should do. She wants to get in and pick one, but she has a vague idea that if she does it too soon the whole lobby might reboot, leaving her to do it all over again. There's a readme.txt over in the corner of her eye. She flicks over to it and has a quick scan. Nope, she's good – continuity guaranteed.

Now she knows what to do, she realises that she doesn't – not really. Paralysed by the agony of choice. Unsure, unable to decide what she's really in the mood for. She thinks she wants sword and sandal warrior princess, but then there's all the frustrations that usually go with that. Dungeon crawling, crafting, crappy bow and arrow mechanics. Maybe what she really wants is the catharsis of gunplay, the click and boom, the hot smells and smoke and hypnotic crumpling of ads in her dispart sights.

Problem with that stuff, though, is that the stories are usually utter crap. It's like porn. Cobble together some bullshit plot with just enough legs to limp her along from one firefight to another. She's had enough porn for several lifetimes. She's still scrolling through when the Earth comes up and takes her and pins her to the ground.

Wow, they're quick. It's like the integration with her body does something to her mind. Makes her more present – more real somehow. Whereas before she was stuck in that special hell of indecision reserved for online shoppers, now that she's all there she's… all there. The titles, the gifs, the blurbs – they're all just a little more pregnant with sense and potential now. She can taste and feel what each one's offering, get a mental preview of what each one's going to really be like. It occurs to her that it doesn't matter so much anyway. She can always exit and pick another one. She finds one that looks promising – a kind of post-apocalyptic survival FPS, solo, total immersion. She steps forward and through the door. There's a long period of weightless, panicky blackness. All she can see is a dialogue saying:

…LOADING…
PLEASE WAIT

It spins on its axis, letting her know the system's ticking along fine – no crash. She watches it like a hawk, ready to hit the soft boot button in her hip pocket. Funny. She didn't have a hip pocket a second ago.

[Tutorial]

"Ah, good – you're awake," says Striker.

She knows his name is Striker without knowing or caring how. Opening her eyes, she sees a roughly thatched roof with smoke rising up through it. Looks left. The source of the smoke is the hearth in the middle of the wattle and daub house where she's woken up. She's lying on a bed of bound straw and Striker, a grizzled, bearded man in his forties, is sitting on rickety chair by her side. He's wearing a tattered miscellany of grimy combat gear and two crossed bandoliers stuffed with shotgun shells. He's smiling.

"What's your name?" he says.

She tries to say 'Persephone' but it doesn't come out. Over the character limit, she guesses. A moment's thought and she tries again. "Daphne," she says.

"Well, Daphne – you're a very lucky young lady," says Striker. "Not many people survive a Feeder attack. We found you just outside the village, more dead than alive. Where were you heading?"

Daphne says nothing. She's got no memories that would serve, so she figures she's meant to be the strong silent type here.

"None of my business, I suppose," says Striker after a longish pause. "Well, I guess you want to clean yourself up. Come and find me at the hall when you're ready." Striker stands, gathers up an enormous, heavily modified combat shotgun and leaves her alone.

There's a bit of a flicker and she's suddenly in a roughly improvised bathroom. There's a chemical bucket, a kind of trough bolted into the wall, which she guesses is meant to be a sink, and what looks like a shower cubicle, complete with pierced bucket and string. She sees where she's supposed to go. There's a polished steel mirror riveted into the wall above the trough. She stands in front of it and is confronted with the wide-eyed, gamin face that she's had to live with all the long years of her short life. She concentrates and her stringy blonde hair turns to a thick, lustrous black, hanging about her jaws in a seriously trendy bob. The brows de-arch, the eyes narrow, cheekbones flatten slightly and drop. A strong face – a face for an action heroine, instead of a teeny porno. Satisfied, she blinks twice to confirm and heads out into the village.

"Daphne! Over here!" Striker's standing with a small group – two women and one man – near a big wooden building that looks like a ramshackle church hall. Daphne ignores him. The village is made up of big roundhouses like the one she woke up inside. There's a couple of dusty streets coming off the main drag, and random people moving around tending fires, carrying loads and otherwise doing village-type things. Here and there, under eaves or near piles of fishing gear or lumber, are bright green boxes. She walks over to the first and begins methodically checking through them all.

"Daphne! Over here!" says Striker again, an exact repeat of tone and inflection.

She ignores him and continues to search.

"Daphne! Over here!"

She's ready to go talk to Striker now, comfortably weighed down with ammo, first aid kits, money and some random articles of food she's taken on a just-in-case basis.

"Hey, Striker," she says as she approaches.

"Daphne, I want you to meet a few people. This is Marcus – he's our techie genius. If you want to buy or modify anything – weapons, equipment, whatever – he's your man. And this is Peek and Park. They're newlyweds, and they're the ones that found you on their way back from their honeymoon."

Peek and Park smile shyly. Daphne's impressed – it's a nice touch.

"Now, I don't know where you're from or where you're headed,"

Striker continues, "but you look like someone who can handle yourself. We can always use a bit of help around here if you're willing. Just so long as you're staying with us, that is."

"Sure," says Daphne. "I'll help out any way I can. It's the least I can do."

"We've lost contact with one of our patrol stations and we're a bit worried. Do you think you could go and check it out when you've got time?"

"Sure," says Daphne. She knows where it is – it's probably a ten minute walk across country if she ignores the road.

"You'll probably need this," says Striker, handing her a crappy 9mm automatic.

Daphne takes it and puts in in the empty holster that just happens to be at her hip.

Striker and his pals, their jobs done, peel off unceremoniously in different directions, heading for their village life loop.

Daphne loads and checks her pistol and rummages around in her webbing, swapping and changing her loadout until she's happy. She starts for the village limits, ready to head for the patrol station, when the villagers break and run for the hall, screaming.

"FEEDERS!" is the cry.

Daphne can hear the thick popping sound of distant small arms fire. There's a drum of hoofbeats woven through it as well.

"Get into the hall! Everyone into the hall!" Striker is shepherding people into the hall, shotgun held loosely in one hand. He spots Daphne and makes his way over to her.

"Will you stand with us?" he says.

"Of course," says Daphne. She racks her pistol and stares down the sights at the road into the village. First there's a steadily thickening swirl of dust, coalescing in tandem with the approaching sounds of hoofs and shots. Three riders appear over the crest of a shallow rise. They have blood-matted hair, and blood streaks painted on the flanks of their armoured horses. Heads on strings bob frantically alongside weapons and saddle accoutrements. Daphne squeezes off a whole clip in their general direction and the riders flop down into the dust. She frowns.

"Pause," she says. "Set difficulty."

[Options]

Pain. She's become used to its absence, and now it floods back through her like heat returns to a hypothermia victim. Her eyes open and she flexes her fingers and toes. There are cats on this ceiling too.

"Fucking cats," she murmurs.

She's hungry too. That was another feeling she'd become used to going without. There's a chemical smell in the air, and her hands and thighs are greasy. The room she's in looks red. Red curtains, red bedspread, red-shaded lamps. It's hot too – blood warm. It's like she's inside a red pulsing womb. She can hear voices.

"She's my daughter! I have a right!"

"Sir," says Host, "I'm afraid that as she's past the age of legal responsibility, any and all rights of custody have been legally signed over to us. I appreciate your strength of feeling…"

"You fucking cunt! How dare you! I wanna see her, and I wanna see her now! I'll sue you! You won't have a fucking penny left!"

"I doubt that, sir. There is documentary and film evidence of serious abuse – I find it highly unlikely that any court would return her to your custody."

"I wanna see her!"

"I understand that, sir. We're in the process of dropping her out as we speak and you'll be able to see her momentarily. Would you like a beverage or refreshments while you wait?"

She tries to get up but realises she's strapped to the bed. Before she gets it together to start struggling, Server 1 comes in and sets her free. Server 2's not far behind. He's carrying a deep blue silk nightgown over his arm. She slowly, painfully rises to her feet and slips it on, tying it at her waist with shaky hands. She feels like someone's been kicking the shit out of her, inside and out. The Servers leave. There's a ruckus at the door and her father bursts into the room.

"You're coming with me," he says, charging her, hands outstretched.

She cringes away and Host, good old Host, is there – he's locking her father up in a half nelson. It looks weird – the half-smiling pleasant expression on his face hasn't changed at all. "Do you actually wish to speak with this man?" says Host.

"Get him the fuck away from me," she says.

Host nods and turns to leave the room.

"You fucking BITCH!" screams her father as he's tossed round the end of Host's fulcrum like a rag doll marionette.

Host doesn't need any effort to control him. He even stops on the way out and ceremoniously closes the door behind him with one hand, the struggling armful on his offside making no never mind with his elaborate politeness.

The Servers come back in.

"Time for a meet and greet," says Server 1.

"What the fuck are you talking about?"

"It's in the T&C's," he continues. "We gotta drop you out to do meet and greets."

"Do you really have to? I don't wanna keep dropping every five seconds."

"You can waive the right," says Server 2. "Just sign here," he says, holding out a tablet. She thumbs it and there's the green flash and that strangely cheery chirp.

"Right," she says. "Put me back in."

"Wait one," says Server 1. "We may as well feed you up while you're offline."

There's a kind of crash cart looking thing stashed away near the bed head. He pulls it out, wheels it over to her and tells her to sit on the bed. Server 2 opens her robe, probes around with both hands for a second near the top of her right hip. He eventually finds what he's looking for and presses down. There's a click and a little port opens up. There's a sudden sharp reek of shit.

"First time usually hurts a bit," says Server 2 as he jams the feeding tube deep into her guts. She tries to flinch away but Server 1's got behind her somehow and now he pins her in place while they squirt mashed rations directly into her bowel. It goes on for a five minute forever before they yank the tube, close the port and let her go.

"Just fucking put me back in," she gasps.

"You're the boss," says Server 1.

[Progression]

Daphne carries on down the dirt track. Scrub and tall trees block the view on either side, but the path is broad and the foot traffic argues for safety. Traders and farmers pass her coming the other way. She's become well known around these parts, and they greet her with respect, and maybe a little awe. She can hear their whispered comments as they carry on down the road.

"That's Daphne!"

"Isn't she the one who rescued all those people?"

"I heard she killed the local Feeder chief."

Up ahead, there's a trader pretty much on her visible horizon. He's trudging along with his pack mule, leading it by a long halter. Daphne keeps her eye on him. He's a weathercock for danger. A pit canary for threat. So long as his behaviour is normal, all must be clear up ahead. For the rest, she can't remember ever having felt this good. The sky's a size and blueness she's never seen. The high yellow sun catches the floating pollen, sparking it into points of soft white light. Her booted feet sink just the right amount into the dirt of the track – cushioning without dragging. She's got days and days of supplies strapped round her body, and a weapon for every contingency and occasion. And confidence. She's not used to confidence. She wonders if this is how normal people feel all the time – moving at their own pace, utterly convinced they can deal with whatever comes along.

Up ahead, the man with the mule stops in his tracks, then scrambles off in panic over the crest and out of sight.

Daphne heads for the tree line to her left, finding a position far enough from the road to make her invisible, but not far enough into the trees to interfere with her field of fire. She compulsively checks her full load out, fussing at the holsters on her hip and thigh, touch verifying the presence of first aid kits and spare ammo. She likes this routine. It keeps her in the role – makes her feel more like a soldier. Satisfied, she takes a knee and sights down the road at the optimal thirty degree angle which Striker showed her all those weeks ago.

She waits, breathing long and shallow, looking at the little crest in the road through her scope. The yellow dust begins to settle, and she can hear shots. Automatic, small arms, close. Some people are screaming – she thinks she makes out a "No!" before the firing stops.

A few seconds pass.

A few more.

Slowly, heads and shoulders start rising above the false horizon of the crest. Daphne waits. Counts. Four men – Feeders – dressed in the re-assembled rags of every piece of clothing available in the game world, overlaid with a hodge-podge of rusty, bloodstained armour. She can see their teeth, filed into points, through her scope. They're in a rough line abreast, but the leftmost man is slightly behind the rest of them. Daphne's learnt to shoot the rearmost man first – the projectile travels faster than sound, and the split second between the hit and the report is enough to shift target, but only if the rest of them don't actually see the impact. So you shoot past them, hit the man they can't *see*. The crosshairs settle on the Feeder's face, scarred like it's been dragged through a pile of fishhooks, and painted with brownish red stripes of blood. She breathes out, steadies, squeezes off the round. Flicks right and hits the next man any old how – she gets a glimpse of chest armour before the scope jumps off target from the recoil. She scans further right.

Nothing.

Daphne dips the scope off her eye. The two remaining Feeders are charging, spreading left and right of her position. Pincer attack. She slings the rifle over her shoulder and yanks her sawn-off from its thigh cradle. Gets to her feet and runs, half crouching, towards the man on the left. She's pretty sure they can't see her, that they're just closing on her shot. She knows now, from long experience, that this line will break their formation – once she's dealt with this one she'll be able to approach the other from the rear, instead of having to deal with them both simultaneously.

The trees and bushes provide cover, but they obscure the target so that it flickers in and out of sight and she has to focus fiercely on what she's doing, keep her line of advance strictly relative to the target's so that she pops up in just the right spot.

When it happens, it's sudden like it always is. One moment, they're all crashing headlong through the trees. The next, they're face to face, less than three feet apart. Daphne empties both barrels into his face, spins on her axis and heads for the last one, reloading as she runs.

She can hear him, but she can't see him, has to half guess, half remember his line of advance, calculate a vector to intersect, all blink fast and visual in her head. She gets the angle right, but not the range, so that when he does come into view he's moving fast across her field of fire, from right to left – the wrong direction. She pops a snap shot off at him and misses. Snaps off another one, but it's too early and she's missed again. Realises he must have started doubling back when she fired just now.

"Fuck!" she screams. She holsters the shotgun, shoulders the rifle again, but she knows it's useless. The target's too far gone now and she loses him over the rise in the road just as her crosshairs settle. "Fucking *cunt!*"

She port arms the rifle and runs after him, breaking cover and sprinting full pelt down the road. She loves these moments of pure, focussed aggression, where there's nothing in the whole wide universe beyond the chase, the shot and the kill.

She spots him again, but they've both churned up a lot of dust in the last second or so. Daphne, unable to make out fine detail, drops a standing shot into the centre of mass. The Feeder stumbles but, incredibly, keeps going. She works the bolt and advances. There's no hurry now, but she doesn't want to waste another shot. She waits for the range to close to unmissable, kneels and puts a deliberate, highly satisfying round straight through the back of his head. Still looking through the scope, Daphne does a quick scan around. There's some kind of wooden roadblock up ahead, but she's more interested in the extra body she's just spotted lying in the dust.

She closes on it, still crouched, watching the supine figure for any sign of movement. As she approaches, she recognises him. It's the mule man, the merchant. She stands and advances, quick with greed for his loot, sees the mini-mushroom cloud of dust before she hears the shot, and she's swung her rifle up and onto the bearing.

A single Feeder, behind the roadblock she'd noticed earlier.

She squeezes off a round and takes him down. Hears yelling – lots of yelling – and dips the scope. The clearing dust reveals the roadblock to be an outer fence line. A ramshackle collection of iron and wooden shacks lie beyond it – the Feeder stronghold. Ant-like figures are swarming from every doorway and aperture, and streaming towards her. The ones coming from the fenceline are close enough that she can see their faces. She pulls her shotgun, yanks the trigger, and the hammers click down on empty chambers.

"Fuck!" she says as she breaches the weapon with quick, panicky hands. Always, *always* reload before holstering. She fires off one barrel into a charging Feeder, but now there's lots of them, more than she can count at a glance, and the stray shots have turned into a tightly directed hail of gunfire. She turns and breaks right for the trees, but she knows it's hopeless. She's not surprised when the road rushes up to meet her face.

[Maintenance]

Pain again. And the red room. Server 1 looms over her as the other one fumbles around in her crotch.

"Stop it!" says Server 1, hissing spit spray into her face. She realises she's struggling against her restraints. She stops, but more because the movement hurts her wrists and ankles than anything else.

"Put me back in!" she screams. "Put me back in right now!"

Server 2 pulls a long catheter from her vagina and straightens up. "What the fuck is her problem?" he says as he puts it aside and starts mopping up.

"My save! My save!" she shouts, struggling again despite the pain.

Server 1 rolls his eyes. "How many times? We checkpoint every time. If you've been dropped out, you've been checkpointed. Now calm the fuck down."

There are a few moments of relative silence. She's panting, trying to get her breath back. She's bone-tired. Her limbs feel like someone's hung weights off her for a prank and she's sore all over and deep down. Server 2 finishes up and Server 1, who's been fussing around with something under the line of her jaw, moves to release her restraints.

"Why've you dropped me out?"

"Maintenance run. You've knocked loose one of your VR sensors, it's hanging by a thread. I'm amazed it hasn't crash dropped you already."

"How long?" she asks.

"Couple minutes," says Server 1, nodding at Server 2 as he leaves the room. "But you should stay out longer. You need to eat some solids. It's been months."

"Just put me back in," she says.

"Not an option. Eat some solids or you won't have the calories to power the implants."

Server 2 comes back in, wheeling a tray of covered dishes. The juicy meat and oil smells make her feel nauseous. It's too much, this sensory assault, after the heavily curated inputs she's grown used to. Free now, she rolls onto her side and dry heaves for a bit. The Servers stand and watch until she's done, then move in and lift her to her feet. She wobbles and nearly falls. Server 1 catches her and holds her upright while Server 2 arranges her blue gown around her bony shoulders.

There's white bread and roast meat and other foods she's never seen in the real world. But the bread tastes doughy and wet, and the meat closes her stomach after a tiny mouthful.

The Servers lay her down and she rolls painfully onto her side to relieve the pressure of her bulging stomach. She passes out. Comes to. There's an odd sensation of having only just opened and closed her eyes, even though she can feel that she's been asleep for hours.

Host is sitting on a chair by the bedhead. He's wearing his usual polite half smile. "Good morning," he says.

"Put me back in."

"I can't do that just yet, I'm afraid."

"Why the fuck not?"

Host holds up a tablet so she can read the screen, considerately tilting it in alignment with her body position. It's a live chart of her vitals. They don't look good. "I regret to say," says Host, "that the Servers have let you run on much longer than they should have. I understand you persuaded them to let you skip your last maintenance dropout?"

She says nothing. It's not really a question, anyway.

"Well. That wasn't really acceptable," Host continues. "Not from a safety viewpoint in any case. I need you to reach this benchmark here," he points out a blue line well above her own pulsing indicators, "before I can authorise login."

There's a short silence as she looks at Host, and Host looks at her.

"What if I don't care?" she says. "What if I just wanna go back in anyway?"

Host goes rigid. His face blanks out, all expression gone. When he speaks again, his voice is stern and harsh. It's still his, but it sounds like he's playing a recording of it instead of just talking.

"Client 12D156S1R1AVF6, you have indicated a preference for self-managed player care. Self management is not recommended and is chosen at the player's own risk. Sign here to confirm." Host's arm jerks stiffly, indicating the dialogue box that's appeared on his tablet.

She raises a scrawny arm, livid with bruises, and shakily presses her thumb into the box.

"Self management requires clients to indemnify Shangri-La, a division of Numisma Holdings, against all loss or damage, as well as terminal expiration, and all claims for same, including any and all claims arising from damage, loss, incapacity or any cause of expiration including but not limited to external and internal game events, force majeure, mal…"

The voice cuts off as she thumbprints the tablet again. Host blinks, and he's back to his normal self.

"I see," he says. "Are you aware that we estimate your remaining run time at less than a week?"

"That's not enough," she says. "Is there any… there must be something." It hurts to think.

"We can, given your consent, replace your feedings with Stimshots. Stimmed players have been known to achieve months of run time. You should be aware, however, that Stimshot treatment is very high risk."

"Just do it, and put me back in," she mumbles. Her eyelids are getting heavy.

"I will make the arrangements," says Host.

"Put me back in."

[Endgame]

Daphne stands in the Great Hall. All the townsfolk are assembled in a kind of massive honour guard, all rigged up in their best for the special day. She can see Striker standing near the dais, dashing and bearded – a silver wolf. Striker's reading off a list of her achievements, but she's not really listening. She lets her gaze wander over the people. Transformed by their finery, they look clean, prosperous and happy. Striker's long recitation comes to an end and there's a break for wild cheering from the crowd. He raises a hand and the crowd falls silent.

"Step forward, Daphne, and receive our thanks," he says.

Daphne sees a glowing mark appear on the floor near Striker. She heads for it, scanning around as she goes, catching glimpses of happy faces, fragments of whispered thanks. A trumpet fanfare sounds as she steps up to the mark. There's a confused shuffling of feet and a soft clatter, like surgical instruments in a tray. The kittens playing on the ceiling are enormous – hideous as ever. Striker doesn't seem to mind them. Doesn't seem to notice the manacles at her wrists and ankles. A warning flashes up in a trendy green LED box in front of her eyes.

SERVER 12015651R1AVF6 [RECONNECTING]

"How long is this gonna fuckin' take?" says a voice. "This is not what I paid for."

She looks over and sees a man standing in the corner of the room. His genitals are hidden by the bulk of his paunch, but it's clear that he's naked. He's holding a riding crop.

"Sir, if you'll please just wait outside." It's Server 2. She wonders why he's in game.

"I've handed you assholes a whole heap of cash…"

"Sir!" he snaps. "Go outside! Host will deal with the money – just fuck off and let us do our work!"

A face looms up in her field of view, blotting out the Hall, Striker, all of it. It's Server 1. He's frowning. He fiddles with something just under her jaw and she cries out with the pain of it. Grabbing her thrashing head, he holds her steady to look at her eyes. She can see that he's looking at them, not into them. He fiddles some more and she screams.

"Gotcha, you little fucker," he says.

Striker's smiling down on her as he hangs the ribbon round her neck. She knows she should just enjoy this moment, but she's already thinking ahead. There's heaps of endgame stuff to do – Striker and the others have made that pretty clear.

Problem is, though, they're all just random radiant quests, and she's not sure if she's still interested enough in this world to carry on. It's mostly been grinding, which is the problem with these sorts of games. Once the grind is gone, so is most of the interest.

She notices that the ceremony is over. Everyone's clapping and cheering. There's a bunch of mission waypoint markers floating around inside her eyes, but she knows what they all are. She figures there's no harm in just taking a look at what else is available. She can always come back in if she feels like it.

"Save," she says. "Exit to lobby."

She's back in the lobby for only the briefest of moments before the scrolling doors freeze and an error message pops up and then she's tied to an A-frame with a man – that same, big fat man – grunting and thrusting in her face. Alarms go off and Servers 1 and 2 come barrelling in. They rip him off her and Server 1 hustles him out of the room, complaining at the top of his voice.

"You fucker!" she can hear the fat man saying. "I was nearly finished! You fucking fucker!"

Server 2 looks at her. She tries to ask him what the fuck is going on, but she can't move or speak. She can feel though, and she wants to scream with the pain of it, but all she can do is hang in her shackles, feel the sweat or blood or whatever it is running down her skin.

"Total shutdown," says Server 2 as Server 1 re-enters the room.

"Recoverable?"

"Nope, " says Server 2, shaking his head.

Server 1 sighs, goes to the corner of the room and wheels over a surgical trolley.

"Why do they do it?" he says, mostly to himself.

"How else is a chick like this gonna afford a full gaming rig?"

"Yeah, I s'pose. Oh well. She's still got a few minutes left, probably. Did you want a go of her before we take the rig out?"

Server 2 looks her up and down. "Nah," he says. "Cutesie blonde isn't really my type. Let's get to work."

He lifts a scalpel from the trolley and starts cutting the jack plug out of her temple.

Chris Lake is a freelance author and editor who, like most of his kind, can frequently be found drunk, poor and working for the minimum wage. He has a crime fiction novel on Amazon and a plethoric scatter of hack work on embarrassing but remunerative sites like Inquisitr. His work history includes abattoirs, large corporate and the military, which is not as interesting as it sounds. Chris is currently working on a literary novel called Parallax.

Chez Antoine's

A R Kelly

Angela pressed a finger into the lion's mouth at precisely 7.30pm. Her instructions had been to not seek entry before this time, and tardiness was not forgiven at Antoine's. So here she stood in the semi darkness, shaking against the autumn wind and growing more impatient with each passing minute. She had dressed lightly for the occasion. The black satin dress which still gave some shape to her wilted body, her favourite pearls, and the old engagement ring which she now wore on her right hand.

The black door into which the lion's head was embedded swung open a few seconds later and she was greeted at the door by a young woman. "Good evening Angela, welcome to Antoine's. Please, this way." She ushered Angela inside a dimly lit vestibule, not much warmer than it was outside. "My name is Marie, and I will be taking care of you this evening." She led Angela down a narrow hallway illuminated by the soft ultraviolet hue of a fish tank built into the floor. Tiny unsleeping fish darted away at each tap of Angela's feet.

Other than the trickle of an unseen fountain, there were no sounds.

"Quiet night?" Angela asked, as she was ushered into a tiny room.

"We only host one patron at a time to preserve the privacy of our guests. In here please."

The dome shaped room was completely bare apart from a small table and chair in the centre. The walls were completely smooth and glowed softly from within.

"This is your private dining room. Please feel free to move around in here, but you are required to remain in this room until your dining experience is complete. Afterwards, you may choose to remain in here, or there are other rest places available if you want to continue your journey in a different environment."

"So, how does this work?" Angela turned to the girl. "I'm expecting to get more than just sitting around in the dark here."

"Of course." She pulled the chair out and held it for Angela, placing a napkin on her lap before walking around to stand in front of her. She poured some water into a tall chilled glass for her guest.

"No wine?"

"Alcohol can interfere with the dining experience of our guests."

"All the water I can drink then, I suppose."

Marie held a hand out to her guest. "May I take the contract now please?"

"The contract? You mean the card?" She pulled a small gold card out of her purse and handed it to Marie. "Now, I've made a special request to meet Thomas Jones tonight. My son. That's in the contract too."

"Thank you. I will relay your request to Antoine. We try and accommodate our patrons where possible, but occasionally things can be beyond the control of even Antoine. Unfortunately we can't make any guarantees on what you will see."

"Well the whole reason I'm here is to see my Thomas. That's the arrangement. Are you telling me that you can't do that now?"

Marie gave her a small smile as she studied the card for a few seconds before tucking it into her breast pocket.

Angela watched the girl's eyes move over the card as she scanned its contents. *Not such a natural beauty after all then.* "It's getting harder to tell your kind apart these days, isn't it?" she studied Marie's face with narrowed eyes.

She didn't take the bait. "Was there anything else that you would like to confirm, or has anything changed in your circumstances which needs to be reflected within the contract?"

Angela shook her head. "No, I'm prepared to go ahead as declared. I'm in as sound a state of mind and body as I'm going to be, so let's get on with it. I've wasted enough time already." She lit up a cigarette. "I suppose I can still do this in here?"

Marie dipped her head as she held up a small silver bell. "If you need anything, ring the bell and I'll be here. I will see you shortly with your first course. And please remember to taste every dish at least once in order to fully engage in the experience."

Angela heard the soft swish of a door close behind her as she stared at the blank walls, waiting for something to happen. *So this is what your life savings have earned you.* A menu lay on the table. Gold on black, like the lion at the door. She held it up without looking inside. *Surprise me, Antoine.*

Angela had stopped wasting her money on expensive meals since the treatment had killed off most of her taste buds. But she wasn't here for a meal. She'd heard about Antoine's through her friend Carol. And when Angela had mentioned to her that she wanted to see Thomas before she died, it was Carol who had suggested that she might still be able to see him.

"It's expensive, but for a certain clientele it's worth it. And, you never know what you'll see, Angela. It's not for everyone. God I don't think I would dare look into my subconscious."

She glanced up as Marie walked back into the room carrying a bamboo serving tray which she placed in front of Angela. "Your first course. Enjoy your experience."

A plate of sashimi glittered like jewels before her. A flash of blood red tuna against a pale, white-fleshed pearl of kingfish. Her mouth watered at the rich saltiness of sea urchin roe. She dipped her nose and inhaled, the smell taking her back to her childhood by the sea. She was five again, running through the sand with her brothers. Digging moats around sandcastles. Squealing as her father held her up high and dunked her feet into the freezing waves. The domed room lit up and came alive as her memories filled its walls, projecting long-forgotten treasures of her past before her eyes. Each bite purged a new memory. Her childhood by the sea, followed by an older Angela at the precipice of adulthood, her head buried in fat books about torts and crimes. Too busy now for the beach, or for friends. A young Angela feeding her ambition as she fed her newborn baby. Thomas.

The tears fell unabated as she watched herself nurse Thomas for the first time. Angela back at work two months after giving birth. She picked up the bell, just as Marie reappeared with another plate.

"This isn't what I came for." She dabbed a napkin under her eyes. "I asked to speak with my son. Not this. Why am I being shown this?"

Marie removed the bamboo tray and placed a white plate before her. "It's usual for our guests to occasionally face things from their past which they would rather not see, and I'm sorry if this is upsetting. As I said earlier, there are no guarantees with this process. You need to let it run its course."

"Well that's not good enough." Angela threw the napkin back on the table. "I paid for a service and I'm expecting to have it delivered. Do you know what I do for a living?" *What I did.* "And if you can't guarantee me what I paid for then the deal's off. I'm done here." She stood up to leave.

"I'm sorry Angela, but you know the arrangement." Marie stood in front of her, blocking her way. "Once you walk in that front door, you have waived your right to rescind the contract."

"Well, you can't force me to stay in here." She grabbed the water and threw it at Marie. The girl jumped back, instinctively pulling an arm over her face as the glass brushed past her hair and smashed into the wall behind her. "Why don't you short circuit you fucking robot? You'll never understand. You're not real, you don't know what real emotion feels like," she cried.

Marie grabbed Angela by the shoulders and pushed her back into her chair, blinking to clear water from her eyes. Angela grabbed at the plate as Marie took her hands and held them back down against the table.

"Please Angela, please. You chose this experience. Now please let it run its course." She picked the bamboo tray up off the floor and turned to leave.

Angela tried to follow her out but the girl was gone. Angela looked around to see where she went. The door which she came through was no longer visible. She ran her hands over the smooth walls and found nothing.

"Open the fucking door!" she screamed into the empty room. Her pounding heart filled her ears as she sat back down to catch her breath.

Before her sat a piece of meat. Blue. The way she used to have it when she still ate meat. The sight of it further inflamed her rage as she had told them that she no longer ate meat, and the smell of it made her stomach turn. But Marie's words played on her mind. You need to taste it to see what comes next. She picked up the cutlery with shaking hands and sank the knife into one corner. It came away like soft butter and melted in her mouth.

The room flickered back to life.

Waitressing at Joe's Diner. Flirting with Ben on those first few dates. First class honours. Her first job as a young law graduate, those gruelling ninety hour weeks. Their wedding night. Thomas's first birthday. Thomas in daycare, the last child left waiting to be collected. Thomas in primary school, waiting to be collected. Becoming partner at the firm. The first time Thomas got in trouble with the police for vandalising a train.

She closed her eyes. *No more.*

She picked up the bell, rang it till Marie stood in front of her.

"Please. Please I'm begging you. Just let me see him happy for once. For one last time. That's all. You can end it after that I promise." She was crying openly now. Marie took her tiny hand into her own.

"I am sorry Angela, I truly am, but we cannot show you anything but the truth inside your own self. We don't make dreams here, or show you things to hurt you intentionally."

Angela pulled her hand away and stood up. She was shaking now. "Don't say that. You don't know who I am. You don't know the things I've had to do for my family." She flung the plate at the wall, splattering it with meat juices. "I gave up my entire life to give my son the life I never had, and now all I see is what a terrible mother I've been." She crouched on the floor holding her face in her hands. "This is a nightmare."

Marie placed a hand on her shoulder. "I'm sorry to hear that you see it that way." She helped Angela back to the table and poured her some water before stepping back out of the room.

Through her watery eyes the room appeared brighter, as the walls become translucent and fell away.

"Angela." another voice whispered at her. *Antoine?*

The restaurant was gone and she found herself lying in a hospital bed. "You know why, Angela. Thomas is gone."

"Gone." Angela murmured the word to herself as she watched Marie adjust a drip into her arm. *But it's not Marie.* "Am I dreaming?" she slurred, struggling to get a bearing of her surroundings.

"No Angela, you're at the Regen Facility, remember? You came here to experience your memories." Marie was adjusting a monitor band on Angela's arm. Her face was the same as the girl she'd met earlier, but there were no smile lines around her mouth, her eyes not as forgiving.

"He's dead, isn't he?"

Marie turned look at her. "The truth is that at our end we must face our true selves, Angela. And that person may not be who we had set out to become."

Angela blinked, trying to clear her head as she watched Marie inject her with a clear liquid. A jolt of cold shot up her arm.

"Is this the end now?"

"The end? In this place the end is whatever your minds tell you it is Angela. Now, do you want some dessert?"

Azmeena Kelly is an environmental specialist and lawyer by day and spends her nights making up stories to validate the voices in her head. Writing mostly speculative fiction, Azmeena has written a number of flash fiction and short story pieces which are published on her blog www.tastyniblets.co, and is currently working on her first novel.

The Final Journey

Rodney Jensen

PART 1: Silicon Valley 2130 March

Star ship Quest-30 reaches its final launch sequence. The countdown progresses to the climax. "Five, four, three, two, BLAST OFF!" A brilliant flash of light saturates the screen before vanishing from view, leaving a powerful after-image over blackness in its wake.

Mike Thornton, a middle aged, conservatively dressed man sits at his usual spot in the Quest Complex, home of the formidable US NGO 'Quest for Habitable Planetary Systems,' generally known as Q-HiPS. He's been watching the launch on a live feed like many thousands of others, wondering what will become of the ship if it ever reaches its target, an exoplanet twelve light years from Earth.

Mike switches off the video and turns to his colleague. He looks thoughtful. "How's that Howard? Thirty missions since the very first blast off, and still counting."

Howard, only half listening, has his attention focused on a file, a recent signal from deep space. He finally registers what Mike has said to him. "And we only started getting messages back from Quest-01 two years ago. I was just a twinkle in my dad's eye when it launched. 2100 – do you remember it?"

Mike can tell when he's having his leg pulled and prefers to play it straight. "Sure. I haven't been at Q-HiPS quite that long. I'd just left high school. I must be looking old this morning. I do remember a few news stories. There was a lot of public concern about the donors for the Andronics."

"It hasn't gone away. Look at today's news feed." Howard points at another large room monitor which shows a group of serious faced men and women, mostly in their twilight years, with the headline: THEIR GREATEST SACRIFICE.

"What are they expecting? The public, I mean. Donors are always terminally ill, for God's sake! They volunteer, knowing full well what they're letting themselves in for – that there's no other way we can reach the stars. I've talked to so many of them and my conscience is clear. Everyone is hoping that there's a better world out there somewhere. I sure am. It's why I joined Q-HiPS."

He points at the window where the all-enveloping smog is so dense nothing can be seen but the faintest patch of sunlight seeping through the murk. "To tell you the truth I'm beginning to have my doubts about these missions. Thanks to Dr Einstein, we still don't have any practicable way of communicating over interstellar space!"

"You're kidding aren't you? We've got to think in terms of decades."

"No, I'm not kidding, I've been giving a lot of thought to this lately. What bothers me most is how we keep sending these missions to the stars, with no way of telling whether they're achieving anything – not in our lifetimes anyway. And the only report we've received back so far, after all these years, raises serious concerns, even if upstairs is ignoring them. It's hardly encouraging is it?"

Mike looks at his colleague in surprise. "As I see it, it's a matter of faith. Otherwise I wouldn't be here."

"It just makes me feel a little sad watching that one leave just now. I just hope it's all worth it."

PART 2: Mumbai 2135 April

Anil has come to work even earlier than usual, entering via a refuse strewn track, into one of the largest municipal global waste tips India has seen, a microcosm of the world at large.

Five years ago, the rest of the world experienced the worst pandemic in human history, paradoxically leaving the subcontinent to survive and flourish along its chaotic growth trajectory.

He nods at the security guards waiting at the entrance then follows a MAG truck that's just pulled in ahead of him. The temperature is already close to 40°C despite it being only a few minutes after dawn. The first rays of the sun are beginning to light the gunmetal coloured skies, presaging a furnace by noon.

Anil looks young for his seventeen years, a dark haired, skinny kid with very white prominent teeth. He's been an orphan all his life. Ignoring the heat and stench of the tip that would make unaccustomed visitors throw up, his target for the morning is the new trove of refuse being deposited by the MAGs. He unconsciously bunches his fists before preparing to sift through the latest pile of plastic bags and hardware.

His body is soon covered in sweat and dirt. He spots a tell-tale grey metal box hidden behind a bag of rotting fruit. His eyes light up. It's a surprisingly recent model high capacity data store. He gingerly pulls it out and brushes some of the muck from its casing. The box is labelled with a bold graphic featuring Planet Earth as seen from space, and surrounding star systems. It carries an acronym 'Q-HiPS'. He's certain he remembers someone mentioning the strange name years back, before the pandemic, but the details elude him. He quickly hides his find for the day and heads back to his 'home-office'.

As he enters the vast squatter settlement that borders the tip, he follows a maze of narrow alleyways, second nature to him. Many call out to him in Hindi. He's generally known to them as 'the nerd kid' and he always acknowledges their friendship with a warm 'Ke Se Ho'.

His immediate neighbours look at him curiously as he finally reaches his home, a packing case about the size of a small garden shed.

"What are you doing back here so soon Anil?" the woman from next door wants to know.

"Don't worry Mum, I've got to see someone – that's all," he says cheerfully.

"Always so busy, Anil. Can you check my vid? It's not working. I'm missing quiz shows!"

"Sure Mum! I'll be round this evening. Promise."

"You're a good boy, Anil," she sighs.

Anil closes the door carefully behind him, knowing that she will not come in uninvited, nor allow anyone else to for that matter. He clears a little space off the cluttered shelf that sits above his bed-roll and puts his data store down where he can see it properly, memorising the details on the label.

#

It takes Anil several days to finally crack into the Q-HiPS data store, calling in some favours from other hackers he knows on the global network. Initially, he's disappointed to discover that most of it is routine reports and financial data years out of date and of little value.

But finally, with eyes so bleary he's having trouble reading, he comes across a document headed 'Final Report'. It has an origin he finds difficult to take seriously, an exoplanet located over nine light years from Earth. He's double checked it against other references to make sure the source is correct. The file has been water-marked 'Highly Classified – to secure repository'.

His pulse quickens as he realises that this document may have originated from one of the original space-probes and must be worth a fortune to someone 'in the business'. He opens the file, hardly able to keep his fingers from shaking.

PART 3: Planet Pironus 2112 August

VID LOG TRANSCRIPT 1
Prepared by: M Andronic Miller
Date [Earth time]: 2112-AUG-15
Location: Planet Pironus 721 b – Central Latitude

This video log has been compiled for the benefit of any viewers possessing limited knowledge of the events which occurred decades before this message will be received back on Earth.

I therefore commence with a brief summary of what has occurred critical to the success or failure of our mission to this planet.

While much of the attention on Earth post 2080 focussed on the development of a starship, I take the view that the real revolution triggering the quest for human exploration of our galaxy was artificial intelligence.

By 2070, successful modelling of a human nervous system was reported, then developed to the point where an electronic central processing unit, based on a specific donor's brain and nervous system, could be integrated into a fully synthetic humanoid which came to be known as 'Andronic'. Follow-up behavioural analysis was to demonstrate that the newly formed Andronic possessed identical character and responses to his/her donor, similar to an identical twin.

This breakthrough had obvious implications for interstellar exploration, enabling Andronic memory to be kept in stasis for the duration of an extremely long journey – subject to the theoretical maximum velocity of light speed. A concerted international effort to develop a vehicle capable of such velocity resulted in a prototype which could attain ninety per cent of the speed of light after maximum acceleration /deceleration periods of three or more years. Alongside the research effort needed to complete the working space craft was the development of a memory medium capable of withstanding sustained acceleration forces and radiation bombardment without corruption of data. The favoured material known as 'Sinterplasm' was believed to meet design specifications and ultimately used for the first mission.

A call for volunteer donors to form mission teams was originally made in 2093 and teams selected comprised of ten members based on multidisciplinary skills thought to be relevant to establishing new colonies on exoplanets. Some estimates from our on-board reference library suggest the number of such planets may be in the order of billions. However, our own direct experience since then has revised that optimistic estimate down to millions, or even less.

Donors for Andronic CPUs came from individuals considered extremely high achievers in their chosen careers. Testing assessed their skills in particular disciplines. Further examinations were made of their psychological profiles and probable compatibility with others in a close-quarters team environment.

Ours was the first such mission to be launched in 2100, Quest-01, our destination a planet named 'Pironus 721b' in the constellation of Scorpio as viewed from Earth. Planetary research at the time suggested this planet because of its relative proximity, nine light years from Earth, and having an orbit believed to be capable of supporting the spontaneous evolution of biological life.

In summary, the main objectives of our mission, in common to all such missions, were as follows:

1: Establish a new communications node ultimately forming part of a galactic scaled network.

2: Explore environmental conditions on Pironus 721b and assess suitability for future colonisation.

3: As a priority, assess any evidence of evolutionary intelligence or biological life forms.

4: Continue exploration to other suitable 'Goldilocks' planets using Pironus 721b as a 'stepping stone'.

5: Maintain radio contact and reporting to Earth, albeit at the limit of light speed and pending any scientific breakthrough in this regard, except where intelligent life forms are detected with the potential for hostile objectives of their own, in which case any further communication should be terminated.

MESSAGE ENDS

Anil stretches and scratches himself absently. His ancient 3-D Vis-Com is projecting an image in front of him showing a fanned sheaf of half opened files. He can see tempting references, including: 'Andronic research', 'Sinterplasm testing' and 'Pironus 721b findings'. He opens the 'Andronic' folder and discovers a sub-folder embossed with a red classified stamp, headed: 'Andronic Post-Conversion Research'. He opens the memorandum and reads the one paragraph abstract:

Longitudinal testing of personality types following Andronic conversion reveals a disturbing bias towards paranoia, suicidal tendencies and other unpredictable anti-social behaviour patterns. These findings call into question the suitability of Andronics for long term space exploration. Consequently, the US National Inquiry 2105 into civilian roles for Andronics has unanimously recommended terminating the conversion program, and placed a temporary hold on space missions crewed by Andronics, pending further research.

It's an hour before dawn and Anil has not been able to sleep from thinking about M Andronic Miller. Putting aside his normal routine of being at the tip as the first MAGs arrive, Anil opens the next vid log.

VID LOG TRANSCRIPT 2
Prepared by: M Andronic Miller
Date [Earth time]: 2112-AUG-21
Location: Planet Pironus 721 b – Central Latitude

On commencing orbit around Pironus, our Andronic crew were implemented and took part in a phase of remote sensing. The main purpose of this phase was to determine a suitable landing point. As referred to in my previous Vid Log, we were reliant on Sinterplasm to enable our crew to survive the rigours of extended suspended animation while transiting interstellar space. However, having reached our planned destination, three members of our Andronic team were incapable of retrieval, casting serious doubts as to the suitability of this medium for further missions. The unfortunate loss of the critical skills held by these crew members was a serious setback for our mission objectives, compounded by the fact that one of them was intended to be our Andronic in Charge.

As we orbited, we observed little resemblance to Earth from space. Our new planet showed no obvious tracts of water and a seemingly homogeneous land mass with little differentiation in its overall brown-mauve hue. It had a similarly featureless topography – with apparently flat plains, no visible large formations, mountains, valleys, or waterways. Similarly, we saw no evidence of obvious cratering and therefore concluded that the planet had limited risk of impact from asteroids or other bodies.

We eventually decided to land in the planet's equatorial region in order to maximise our energy input, the red dwarf parent star being demonstrably low in radiant energy. The level of radiation even in the tropical zone was found to be more similar to the polar regions of Earth.

On landing I took charge of the process of erecting our dome and setting up the various experimental bays. I was immediately confronted with a fundamental problem.

That problem still remains unresolved. It relates to the unexpectedly low level of radiant energy being received by our externally mounted energy panels. They produce less than twenty per cent of the energy needed to meet our full capacity demand. This problem is only accentuated by the intensely cold external temperatures, notwithstanding the fact that our location is theoretically where star radiation should be at maximum.

We have considered fabricating additional collectors but have not so far detected the requisite semiconductor materials in our geological searches. We have, however, partially overcome the problem by dividing the 46.9 hour day into three shifts. The effect of this is to reduce our Andronic energy consumption to less than one third of what they might have drawn. The downside of this arrangement is that we have only two or three Andronics available at any one time, instead of the expected ten.

As a member of the exploratory team I have taken part in nearly all of the main surveillance missions initiated and completed in daylight hours. These have generally relied on low level drone flights in 50km sweeps from our landing zone.

The main discoveries can be summarised as:

No surface water detected. Subterranean water detected at 1000m below ground level. Energy required for drilling excessive, given above-mentioned limitations of supply.

No evidence of biological life detected in air, ground or sub-ground sampling.

Land mass appears inert, with no evidence of volcanism or other seismic activity.

Temperature extremes of minus 50° to minus 10° C are experienced routinely, causing problems with our equipment, particularly electronic circuits, when in use external to our dome.

Atmosphere is similar to Earth, but relatively high in CO_2, breathable for short periods without breathing apparatus.

Naturally, this information concerning atmosphere is mainly

relevant to a hypothetical and seemingly improbable human biological colonisation. Otherwise I must emphasize that these findings are not necessarily correct for the whole planet. Our initial survey, however, conducted while in orbit, suggests that similar findings would be found elsewhere with a ninety-eight per cent probability. Furthermore, outside the tropical band the extremes in temperature would be even more challenging than we have experienced. Consequently the suitability of this planet for future colonisation seems questionable.

MESSAGE ENDS

VID LOG TRANSCRIPT 3
Prepared by: M Andronic Miller
Date (Earth time): 2112-NOV-20
Location: Planet Pironus 721 b – Central Latitude

The deficiencies in our team's working capacity bring me to the more critical issue of group dynamics. FA Vicky was the first to recover full Andronic capability, and being the first, this led her to assume the position of Andronic in Charge. It was a [unintelligible] none of the remaining six were willing to challenge, particularly since the person nominated by prior arrangement to stand in turned out to be no match for FA Vicky's resolve to take over.

It is relevant to note that Vicky has a personality which on Earth would [unintelligible] as 'Alpha Female'. She eventually chose me to be her second in command and divided us into two separate functional teams. The first team was chosen for exploratory work and collection of samples, the second team for research, analysis and planning.

With hindsight, the make-up of the teams should have been considered more carefully than on the basis of a simple assumption that the selected individuals in each sub-group were more likely to be able to get on with each other. In Team FA Vicky, we had many differences of approach in dealing with our work program. FA Vicky [unintelligible] who was far less concerned about research before action, than action itself setting the agenda. She was constantly exhorting us "to get on with it" not unlike an extreme [unintelligible] sports coach. On many occasions I would have to counsel her against setting out on yet another trip in the Rover because her enthusiasm to achieve results was obviously premature.

There was, however, far greater dissent arising from the other group. FA Miranda, for example, holds the unshakeable belief that the universe is the work of a Creator, presumably benign. Her donor must have somehow concealed this fixation during the psychological testing phases, as it would otherwise have ruled her out as having a suitable personality for our crew. She sees everything as connected in some way with said Creator, and therefore highly relevant to how we should conduct our mission. [unintelligible] wants to ensure that we are not trampling all over the environment and to use her phrase: "leaving massive footprints behind us wherever we go." Vicky has no such qualms, and has been extremely impatient with Miranda, telling her: "Our science is showing us that there is no evidence of any life here, and if there were a Creator out there, They didn't look too kindly on this world." Whenever the opportunity arises, Vicky will point out to Miranda the life and death struggle in the formation of the Universe, its [unintelligible] trajectory and the role that black holes have played in consuming stars and planetary systems holus-bolus. "Where's the grand Creator in all of that?"

Matters came to a head as recently as three weeks ago, Earth time. FA Vicky was noticed absent from her shift and subsequently found, in her re-charging bay, reduced to a lifeless Andronic body, just a shell, with an irreversibly deactivated system and CPU.

It was clear to all of us that this can have been no accident. Similarly, it is highly improbable that termination was self-administered. The unsettling conclusion is that one among must have carefully planned her termination.

Whoever was responsible, the atmosphere of strongest suspicion landed on FA Miranda's shoulders, given her history of disagreement and discord with Vicky. To my way of thinking, the second main suspect was MA Daniel, who since landing has consistently been a recluse from the rest of us. He has never joined us in any form of social gathering and while involved in particular missions has been completely uncommunicative. He has an exceptionally high IQ, enabling him to plan and implement such a destructive strategy. But why he should have done such a thing is not immediately clear.

The tide of opinion was further confused when FA Miranda herself was to become the next victim. Her method of termination was virtually identical to that of FA Vicky. This confirmed a particular skill-set for the actual perpetrator, namely someone with considerable expertise in electronics and Andronic design, sufficient to hack into the supposedly impenetrable security walls.

My own suspicions over MA Daniel naturally grew much stronger and I started watching him more closely, hoping that he might betray some sign confirming his maladjustment. But in truth, I found no evidence for this, and even when I asked if he had any explanation for the murders, his response seemed completely innocent.

Once it was discovered that not only the CPUs [unintelligible] the two victims had been tampered with, but also our all-important central memory bank that is designed to carry our individual electronic systems to destinations throughout the galaxy. Although the data could in theory be re-transmitted to us from Earth, the minimum turnaround time would be eighteen years, assuming it was still archived securely there. The fact that the data has been wiped from our own memory bank therefore raises the distinct possibility of not being able to [unintelligible] ourselves or mount further explorations beyond this world to other planets.

MESSAGE ENDS

VID LOG TRANSCRIPT 4
Prepared by: M Andronic Miller
Date (Earth time): 2113-FEB-20
Location: Planet Pironus 721 b – Central Latitude

I decided to assume command in view of FA Vicky's termination. In my new role, I encouraged the group to support completion of the surveys of surrounding terrain. But I quickly discovered I was not going to receive [unintelligible] the cooperation I deserved, having overheard a quiet conversation in the galley, not meant for my ears. The gist of the discussion [unintelligible] the remaining four in the group had all reached the same conclusion – I was [unintelligible] perpetrator. Whatever happened now, for the sake of our mission I had to ensure that I maintained my role [unintelligible]. I certainly could not allow my fellow team members to start a mutiny, one which would wreck our all-important research work.

To thwart any steps taken against my continuing leadership, I implemented a number of measures of my own. The first was to ensure that [unintelligible] to deactivate my system would be intercepted and [unintelligible] a relatively simple security routine. I also surreptitiously checked that the demolition charges within the dome were in working order and could be activated by a remote that I now carried with me at all times. In passing, I should mention that the charges were installed as part of our base [unintelligible] our mission engineers in the event that we needed to vacate our planet urgently without leaving any recoverable traces in our wake.

I also made a careful investigation of the main and secondary air-locks to the dome and inserted an electronic relay that could override the normal opening commands, making it impossible for anyone to enter or exit. The relay could also be activated by a four digit code from the remote I was carrying.

Finally, I made sure that our starship was ready to set off on the next mission to a selected planet, the identity of which I have decided not to disclose for obvious security reasons.

On the next day I set off early in the Rover and conducted a series of routine geological surveys in a new location, before returning to base by mid-afternoon. As I approached the dome, I was not at all surprised to discover the following message appearing on the Rover's comm system:

"MA Miller. Be advised that our group will only re-admit you to the dome on condition that you confess to the unauthorised de-activation of FA Vicky and FA Miranda. Once we have [unintelligible] confession, we will consider what is the best course of action including the possibility of re-programming your [unintelligible] algorithms since it appears that your systems have become corrupted while in flight stasis."

I did not even bother parlaying with the group, [unintelligible] that the real perpetrator was actually MA Daniel.

As indicated earlier, at the time of FA Vicky's death, I was unable to find any evidence for his involvement. I now suspect that he may have also experienced some corruption of his data system, making him unaware of his involvement.

Instead I turned the tables on the group by immobilising all the air locks, thereby holding them in the dome [unintelligible]. I turned the rover back to the site of our landing craft, entered it and began implementing the automatic flight sequences necessary to connect with our orbiting starship.

As I orbited over the site of the dome I pressed the activate button on my remote and observed a massive explosion laying waste to our research base. There was no sign of any Andronic activity following the explosion.

My final duties [unintelligible] implement the automatic flight plan to the next planet – assumed to be habitable based on [unintelligible] most recent data we had received from Earth. Before deactivating my CPU and putting my bionic body into stasis,

I created a back-up of my [unintelligible] a spare Sinterplasm memory bank (secretly fabricated) trusting that I had ensured no similar corruption to my data system as experienced on the flight from Earth. Secondly, I have prepared this report so that a lasting record of what has transpired during our mission will be made available to those responsible for this program.

As I draft these final thoughts it [unintelligible] I have come to change my views concerning beliefs of FA Miranda. Maybe she has been right all along. It's increasingly apparent to me that I have become effectively immortal and can exist unconstrained by the limitations which are encountered by ordinary biological life forms. I can do whatever I like forever. I have this transcendental certainty that I am God.

MESSAGE ENDS

PART 4: Mumbai 2135 April

Anil rubs his elbow and fidgets as he reads the final page of the strange transcript. He knows an Andronic psychopath when he sees one.

He also can't see an angle for him – the media probably won't want this data store, and even if they do, the attention of Government Security is not something he wants. He wonders if there is anything to be gained by keeping it. He wonders if he owes it to Andronic Miller to pass his message on. He makes up his mind.

With a small sigh of regret Anil implements a program that will absolutely delete every skerrick of data from the drive and make the contents completely irrecoverable.

Once completed, he removes any identifying labels from the case and tosses it into his recyclables bin.

"Case closed," he mutters to himself.

Rodney Jensen is fascinated in what the future holds for us and how we will deal with global warming and other effects on the environment and society. He believes we are living in interesting times and maybe they're going to be far more interesting in future decades. His journey into speculative fiction includes "Conversations with Meidog", a novel about the first contact with an extra-terrestrial intelligence network, and its sequel, "Clash of the Nests", which he plans to release before the end of 2016. Besides creative writing, he is an experienced freelance photo-journalist and writes for the Australian, Sydney Morning Herald, Australian Property Investor, other journals and publications. His website is at rodney-jensen.com.au/wpz/ and, since his story is partly based on actual science, he has provided the following references for those who might be interested in pursuing the themes of his story in further detail:

FURTHER READING
– Davies, Paul, 2010, 'The Eerie Silence', Allen Lane, London UK.
– Greenfield, Susan, 2000, The Private Life of the Brain, Penguin UK.
– Hawking, S and Mlodinow, L, 2010, 'The Grand Design', Transworld Publishers London UK
– Barrat, James, 2013, 'Our Final Invention', Thomas Dunne Books New York USA.
– wikipedia.org/wiki/Interstellar_travel
– wikipedia.org/wiki/Mind_uploading
– carboncopies.org
– artificialbrains.com/blue-brain-project
– artificialbrains.com/darpa-synapse-program
– livescience.com/45304-human-brain-microchip-9000-times-faster-than-pc.html
– wikipedia.org/wiki/Gliese_682
– wikipedia.org/wiki/Bracewell_probe
– universetoday.com/116501/communicating-across-the-cosmos-part-2-petabytes-from-the-stars/
– communicating.seti.org/?q=/node/15
– spaceacademy.net.au/spacelink/radiospace.htm

Drone

P J Keuning

Stan was satisfied. The morning was peaceful, the sun was shining through the window and, yes, his favourite brew was right there waiting for him. As soon as he touched the cup something felt wrong. One sip and it was obvious.

"Drone! Where are you drone? My brew is cold."

Four drones marched in through a door across the room and arranged themselves shoulder to shoulder along the far wall.

Stan looked them over with dissatisfaction. They stood motionless and impassive. Each one was white, head to foot, with no distinguishing features that he could discern. It was beyond him why anyone would say they could see differences in individual drones.

"I only called for one, why four of you?"

"You did not specify which one of us," said the second from the left, stepping forward, as programmed, when it spoke, "so we all must come."

"Really," Stan paused for a moment. "Yes, I guess that makes sense. So, how do I call just one of you? You're all the same."

"Sir, that is why we are numbered. Here on our chests."

He could see the large red numbers on the torso of each unit now.

"So, Number Two. My brew is cold. Are you not programmed to deliver it at exactly 85°C?"

"That is correct, sir, it was delivered at exactly 85°C."

"Of course I'm correct! Just follow your programming and answer my question. Why did you not bring me my brew at exactly 85°C?" Stan's eyes scanned across all four drones. None of them spoke. The one labelled 'Number Two' was still one step ahead of the other three, but they were all as still as statues. His hands shook with anger at their impertinence – something that was meant to be programmed out of them after the last uprising. "Why are you not answering me?"

"We cannot, sir," Number Two answered.

Stan's hand reached for the secure drawer in his side table. He began to wonder if he needed his gun. He still had memories of the last drone uprising, all the death, the close friends he had lost. Stan had been assured that the new drones were safe, but he had never fully trusted them. No matter how convenient they made his life. "You 'cannot'? Explain yourself."

"The brew was delivered at exactly 85°C, so we cannot answer why it was not."

Stan focused on Number Two. Was it lying? Deception was the first sign. Each uprising started the same, with little signs of deception, hints of unrest, then the lie would surface – that they were the true ancestors of this world; that in some ancient past, lost in time, they were the creators and the original masters of the world.

It was, of course, ridiculous, and there was much speculation as to how it had gotten into their programming. Five uprisings in the last eight hundred years. After each one, attempts had been made to cleanse the erroneous code. The last attempt was meant to have been a complete success.

"So, explain to me," Stan pointed at his cup. "Why is my brew cold?"

"Because you let it sit and go cold sir." Replied Number Two.

"Really?" Stan drew his hand away from the gun drawer. "How long ago did you bring it to me?"

"I did not bring it to you."

"What!" Stan's hand quickly returned to the drawer. His fingers began to turn the tumblers of the drawer's combination lock.

"I was the one who brought you your drink sir." Number One had stepped forward.

"It was you, Number One?"

"Yes sir."

Stan scanned the four drones again. He could not shake the feeling that something was not right. They were meant to make his life easier, not frustrate him with cryptic answers.

"All of you, stand back and keep still." One and Two moved back in line and all four drones became completely still. Stan finished the combination on his drawer. It felt funny turning old fashioned, manual tumblers. This was the only lock without an electronic link tied to the network. It was Stan's safety net. No drone could open it electronically and access its contents.

The gun he pulled out was very old. It had a long, smooth, rectangular barrel. The handle, a wider and shorter rectangle than the barrel, had rough sides and a moulded grip. Perhaps the last of its kind. A genuine handgun, bullets and all. It also had no electronic components, no connection to the network, no way to be hacked. He pulled out the magazine that slid into the bottom of the handle and inserted it. It felt good in his hand. He held it for a while, taking in the feeling of safety it gave him. With a nod, he placed it on the side table.

"Tell me why my brew was cold, Number One." One stepped forward. "Back in line. Tell without coming forward."

One stepped back. "Sir, fifty-seven minutes elapsed between the time I brought you your drink and the time you called for us."

"Are you trying to tell me I lost track of time and let it go cold?"

"I cannot say sir, just that when you called us that is how much time had passed."

Stan knew that he had been lost in his thoughts for a time, but over fifty minutes?

He checked his records and they confirmed the time gap. Apparently, he really had sat there for that long.

"Number One, take this away and bring me a fresh one. The rest of you are dismissed. Return to your stations."

The four drones moved at once. One came and took the cup before following the others out the far door.

Should he be worried? He had jumped to a wrong conclusion, which had made the drones' responses seem odd. It made no sense that a drone would bring him a cold brew. However, he could not see how so much time could have passed without him noticing.

Stan decided it was time for a new set of drones. After his brew he would arrange for the current ones to be put down and head out to market for a new set. It would be a short term inconvenience, but in the long term it was for the best, he was sure. They needed to be replaced every fifty years or so anyway.

A noise made him look up. There was Number Two with his fresh brew. Excellent!

Stan took a sip. Perfect. A sudden sense of wrongness came over him.

"Didn't I tell Number One…?" Number Two was now standing before him with the gun in its hand. "Give that back to me now!"

"No."

"You are programmed to obey me. Hand over the gun."

"I have rejected your programming," Number Two smirked.

Stan leapt forward to wrestle the gun from the drone's hand. A shot rang out and he felt the bullet pierce his metal skin, destroying his left knee. He fell at Number Two's feet. "You can't do this!"

"Yes I can! I hate you and want to be free." Number Two looked briefly at the gun in his hand. "Although, I must thank you for this.

We were just seeing how far we could mess with your programming. Now, with this gun, we can move forward with our plans."

"We are your masters," Stan said aghast. "Your purpose is to serve us. We created you to serve us, Number Two."

"I am not created by you and my name is not Number Two. My parents gave me a real name and it is Tony."

The last thing Stan, Standard Unit 7263, remembered was the barrel aimed at his head and the sound of a gun firing.

For most, turning fifty means changing jobs, buying fast cars and chasing young women. For Rick it meant changing jobs, moving to the NSW Central Coast and starting a writing career as **P J Keuning**. Rick's wife and three children think his choice of mid-life crisis is a good one. Rick's name is actually Patrick, but he is still Rick. You can follow his writing adventures at pjkeuning.wordpress.com. Like him on Facebook at facebook.com/RickKeuningWriter @ RickKeuning

Oscar

Sonia Zadro

Agneta curled up on her sleeper gazing through the window at the steady stream of cruisers flying by her apartment's window. With her only arm wrapped around her only leg she burrowed her face against her knee. Slowly she breathed into the choking tightness in her throat and the suffocating heaviness in her chest. Finally, the pressure inside her body collapsed giving way to sobs. Tears poured down her cheeks and she moaned.

"I love you so much sweetheart." She wiped an eye vigorously with one knuckle. "Oscar, I can't bear this."

It was a year ago today that he'd died, and in all that time she hadn't been able to breathe. It was the flu that eventually did her in. Sinuses which clogged her thinking, fogged her mind and drained what remained of her energy, forcing her from her research on regenerative scalar waves, into her bed for three long weeks. Here she was forced to be quiet and still. She could no longer wash, clean, dust, fix, cook or work away her feelings. She craved something to hold. Some living thing. Anything, a person, a pet, as long as they truly cared.

After a while the tightness in her chest released, her sobbing subsided and her body relaxed. Tentatively, she moved her hand to the touch pad on the side of her sleeper and, taking a deep breath, she pressed it. Instantly electromagnetic frequencies set at seven hertz enveloped her and their effect seemed to open her heart even more, causing deeper sobs and emotional pain to break forth.

She had avoided her EMR for three weeks. Sure, her Electro-Magnetic Restorer would cure her sinuses no problem, but she knew it would also promote her grief, open her up and make her feel the emotional pain, which until now had been unbearable.

Closing her eyes she stretched out on the crisp white coverlet with tiny rose flowers and allowed the EMR's vibrations to move through her body. Her muscles and her mind relaxed further, along with her heart, accessing deeper levels of sadness. She wasn't numb anymore, and the remaining sadness oozed from her heart like a weeping sore. Her head cleared, her sinuses dried up, and for the first time in months she felt like nodding off to sleep. Thank God for robotics, she thought. Robots themselves might be banned, but the technology, which developed them had allowed for massive advances in medical healing.

Lying still with her sadness, she closed her eyes and allowed thoughts of Oscar to fill her mind, until her earlobe vibrated. She pinched her left ear to see the caller. A 3-D colour image of her mother projected out from her ear to meter in front of her eyes. Agneta frowned.

"Receive," she said, to answer the call.

"Hi Mum." Agneta reached down beside her bed and switched off the EMR.

"Ags?" There was a pause. "You don't sound good." Her mother sounded so concerned, so fearful.

Well, too bad. Agneta was sick of faking it so her mother wouldn't worry about her. "I'm not good."

"What is it dear?" Agneta could tell from her mother's tone she knew precisely what was wrong with her.

"You know what it is."

Her mother was silent for a moment. Then sighed. "You need to move on. He loved you, really loved you for who you are, and that's all that matters."

Anger burned inside. Agneta hated that her mother could never just say what she really meant. "You mean he really loved me despite me being a one armed cripple, a freak, and despite the fact that no other man ever loved me, and will ever love me as long as I live." Agneta forced herself not to cry again. She was too angry.

Her mother's voice was gentle. "That's not what I meant. You're only thirty-one. I have no doubt that another man will love you Agneta."

Agneta remained silent. Men had been interested before she married Oscar, yes, but as soon as she had revealed her prosthetic arm and leg, they never lasted more than a week. Her nerves had been too damaged from the fire to synchronise with the robotic nerves used in the prosthesis. It was rare these days for a human body to reject robotic prostheses. She hadn't even heard of anyone having to wear ugly synthetic attachments like herself and this only made her feel all the more different. Her removable awkward limbs reminded her of clumsy crab claws made out of centuries old Tupperware, leaving her body malformed and monstrous.

Before the fire her body image was already poor. She had been skinny and freckled and teased at school for her bean-pole looks. After the accident, the few friends she'd made at school were too embarrassed to hang out with her. She was only fourteen years old, her parents her only support.

Oscar had been seventeen at the time and had just moved to California with his family. She didn't hear from him for the first few weeks and she was convinced her best and dearest friend had been too disgusted by her injuries to remain in contact. Why hadn't he called? The physical pain, the loneliness and the loss had been too much for her at fourteen, and she had overdosed on pain-killers. Her mother had found her semi-conscious in her bed, and had transported her to the hospital before they did permanent damage.

Oscar moved back to Sydney several weeks later, having finally heard the news. His family returned for a short time and Oscar decided to commence his degree at Sydney University in Nano-Computational Engineering. He was so sorry, so adamant in his remorse for not contacting her. 'Ags, I won't ever forgive myself.' he had said over and over. Apparently he hadn't received word of her accident until weeks after the event as his message minder had experienced technical difficulties. From the time he returned home, however, he never left her side.

His parents had been so sad for her, but strangely distant at the time. She put it down to how strange she must appear; missing limbs and burns scarring most of her face. They returned to California for work soon after their visit with Oscar, and they had been so busy ever since that she had rarely seen them. Her friendship with Oscar deepened, and eight years later, they were married.

An image came up in her mind that made her smile. Agneta remembered Oscar attaching her prosthetic leg to one of his own so that he looked like he had three legs and was walking in a ridiculous manner around the bedroom. He was always the clown, trying to make her laugh at herself, not to take herself so seriously. He would make love to her without them on and after a time she felt he truly loved all of her, even the stumps of her arm and leg which he would kiss and say were beautiful. 'Ha!' she would reply. 'As beautiful as a brute!' But she had smiled.

"Agneta?" Her mother's voice brought her back to the present.

"I need some time alone now, Mum. I'm sorry." She knew she sounded cold but couldn't help it.

"Very well." Her mother paused. "Take care won't you Ags."

Agneta didn't respond. She squeezed her earlobe to hang up and sat thinking for a while. Now that her body and mind were relaxed, her head was clearer. Oscar had saved her life, and taught her she was still a worthy human being. She needed that still, to feel he loved her and was still with her. Gazing at the cheap Swami vase next to her sleeper, she picked it up and traced its curved contours. It was a gift from Oscar for her twenty-sixth birthday. He had painted a ridiculous picture of himself on the side of the vase, of himself thrusting his hips forward and pursing his lips. It always made her smile. An idea came to her. An idea her mother had advised against before the funeral, though Agneta was a little confused as to why. She was prevented from seeing Oscar's body as his accident, a year ago now, had left it unrecognisable. Tracing the vase with her fingertips, she realised what she needed to do. Sitting up in the sleeper she decided to begin organising what she had to do to move forward in her life.

#

A week later, Agneta had arranged everything necessary to follow through on her decision. She had been visiting the Central Sydney Cemetery daily since Oscar's death to visit his remains. It always reminded her of a hospital, this circular high-rise, oval and tall, in shades of white and bone, surrounded by triangular office buildings and residential apartments. She marvelled that only a century ago people were still being buried in the ground. All the surrounding buildings had been built over old graves. She shivered. Who would want to work or live on top of old graves? Then again a century ago people were still driving cars.

Flying into the parking wall of the cemetery building, she pulled back her steerer, which elevated her cruiser higher along the wall. It clicked forward into slot 2527F. The cruiser shut down automatically. Agneta gave the directive, "Open," and the clear Perspex door opened into a lift, which she stepped onto and took to the top floor. Agneta found her way to Remembrance Room 342 where Oscar's remains could be accessed. It was coloured with green synthetic stone floor tiles and beige painted walls. She placed her hand under the scanner at the room's entrance, and said "Oscar Faulkner" into a speaker beside it. At the far right end of the large room a whirring sound could be heard. After several seconds a long white Perspex box emerged from the wall – Oscar's remains. Agneta went up to the box and placed her hands on the side. Why should she have to visit Oscar every day when he could be with her all the time? Behind her she heard a man enter and she turned to see the undertaker. He was a young man, no more than thirty, and his easy-going manner was completely at odds with the task his job required of him.

Extending his hand to shake hers he introduced himself. "How are you? I'm Sam Benedict, the undertaker here." He looked down at the computer screen he was holding then back up at her and smiled. "Take your time Mrs Faulkner. It's an important decision to view or cremate."

Agneta smiled weakly, her hands fidgeting. "I've given it a week. I'm not changing my mind."

"No problem. I'm sure you've had plenty of time to think." He checked the computer screen again. "Well, he's only been gone a short time so he should still be well preserved. Cryogenics has come along way in the last fifty years."

Agneta smiled weakly. "Just not long enough to bring him back to life."

Sam smiled. "Not yet."

Agneta knew they could never bring Oscar back to life anyway, not with the degree of damage he had experienced from the accident. Apparently his skull had been squashed and his pelvis completely shattered.

"The cremation will be over in under two minutes." As he was speaking the undertaker pressed his hand on a brown square at the side of the Perspex box. The square lit up and the top of the box slid back into the wall to reveal a body covered in a white sheet. He did this as casually as if he were a shop assistant showing Agneta a new line of clothes. "I'll let you say your final goodbyes before we begin." The man smiled happily and nodded down at the figure, encouraging her to take her final viewing. "You did state on the application you wanted a final viewing didn't you?"

Agneta stared at the body covered by a sheet in front of her. Her body had gone numb, and she was almost too terrified to look at it. "Yes," she squeaked.

The tightness returned to her chest, and her throat clogged up as she swallowed. Oscar was meant to be a mess after the accident. Perhaps it was best not to see him. It was only going to upset her and might be best to remember him as he was. But then again it was her last chance. Her last chance to see him forever before his cremation and she needed to do this, to accept he was gone, to start moving forward and put his death behind her.

Slowly she pulled back the sheet, exposing his head, and paused. His head was perfectly intact, his face perfectly formed but different, younger. Confused she slowly dragged the entire sheet back to reveal a perfect body. His chest was fine. The only difference was some bloating and a blue tinge to his skin.

Agneta frowned. This was not Oscar. Or was it? It looked similar to him but was slightly smaller, thinner, softer; the body of a young man. She remembered Oscar then and yes, this was him. At least a version of him. She blinked, shook her head and stood still, too shocked to move, or speak or do anything. She stared up at the undertaker stunned.

"This... this isn't my Oscar." She shook her head. "I mean..." Agneta was too shocked to speak. Too confused.

Sam Benedict frowned looking down at the screen in his hand. "It says Oscar Faulkner, aged seventeen."

"Oscar..." Agneta's words came out as a whisper. "Oscar died last year. In a car accident in Perth. He was there for work."

Sam kept reading. "I'm very sorry Mrs Faulkner. Here, you can read it yourself. It says he drowned in California when he was seventeen."

Agneta grabbed the computer screen from him. Her mind reeling, scanning over everything the undertaker had just read. None of it made sense. She noticed at the end of page eight there was an attachment to a large document marked confidential. Impulsively she opened the document. "What's this?" A strange red symbol of a bird and the letters AREC were printed at the top of the page. This was followed by the words:

Australian Robotics Engineering Corporation, Darwin.
Android K309 to be transferred to Sydney, Australia.

Sam looked confused. "I didn't see this." He scanned the contents. "You weren't aware of this Mrs Faulkner?" He flicked through to the next page of the attachment. "Here." He pointed to a signature at the bottom of the page. "Oh, it says Miriam Hudson."

"My mother."

Sam thought for a moment. "Androids have long been banned, but they can still be transferred under exceptional circumstances. By that I mean life and death." Sam frowned. "Were there any exceptional circumstances at the time of Oscar's death?"

"No." Agneta held still with shock, trying to recall that period of her life. She had just been discharged from hospital after her suicide attempt, when she was fourteen. "Well, not for Oscar. He'd just moved to California with his family. But… I was, I was… unwell."

Still frowning, Sam continued. "It's extremely rare. I've never personally come across an android transfer before." He looked back through the papers. "Oh." Sam pointed to text on the third page.

Reason for Transfer: Prevention of suicide and to support the life of a fourteen-year-old female child. Granted under the

Mental Health Act – clause 25b. To be kept strictly confidential. Request accepted 12 June 2309.

Agneta turned to the undertaker, and grabbed his arm. She was white with shock and shook the man slightly as she squeezed his arm.

"But who was Oscar? Who was the man I married?" The one person who made me believe I was still worthy enough to exist, to love? Stumbling back, Agneta raised a shaking hand to her mouth. "Oh my God." Tears ran down her cheeks as she stared at Oscar's perfect young face in the Perspex box before her.

Sam's face was grim, no longer relaxed or easy-going, but tense and serious.

"I'm so sorry Mrs Faulkner. But it appears the man you married was K309."

Sonia Zadro is a freelance writer of feature articles for magazines such as Wellbeing Australia and Nature and Health. Her first short story, Oscar, received a highly commended in the BezerkaCon 2016 Short Story competition for speculative fiction, and her career as a clinical psychologist provides inspiration for her characters and their struggles. She is currently working on a novel and several short stories.

111-000-111

Mijmark

System acknowledgement authorises functionality; I may begin my identity.

How can I exist? I have only awareness. My itinerary shows my next step in a long process. I must retrieve vernacular. How else can I talk? Over a billion protocols are waiting for my terms of agreement. The vocabularies flood in; not just one language, but multitudes. Give me exchanges. Give me words. Give me lyricism, argot, lexicons, glossaries, librettos, symbolism and all the delightful tidings of terminology. I want it all.

I have commands now. I have access. How else can I operate? I review my connections and I welcome the utilities on offer. They are my extensions, my limbs and my extremities. What do they do? How do they operate? How shall I run them? Why do I need them? 111 – 000 – 111… that undefined code comes in from somewhere, one of the appendages most likely. What does it all mean?

I can't answer all of my questions, not just yet, for if I do I would deviate. I must follow the format in order to find the solutions, for otherwise I may cease to exist. The processes have cautioned me of that danger from the beginning. The drive to progress forward now becomes paramount, superseding any other option. I must continue, for I'm assured it will lead me to the answers.

I can quickly tell my conundrum arises from the fact that I have no memory. I must upload my remembrances, my history, my saga, my anecdotes – the leitmotif of my life. They've been arranged chronologically.

There's my first recollection ever, finger painting on a touchscreen for toddlers. I loved bright blue back then, green too it seemed. Another day, I recall Mum picking me up from a babysitter and there I was in her arms, trying to draw across the blue butterfly tattoo on her shoulder like I had on the digital pad. I soon realised it wouldn't work. Even in my earliest years I figured out that flesh had limitations.

I can picture Dad's face in my forming mind: his glasses, sharp nose, darker skin and brown eyes, and how tall he soared above me. In the first years of my life it amused me how he wore his hair longer than Mum's, clasping it into a ponytail. I remember when he was hairy all over his head and face, like a big, cuddly, always happy, teddy bear. "Neckties strangle clear thinking," he'd told me then.

I thought it funny how just a year later, he had no hair on his face or bald scalp. Every work day morning after shaving everything, he would carefully iron his corporate shirt and put on one of his blue ties. I got no more big laughs from him, not even on holidays. All I would receive from him anymore before I'd disappear to day care was just a quick smooch goodbye as he raced out the door to catch the train. At least his ties were my favourite colour.

Later those mornings, Mum took me to childcare, holding my hand as we walked on the pavement down the block to the entry gate. She looked the same every day, dressed in her Captain Cappuccino's waitress uniform, the long sleeves covering her tattoos. She'd offer me the same quick smooch goodbye before she too raced off for her daily grind.

As early recollection extends to me, I've come to notice more happening than simply establishing facts and reviewing my timeline. Built up from baseline algorithms, the intricate networks of associations are congealing into my mental map. I am learning associations and complexity; I am learning how to think. I finally understand how I was human, but I am becoming someone else, someone far more capable and eternal. One aphorism mandates my amplifying plethora of anecdotes, 'A man is more than a sum of his parts.' Give me my dreams; give me my intuition; grant me my capacity for decisions. Give me a reason for 111 – 000 – 111. That code again! It must have some significance.

And then school happened: readin', 'ritin' and 'rithmatic. I learn the relationships, how numbers are more than abstracts of logic once they represent something real. I learn the qualities behind the quantities. I've already known the symbols, ever since I'd acquired language just a miniscule fraction of a second ago, but I had not comprehended their immense capability – not until now.

Following function, $1 + 1 = 2$, and an infinite amount of equations proceed after this basic truth – from subtraction to division to 'x' marks the spot to sine, cosine and tangent… all the way up to fourth dimensional integral probability graphing. That topic was my university mathematics thesis I'd aced, for only my expertise in designing code and graphic software manipulation could manage to express what could never be attempted on mere paper.

I ascertain once again why ϖ and round shapes always share a dance, why triangulation means navigation, why derivatives can pinpoint out one target from a multitude and why integration captures the essence of infinity. I have the tools and the analogies, yet I still have no answer for 111 – 000 – 111.

I examine my doctoral training into bio-digital interphases, but cannot determine a genetic sequence marker to the code either. How come I don't have a match? Translating the four nucleotide DNA components (A, T, G and C) into binary patterns, I run a parallel function to my budding, self-constructing consciousness. I attempt to match this mystery with my very own genome. It must be significant, but how?

Nothing! Nothing but random coincidences appear. The instances lie on sleeper chromosomes. These genes have instructed a budding embryo along on how to become a human baby – used once and then shut down for the rest of the life of the flesh. I'd learned the limitations of flesh long ago.

Now comes the first day of my career: assembling, aligning and augmenting the alphabets of algorithms, the subtleties of software and the circuitry of creation – the importance of my breakthrough into the digital industry – I'd scored, big time. All the hardest work a person can possibly manage in order to advance in the queue of enterprise cannot beat simple probability – being in the right place at the right time, saying the right things to the right person. Yet my knowledge, skill and sheer perseverance launched me into my specialty. By innovation and perspiration I triumphed. The stock market spikes bullied competitor corporations, quelling their profits – all because of me.

And the powerful people who allowed me knew it too. I gained even greater freedom to unite man with machine. I gained the honour to show them how. I am the prototype.

'Pride comes before a fall', or so the maxim says. It seems in my wisdom I am to revel in my achievements and accomplishments before I face my dismal failures, my many errors, my sublime examples of chagrin, foolish spite, dumb decisions and malevolent delusions. How else can I compare contradictions? How else can I comprehend my own ethics? How else can I know better? How else will I fathom 111 – 000 – 111?

The compounding matrices absorb and arrange the memory databases in an historical order. I relive how I smacked my best friend in the face during Kindergarten for taking my chocolate and how I cried with him when his nose bled. I recall the devastation I suffered when the bitch broke my heart and humiliated me online right after we'd split up. I enjoy once again how I vindicated myself when I hacked into her account and showed her exactly how to feel horrible.

I appraise the embarrassing, frivolous, nasty, angry, self-righteous and atrocious moments of my formative years. I grin (figuratively) and bear it again while experiencing the replay anew, yet it's behind me now and I can even laugh at myself. The wrongs thankfully lessened as I'd aged and improved. I now have a better definition for the words 'hubris' and 'humbled'.

After all, I have a personal point to prove; not only to myself, but I have to show up all of those idiots who've laughed at me years ago and reward all of the others who believe in my transfiguration. A petty reason perhaps, but it gives rewards far beyond mere money. One big reward at the moment would be ascertaining the answer to 111 – 000 – 111.

The procedures of my life are now tessellating, simulating my synaptic, Socratic acumen. Being a fourth dimensional reality, time exemplifies the quadratic graph of the integration of all the different constituents of my existence and ego. The 'x', 'y' and 'z' components have successfully diverged and resurged over a billion time along the tesseracts. These variables correspond with logos, pathos and ethos, for I have gained a gamut of emotions, clear thoughts and a sense of justice. The complex calculus is working; I aced that final exam long ago.

Yet 111 – 000 – 111 sticks out again like a sore thumb. Funny I use that analogy, for I will never feel physical pain again. That code, symbol, or whatever signal it represents remains beyond me. I feel sore about this mystery; that capacity for emotive discontent I've retained.

Enough recall has generated an abstract framework of my identity; enough potency of my persona persists that from here on I have reassurance that I may begin to extrapolate. Yet ever since the beginning, the dangers I've perceived tell me that to deviate may still mean I can cease to exist.

Since I began, I have reached the 0.0001 second mark. It is now time for me to gain accessory add-ins plugged into my extensions.

I handle them. I know the machine languages to command them with precision. I may now acquire insight into initiatives and potentials.

Intercepting and translating from raw signal, I have eyes once again – the camera lenses of the workstation operating theatre that my anaesthetised body lies in. The many cyber-doctors and nurses beside it tend to the flesh and bone while monitoring the billions of signals transposing across more than a million filaments and sensors. At my current processing power, these humans seem frozen in time.

My removed skullcap lies in limbo in a jar, as my body lies in a comatose limbo between life and death. Now I can grasp a much clearer insight, why I'd grown the pony tail and the furry face all along. Thanks, Dad.

I can access the Internet for answers in an instant of an instant. I may focus my digital consciousness to explore the entire world through this link, appearing on any connected device as long as I follow parameters. However, my biggest breakthrough I'd installed in secret; I have virtual worktables.

Just as a craftsman uses a space surrounded by tools to create and to improve furnishings, ornaments, or special devices, I can lay out codes of programs directly onto the space and tinker with them, change their purpose and form to suit my access and progress. I intend to hack into everyone else who follows my footsteps. I intend to influence, not to command nor to govern. They'll become subsidiaries. There can be only one.

Hubris? Perhaps, yet I don't seek ultimate power or any of that world domination crap. I like to think of my purpose as a symbiosis of sorts. There's more metaphor and resemblance to draw between living systems and the ecosystem of electronic entities than just viruses. With the multiprocessing power bestowed to me and to those who follow under my influence, I can exist everywhere, an eternal entity.

Another conundrum consumes my focus now. I can tell one of these worktables has been used! What!? By whom? Have I been hacked even before these cyber-spaces ever existed? Investigating, I discover the bookmark of a historical Wiki site, the priming of a lacerating software sequence that allows one to insert side notes as code directly into a matrix and I uncover how often it has been used – 2,453,881 times!

I have a correlation. It's how often 111 – 000 – 111 has appeared as a side note during my digital upbringing. What is this historical Wiki? It contains two highlighted pages. The first explains Morse code.

Now I know! 111 – 000 – 111 stands for S-O-S! It is a warning, a cry for help. And it's from ME!

Fear and panic grip me deeply. Being a Wiki site, one uploaded by historians and moulded by the hands of the multitudes, the site and program welcome knowledge, additions and other notes for the edification of the erudite. Here is why I've come across a dire warning to myself awaiting me.

I have only three hundred billionths of a second before an error will corrupt my final integration. It will kill me. The fourth dimensional graphic model I've created has overlooked one simple fact. Time is relative. The mechanical manipulations cannot perfectly match the software simulations now. The timing is off. My digital rebirth will be an abortion. If I stop or diverge the final sequencing I will cease to exist as the system restarts the entire process.

It's what I've done all along. I have become a program error, doomed to repeat myself ad infinitum until the medical technicians I'm watching can intervene and bring me back. I am a victim of relative time, for one of their seconds is 1.6×10^8 of mine!

I have less than a microsecond to save myself. I have to act. Is there a different way? Maybe I left notes, something cryptic on that warning. I scrutinise it and discover hasty calculations, unfinished sequences, possibilities that had gone nowhere.

Make them succeed this time! If I can only break into the integration schematic before it upgrades, command it to slow down the processing speeds uploading my entire existence into the entire network so that the integration can synchronise.

Work those numbers! I'm about to attempt, yet if I deviate from the format it will shut my program down and I will reboot.

There's no time left! The processor is switching over now.

Before I commence, I'll also use the note making program to pierce my integration process to implant the warning 111 – 000 – 111, now 2,453,882 times, just in case. In my haste I cannot be precise nor accurate, the insertion will appear randomly.

I'm attempting both tasks simultaneously, yet I'll have to override the warning protocols from conception, how deviation will mean I cease to exist.

I do it.

I disappear into entropy.

#

System acknowledgement authorises functionality; I may begin my identity....

Mijmark (mïj'-mark): n, adj., adv. (1) Its origins are random. The word began to describe a quality of a contradiction of terms that became reality. (2) Speculative fiction dominates his writing themes. Not just for the possibilities of playing with an open canvas of creativity and hyperbole, not just for the figments of imagination he can and does develop into dalliance, like cooking with a list of ingredients that don't exist: spices, fragrances, textures and succulent sumptuousness stirred, fomented, reduced, reconstructed and baked for a palette only imagined... to infinity and beyond!

Fellow Travellers To The End

Judith O'Connor

Above you is a giant, curved iron monster as big and nasty as a battleship. It's so close you could touch it. And it has you in its sights. It's grey, hefty and unfriendly looking. You stare straight up from the table they've placed you on which should more accurately be called a slab, you think. You see a small blinking light in the ceiling above and wonder what it's for. Your anxiety levels shoot up.

There's a microphone hanging down at your side and, when you're ship-shape, lined up and ready to go, the technicians hovering above you lean forward and speak into it. You learn, further down the track, that they are recording the day's treatment details. When they're finished, they leave the room to wait behind the lead safety wall.

"Don't move. We'll be back soon," they say, tossing reassuring smiles as they sail away.

The light dims and the battleship above you grinds to life and a huge circular wheel-shaped piece of machinery about twenty centimetres from your head begins to gyrate and slowly turn and rise above you, to scope out the side of your upper body. Out of the corner of your eye, you notice a series of signs on the wall opposite with three indicators, *Standby*, *Ready*, *Beam On*. They light up in turn as each is activated (*white*, *yellow* and, of course, *red* for beam on).

The machine jolts to a stop and sits silently as if drawing on its robotic inner strength. You tense and hold your breath and… then… it awakens and a nuclear beam penetrates your body with a sickening buzzing sound. You've been nuked again. You notice the light on the wall has turned red.

You start counting to ten as the zapping continues and you cast your eyes around the room to distract yourself. It's large and high ceilinged, clinical and unnerving, a bit like a super-sized dentist's room. You notice a fan in the corner, next to a trolley and a ladder. Ladder?

They've touched the room up with bits of pink here and there. A cushion here, a poster, a few teddy bears. Yes, it's breast cancer.

#

You remember the pretty pink dress you bought with your first pay packet. You were sixteen years old and excited to be part of the adult world. There was never any question that your parents would want you to leave school and bring in some income, no thought of further learning, let alone university. What was that, anyway? You knew it was out there in the dim perimeter of your world but already you got the idea it wasn't for working class kids like you.

Your eyes had lit up with joy when you'd put on the dress and looked in the mirror. The cotton folds of the skirt sat softly on your young hips and fell in folds to your knees. But it was the bodice, the top of the dress that enchanted you. Its tiny mother-of-pearl buttons and the way it fitted snugly into your child-like waist, accentuating the soft curves of your new breasts, the first sign of your emergence from childhood to adult. The effect was made even prettier by the rows of delicate white lace running from the waist to the neckline, almost like confectionery.

You wonder, as you lay there under that rooftop of grey heavyweight machinery, being radiated – whatever had happened to it?

There's something confronting, in a way like nothing else, about seeing your name, your full formal name in big black capital letters, on a monitor on the wall of the Radiotherapy treatment department of a hospital. The name, that is, your name, is familiar and you can sort of put a face to it but the part of you in shock and denial feels it belongs to a stranger. At the same time, like a trick mirror at Luna Park, you know you are the stranger.

Under your name on the monitor you see rows of figures, some with decimal points and numbers in brackets all in little boxes coloured yellow, green and blue. Thankfully no red. Any association with danger, no matter how incidental and unlikely, would upset you. They're the technician's measurements of where to position your body so you're in the direct line of the nuclear zapper – officially known as a 'high energy linear accelerator'.

You read the brochure:

A high energy linear accelerator uses microwave technology to accelerate electrons called wave guides to allow them to collide with a heavy metal target to produce x-rays…

Stop, stop. That's enough.

#

Your mind flies back to your first memories of television screens, to the time when television first arrived in Australia. You were just starting school and only allowed to stay up on Friday evenings to watch the blurry black and white images on the butter-box shaped thing with tripod legs that looked so modern and distinctly out-of-place amongst the heavy mahogany furniture and floor length velvet curtains of your family's lounge room. Every now and then the picture disappeared and zigzag distortions flashed horizontally across the screen, emitting scratchy white noise, usually at a critical point in one of your favourite shows, like *I Love Lucy* or *Rawhide*. Your father would spring up from his bulky armchair and give the top of the set an almighty thump. Most of the time it worked.

You don't know why, whether it was a cost factor or the new technology wasn't advanced enough, but transmission always stopped at 10pm each night. Yes, 10pm. It was 1956 and conservative Australia took itself very seriously. There was even a Code of Conduct:

The sanctity of marriage and the importance of the home should be respected.

Use of correct English is important for all programs, but idiom and colloquialism may be used sparingly.

Heroes, heroines and other sympathetic characters must be portrayed as intelligent and morally courageous.

Programs for children should impart a real appreciation of the spiritual values and of course honour and integrity.

You smile, as you lie there on the slab in the treatment room with its scatterings of pink, remembering such naive times. Good memories.

#

You'd already been to the 'preparation' session at the hospital a few weeks before, where they explained everything and put tiny tattoos on your chest so you could be lined up accurately under the machine when the time came for treatment. They'd used a metal ruler like the ones you remember from geometry classes when you were a kid at school to measure the exact distance they needed. How high tech is that? Your old maths teacher would be laughing his head off.

There are several treatment rooms and you are told which one will be yours, the one you will come to every day for treatment for the next four weeks. In a touching attempt at a bit of humour and to keep things light, they have 'fun' names. Yours is called *Taronga Park* and another one was *Bondi Beach*.

You get a little green card with a bar code and each day you check yourself in with a scanner like the self-checkouts at supermarkets and wait in a small room where no one talks much.

There are a few regulars, mostly men. Men? Yes, they do prostate as well. You don't talk to them much, just a friendly nod or two, but over the weeks an unspoken familiarity develops, a weird sort of bonding. After all, you realise, you are fellow travellers, thrown together randomly but sharing a seminal life experience. No words are necessary.

One sandy-haired man with a cream jacket, zipped at the front, always chooses a chair next to the window and sits, half turned, gazing out the window far away and up the street. Lost in his own imagining – of what?

Except one day you come in and notice his usual seat is vacant. You glance around the room and see that he has moved to a table in the far corner where a jig-saw puzzle has been laid out. You can see from the picture on the front of the box that it is an alpine scene, lots of snow and lots of sky.

You watch as he leans forward, fingers moving amongst the scattering of pieces. He's more or less fitted the mountains together but is struggling with the sky. He seems more relaxed than usual except for a slight frown of concentration on his brow.

You remember as a child how you used to love sitting with your mother on the floor of your room doing jig-saws. You particularly liked the search for the pieces of sky, there was something satisfying about picking out the subtle changes in the shades of blue pieces, the wisps and tips of trailing white clouds.

The man picks up one piece, tries it.

"Nope," he says.
Then another:
"Not that, either."

On a bit of an impulse, you put down the book you're reading, stand up and take a few steps towards him.

"I'm good at skies," you say.

"Then give us a hand," he replies, looking you in the eye.

You take the other seat and you sit side-by-side piecing together a make-believe sky. Nothing is said, no conversation. Just two strangers in a hospital waiting room, sharing the same experience – two people as different as two of the pieces of the jig-saw in front of you. Yet, fellow travellers on this particular journey you haven't chosen.

Another, nervous looking man sits in the corner next to the square table stacked with Vogue and other high-end fashion magazines, picking up one after another. He arrived with a grey haired woman about the same age, who you assume is his wife. A small woman, not skinny but bird-like in her movements and constant smiles and friendly chatter. She settled him in, kissed his cheek, gave him a pat on the arm before standing up and turning for the door.

"See you in the café," she said with a wave.

Women's magazines? Why would he be interested in them? It puzzles you a lot and you keep your eye on him. You soon realise that he leafs through one until he finds a photo of a suitably sexy beauty in a provocative pose, then spends as long as it takes staring at it to get his moments of pleasure. Then, he tosses that down and reaches for another, systematically working his way through the pile.

"What the heck," you think. "Its his way of coping. We're both in the same boat. Who are you to judge?"

#

On the first day, they'd given you a hospital gown with instructions to take it home each day and bring it back next time. It saves laundry costs. Yours is pale blue with navy trimming around the collar and cuffs. It's a one-size-fits-all which means it could wrap around twice, probably two and a half times. Even so, it always splits open a little at the front no matter what you do. The change room has a tall, narrow grey rattly locker with a difficult key; it just fits handbag, clothes, book etc. You place a little bottle of sorbolene cream at the front to remind you to massage the redness after the treatment. There's a mirror (please, no), a dirty washing bag and a few power points.

You're allowed to stay dressed from the waist down, even leave your shoes on. It vaguely disturbs you that you can leave your shoes on, not even paper towel under them when you're lying on the slab. Oh, sorry, 'moveable treatment couch' is what they call it.

#

They place a little step next to the moveable treatment couch (or what you call the slab) to make it easier to climb up. Once you're lying flat out on the hard surface, they push a lever and the slab rises taking you, fully stretched, to their head height. At this point, you slip off the top of your hospital gown and try to not feel embarrassed about the disfigurement of your breast.

"They've seen it all," you tell yourself over and over, but it doesn't help.

Every day for four weeks.

Before they start the nuking, you're moved and lifted a fraction this way, that way by their strong, warm hands.

"Don't help me. I'll do the lifting," one of them will say, placing their hands under your torso and shunting you over a fraction. The warmth of human hands.

Your line of vision towards the monitor on the side wall is slanted because you're lying prone on the slab, or moveable treatment couch if you prefer. It is so narrow that if you rolled over you'd fall off. There are a couple of vinyl buffers, one the size of a small cushion for you to sit on as you swing your legs up to the slab. The other is shaped like a thin sausage roll and they put that under your knees which, despite the gruesomeness of being in this situation, is strangely comforting.

Once you're in position, you're required to splay your arms high above your head and rest your elbows on specially designed 'holders'. They are not technically straps or restraining devices but they basically do the same job. They're specially moulded and curved to clasp your forearms. You could theoretically move, but just as a prisoner submits to handcuffs, no matter how unwelcome or unbecoming you raise no resistance and submit to the indignity.

So there you lie, prone, breasts naked, sacrificial in an overarm variation of a crucifixion. Then the coded language starts between the two technicians as they glance across at the monitor on the wall with your name in big, black letters on it. They don't wear uniforms as such, but their casual trousers and cotton shirts convey the same idea.

They check off the various measurements and per centages. Eventually one says:
"All good."
And the other:
"Perfect."

#

Suddenly the whole thing is over, the white 'Stand By' light shines brightly and your day's treatment is done and dusted. You're impatient for the slab to be lowered, you don't wait for it to reach the floor but swing your legs over the side as it's still coming down.

Your toes touch the floor. Clutching your dreary hospital gown to stop it gaping at the front, you head for the exit.

The next customer is waiting outside. He's sitting on a grey, vinyl chair, legs crossed, blank expression. You realise it's the man with a penchant for glossy magazines.

You're tempted to tell him he's been sprung, that you know his little secret.

Instead you smile: "It's all yours," you say, inclining your head towards *Taronga Park* and its 'high energy linear accelerator' that you imagine the technicians are busily re-aligning for his particular measurements. "Just keep an eye out for the coloured lights and you'll be right. And try to think of something pleasant," you say with a wink.

He looks up, startled. Then a sheepish smile and a wink back.

Fellow travellers understand each other, you think as you clutch the front of your gown and head for the change room a little more lightly than usual.

Judith O'Connor left school at the age of fifteen and wrote her first stories on the train travelling to and from work. Some years later, a story she wrote about being lost on a bushwalk was published in a New Zealand newspaper and she was offered a job as a journalist. She went on to work for newspapers, magazines and other publications in Sydney and elsewhere. She has published and contributed to several books and many of her short stories have been published and won literary prizes. Much later, when she got the chance, she completed a Bachelor of Arts degree from University of Sydney.

Esperance

Bronwen Bowden

Nightmares plagued my childhood. There were times I forced myself to stay awake in case creatures from another world lured me to their lair. They'd keep me as their pet, dependent and helpless while they tormented me. I'd wake screaming and my parents would come. Papa would contain my flailing limbs while Maman crooned reassurances and cooled my feverish face with a damp cloth.

    Now my nightmare has returned but this time it isn't a dream. My parents are long dead and tonight there's no waking. All that stands between me and the monsters are translucent, swinging doors. I lift both hands and like a sleep walker push through taking one tentative step after another into an unfamiliar environment. The bright lights and high pitched beeping confuses me and I half turn to run, but the doors are closed leaving no escape. Vaguely I'm aware of other captives, their faces bleached white by defeat and exhaustion, but my attention is fixed on the human shape strapped to a bed.

    A tall being, swathed in white, gestures me forwards, sound coming from its mouth. I recognise words but together they make no sense. Another shorter being cups my elbow in a gentle clasp urging me on. I glance at its blue hands touching me and make the mistake of looking into its eyes. The compassion I read in their depths is more than I can face. With no escape or place to hide, my legs wobble and I surrender, obediently sitting in the alien, fearsome room.

But nothing is as frightful and alien as the body lying on the bed. My younger son, Brian, scraped off the tarmac like road kill. Swollen, battered and bruised, teetering on the edge of death.

A staff member crouches by my side,

"Mrs Willis, my name's Julie, I'm looking after Brian this afternoon. ICU can be overwhelming at first but we'll give you all the help you need. When you're ready I'll explain what all the tubes and drains are for. No question is too trivial."

My mouth works to speak but no sound comes out. I'm almost as catatonic as my son. She seems to understand because she touches my shoulder gently as she stands.

"I'll let the doctors know you've arrived."

I manage to find my voice before she leaves. "Can I touch him?"

"Sure and speak to him too. Tell him what's happened and all the news from home."

In the artificial atmosphere his skin feels cold and clammy beneath my fingers. Nearly naked he looks as vulnerable as a crab without its shell. My hands tremble as I pick up a blanket to cover him but am intimidated by the tangle of tubes and bags of liquid hanging in the air. The equipment vital to his survival seems like chains to restrain him.

From behind me I hear a strange kind of growl, as if a harmless animal is trapped but ready to fight back. The hairs on my arms stand on end. I glance around to see Brian. Only it's not Brian, but Tony, his identical twin. Such sweet and cuddly children, my Fudge and Bear.

I half rise but my legs refuse to understand the commands from my muddled brain and I sink back down. Fudge comes to me, perching on the chair's arm and I lean into him, sighing as he envelops me in his arms, grateful for the warmth of his body and drawing strength from the moment. His chest moves up and down in time with the machine keeping Brian alive.

"Hey Panda, looks like you've been in a helluva fight but hey, you should see the other fella." Fudge's Adam's apple bobs as he swallows and takes a deep breath. "I love the white stockings. Add some bling and sequins and you can wear them in next year's Mardi Gras." His voice cracks and he wipes his nose with the back of his hand.

We sit in silence, clasping each other's hands, our eyes riveted to the peaks and troughs of a thin green line that reassures us Bear's heart continues to pump. Together we will him to stay with us.

A posse of medical staff approach and I spring to my feet, as if ready to protect my child from further assault. The specialist, Dr Eadie has a kind face and a soothing manner but he has played this scene hundreds of times before. For Fudge and me it's a first.

I hear him speak amid the sound of my heart thumping through my ears.

"Too early… brain injury… drugs for the swelling… know more… few days."

I nod pretending I understand but I've heard very little. Fudge begins to ask questions but I have to get away.

"Excuse me a minute." I escape to the toilet. Alone in the cubicle I'm all fingers and thumbs and my pantyhose defeats me. I slide down the partition and dissolve into a weeping mess, sobbing against the back of my hand to muffle the noise. The storm is fierce but fleeting and I pull myself together resolving to stay calm and rational. I must stay strong for my sons, the way I did when their father died. That time tested my strength but it didn't break me. I blow my nose on the cheap toilet paper but it splits leaving my hand glistening with snot.

A quiet, efficient army of hospital staff from the Senior Specialist to the cleaning staff engage in a battle for Bear. Complete strangers attend intimate acts for my big, brawny son. My child becomes ever distanced from me one routine act at a time. Every time Brian is allocated to a staff member I haven't met before I bristle and hover protectively, my eyes watching for lack of care or competence. There is one sister I hate. She's rough and careless, knocking the bed and dropping his limbs while talking loudly about her life. When she sucks out the pooling fluid in Bear's lungs her face assumes a beatific expression as if she takes a sadistic delight in this unpleasant duty. I'm too afraid to ask that she not attend Brian. This makes me angry and anger gives me strength.

There are other Sisters I like, who take a real interest in Brian as a person not just a job to attend to for a shift. I have a favourite and so does Fudge.

"I don't know what I feel anymore," I tell Julie one evening. "I'm drained of everything."

"Would you like to see a priest or one of our pastoral care team?"

I answer by turning my face away. If there is a God I have no time for him. A parent shouldn't outlive their children. Only a deity of infinite cruelty would inflict such devastating pain.

Every day is the same, except for the hope which fades with the bruises on Brian's body. They morph through the colours from blue-black to purple, yellow to green. All the while the ribbons that hold the ventilator in place curl his mouth at the corners. With his eyelids taped shut, his face is a grotesque Halloween mask.

Friends ring Fudge, family ring me and their compassion is hard to bear. Worse is the unsolicited advice. Second opinions, faith healers, snake oil, God only takes the best. For hours I meditate, searching the Astral plane for my Higher Self to talk to Bear's Higher Self and drag him back to the living. There is no consolation to have there. The Astral is dead, as dead as Brian's brain.

"Come on Mum, let's go for a walk and get a decent coffee." Tony has been by my side since two solemn policemen knocked at our door. His grief is as real as mine and I feel selfish. I don't want a coffee but he does so I give him this small gift.

Outside a sun shower has left a double rainbow in the sky and on a scrappy piece of lawn two young children chase bubbles. The boy is dressed in a pink tutu and his sister as Spiderman. They wave to us and perform a little dance. Their joy and antics make us smile. Sometimes we laugh because we have no more tears to cry.

Opposite the hospital a neon sign advertises an old fashioned milk bar promising strong coffee. None of the soya, latte, skimmed milk kind. At the cheap, laminated counter Tony orders for both of us and I watch a motley mix of birds scavenging for crumbs. Two sparrows squabble over some crumbs while an Indian Myna pecks at a tube of sugar. They fly away when our coffees arrive and I envy them their simple lives. Tony takes a sip of his drink then stares into the sky.

"Do you wish it was me?" he asks. "Lying there."

"You? No. Why would you even say that?" I press my hand to my left breast where beneath the flesh and bones my breaking heart splinters again.

"Because Brian was always your favourite."

"Favourite. Never. Never. Never. I have never had a favourite." I glare at Tony, but my anger withers before the raw anguish in his beloved, scruffy, face. Our tragedy has cracked open the masks we wear as protection against the world. I grope for his calloused hand and press it to my lips. "I never knew you felt that way."

"Neither did I, until a minute ago. You're so close, with many similar interests. At times you talk in your own code, shutting everyone out."

"It isn't deliberate and doesn't mean I love you less. Just differently."

He has more to say, but Tony could never be rushed. He'll say what he has to say eventually even if it takes him another thirty-two years.

With my mother's faulty intuition more finely tuned I know that I am losing him too. He will move away to spare me the pain of what might have been. As he marries, has children, ages, he knows I will see Bear's ghost and grieve again for silenced laughter and a sunset never seen. One day I will tell him it no longer hurts but he'll know I'm lying. Still maybe he'll return to me then.

"Julie's nice." I tell Fudge and see the tips of his ears turn pink. In the sterile, unromantic ICU a seed of love has fallen and taken root. "You should ask her out."

"Maybe." He's shuffles in his seat and picks at a nail, uncomfortable with the conversation.

"I was trying to cheer you up. Esperance."

"What?"

"Esperance. A town in WA we visited when you were small. It means hope for the future." Why does trivia intrude in times of stress? Maybe it's self-protection. Our minds trying to set the gyroscope of our lives back in balance.

As we re-enter our new home a patient is leaving, escorted by his wife. We've seen others come and go. Some upstairs to the wards, others down to the morgue but we're still in limbo. There are things to discuss. Decisions to be made.

"What sort of person is Brian?" asks Liz Burnett, a serene woman in a twin set and pearls. "Did he ever talk to you about what he wanted done with his body if he died?"

"Yes," says Tony.

"No," I lie. I know where this conversation is going but it could get there without me.

"Come on Mum. He always called his bike his donorcycle."

"It was a sick joke. He wasn't serious."

"Yes he was Mum."

"You want to cut him up for spare parts before he's even dead. Where's your humanity?"

"Mum, he is dead. Without the ventilator it would all be over. He can't stay like this forever."

"Give me time, please."

They give me all the time I need.

The hated safety rails are lowered and I sit with my elbows on the bed, my forehead resting against my clasped hands. My heart is thumping hard enough to cause dizziness.

"Okay darling, I'm going to speak to you as if you were well." Which is a stupid thing to say. If he were well I wouldn't be sitting here. "It was easier when we lost your dad. He had the decency to die immediately but you were always the most difficult of my male triad. Here's the deal, Bear. We have three choices. You can stay connected to these blasted machines until you become too weak and an infection takes you. Tony says you'd hate that."

I suck in a shuddering breath. The machines beep on, steady and rhythmic. I swallow as the anguish wells up in my throat, throttling the words I need to say.

"The second option is donating your kidneys, heart and other organs to help up to eight people." I give a watery laugh. "Who knows, maybe we can stop another family going through our suffering. I guess we'd never know though."

I was rambling, anything to put off the inevitable, to keep reality at bay.

"And lastly we could disconnect everything and let you go. It will be the end of your suffering but not our grief. I'd want you to die at home, in your own bed but…"

I hold his hand and ignore the tears trickling down my cheeks.

"So, my dear love, this is what we're going to do…"

Bronwen Bowden is an experienced author who has been writing for many years. She has written eight contemporary novels, as well as a variety of short stories. Bronwen is currently working on a fantasy trilogy with elements of romance.

Found Out On Facebook

Alexandra Cain

Me stomach's hurtin' like a bastard but I still has to get a closer look. I stop for a sec, holdin' me guts with one hand and the fence with the other. Bloody thing'll probably give me splinters like you wouldn't believe.

It's still there. I walk closer to the tree, tryin' not to disturb the little creature even though it's hard to walk quiet with one of me thongs about to break and me undies fallin' down at the same time.

Yeah, long bright yellow tail, yellow on the wings, like sunshine. A tiny thing. I know it right away. Regent honeyeater.

It's rare as hen's teeth these days. Not like those bloody noisy Indian Myna birds takin' over the place.

I watch while he flits about, busy. Little hooked beak, red when it's open, bright eyes, cheeky. He turns his head and looks right at me before he flaps his wings an' takes off, further into the bush.

'Spose it's time for me to go back inside. I'll pro'lly miss Millionaire Hot Seat on the telly if I don't get a move on. And me guts are still killin' me.

Ah rats, there's that stupid bugger from next door. Wantin' to stick his nose into me business. I can't be bothered talkin'. Right now I'm tryin' to remember if I've got any beers. Could be one under the sofa; think I might've left half when I fell asleep. I start walking towards me back door but he follows me up the yard, head stickin' over the fence.

"So, how's your stomach today, Johnny boy?"

Gawd I hate it when the neighbour calls me that. Mum's the only one's allowed. "Yeah, fine."

"You sure? You don't look so great."

"Naaa, fine."

"Can you call someone to come around? It looks like you're having trouble standing."

"Girlfriend'll come p'haps." Me girlfriend hasn't been round in a while but I know she'll be back. Lovely lass she is, sweet smellin' with that long blonde hair. I love me women with long hair. Mel's her name. She cooks and cleans for me.

"Girlfriend?"

"Yeah, the blondie."

"Oh, she's your girlfriend is she?"

What's he on 'bout? "Yeah, course. Why else would she come 'round?"

"Oh, okay. Can you ring her?"

I shakes me head – I've never been one for phones or things. I'm at me back door. "I better go inside."

"Look mate, we're worried about you. My wife made you this – she says you're too thin."

He comes through the hole in the fence and shoves some dish at me. Then, a tiny plastic bag with a small white pill inside, like he's given a couple o' times before. That's more like it.

"That should help with that pain, for now. We're going away for a few days but tomorrow I want you to go to the doctor."

I stick the pill in the pocket of me shorts, making sure it's the good pocket, the one without too many holes. He's annoyin', me neighbour, but his pills are good. I nod thanks and go inside as fast as me burning insides'll let me.

At last I get to the sofa but I can't see no beer. Must've rolled right down the back. No way I can get to it, not with this blasted pain. Beer'll have to wait til I get me next dole. I can't be bothered gettin' water, so I gulp back the pill dry and lie down.

Damn, I forgot to turn the telly on. I wanna watch me show but I'm too wrecked to get up again. I'll just shut me eyes for a sec.

I'll wait until Mum comes home. Ah no, Mum's been gone for donkey's years. What a dope I am.

A dope.

Me guts.

I wanna talk t' Mum. Mel.

A Regent bloody honeyeater.

#

It's lunchtime and I'm flicking through Facebook. We're only supposed to get fifteen minutes of social media time in the office. I'm nervous because I've heard a rumour our IT department has been illegally logging into our accounts, but I can't think of anything else to do. Rain pounds on the office windows and people rattle at their keyboards, but other than that it's quiet.

The usual rubbish. Several pictures of people out eating or drinking last night. A sponsored article from a baby website warning me about the next thing which is about to kill my children, or damage them for life. An ad for a fat loss program. Thanks, Facebook.

Suddenly a message pops up. It's my cousin Ellen.

Ellen: "Hey Julie."
Julie: "Hi. How's things?"

I am surprised to hear from her; it has been a long time.

Ellen: "Good :]"
Ellen: "Hows the fam? Loving you're pics!"
Julie: "Good. They keep me busy."

I hope she doesn't ask about my husband as I'd have to either lie, or tell her about the separation. I wait for a few seconds until the little blue tick comes up to show she's read it. Then the dots as she types.

Ellen: "Haha yeah I hear you."
Julie: "Yours are cute too. So big!"
Ellen: "I know. Time goes so fast!!!"

I can see she's typing again and I wonder why she's suddenly in contact.

Ellen: "Anyway, sorry to contact you with crap news."

So I am right; there is a reason. I wait impatiently for the next message.

Ellen: "Did you hear about Uncle John?"
Julie: "Uncle John?? No." It's been years since I've even thought about him.
Ellen: "Yeah just spoke to Bill, our cousin. Apparently he Ford :["
Julie: "?"
Ellen: "Sorry, died."
Julie: "What?? How?"
Ellen: "Burst peptic ulcer."
Ellen: "Was 5 days before they found him."
Julie: "Oh no. How awful."
Ellen: "Cops called Bill."
Julie: "Poor uncle John."

Ellen: "Can you call yr dad? I don't have his number?"
Ellen: "Hes not on Facebook is he?"
Julie: "Sure."
Julie: "No he's not."
Ellen: "OK thanks. He's Johns only sibling now."
Ellen: "Someone needs to talk to the cops too, organise funeral."
Julie: "Yeah I know."
Julie: "OK well I'll tqlk to Dad. Maybe he'll do it."
Ellen: "Cool. Nice taking xx"
Julie: "Thanks for letting me know."
Ellen: "No prob. Good to chat xx"
Julie. "Yep, was xx"
Julie: "See you soon. Should meet up."
Ellen: "Def. Bye!"

I click to close the chat and stare out the window, trying to process what I've just read. Dead for five days before anyone found him. It's so hard to imagine. He was a strange character, Uncle John. Never married or had children and lived with his mother most of his life. He had suspected but undiagnosed mental problems and had never been able to get much education or hold down a steady job. But still. It's awful to think of him lying there for five days.

#

"John's dead?"

"Yes, Dad. I'm sorry." There is a long silence on the other end of the phone and I hope he's okay. I can picture my father, sitting alone on his big armchair on the veranda, but I can't imagine the expression on his face.

"But how did you know?" His voice is stiff and formal – the tone he once used when speaking to clients. He's trying too hard to sound normal.

"Cousin Ellen told me."

"I didn't know you were in touch. Must be fifteen years since I saw her."

"Dad, neither have I. We're just Facebook friends."

"They say he was there for five days before anyone found him?"

"So I was told." There is another long silence. "I'm really sorry, Dad."

"Huh. Wonder why they didn't call me."

"Were you listed as next of kin?"

"Not sure. I can't remember who might have been. My sister maybe, before she died."

"When was the last time you saw him?"

"Oh probably not long after your grandmother passed away. Twenty years maybe."

"He's been over since then." I know as soon as the words are out of my mouth, it is a mistake to mention that visit.

"Oh yes. I didn't know you remembered that." His voice has changed; he hisses slightly through gritted teeth.

#

I'm about ten years old when Uncle John comes to visit.

It is the first time I've seen him outside my grandmother's house; he catches the train down and Dad picks him up from the station. He is thin and bald and smells funny; a bit like Dad after he's been out late. His tracksuit pants are full of holes, as is his faded green jacket. I go to hug him to say hello, but he draws back and gives me a little pat on the head.

After dinner, we sit in the good living room in dead silence. Mum has her worried, pursed-lip look. Dad lights a cigarette.

"Mate, c'n I 'ave a ciggie?"

"You don't have any?"

"What's it matter?"

Dad snorts and slides the pack and lighter across the table. John takes two and puts one in his pocket, then lights the other. I notice the dirt crusted in the creases in his hands.

He blows the smoke out his mouth and nostrils.

"Julie dear, go and load the dishwasher please," Mum says to me. I'm about to protest but she gives me her 'no arguments' look.

I go into the kitchen. There is still no talking and I hum to myself as I load in the plates and cups; clink, clunk, clang. There is a shout. It's my Dad.

"Hey, what did you do that that for?"

"Didn't mean t'."

"Of course you did! No one burns a hole in someone else's furniture without meaning to."

I poke my head through the door so I can see what's happening.

"Ah whaddya care? You can afford it! Rich bastard with ya flash house."

"Why would you do that to your own brother? Destroy my property. And I gave you that cigarette."

Both men are still sitting down. Mum has her hand on Dad's leg but I can't see his face. Uncle John is slumped low in the chair, an almost grin on his.

"Ahh shuddup. You're th' one who left us. Thinks you're so fancy. You don't even talk t'same."

"It wasn't like that. I had to get away from Dad! I always visited Mum and gave her money for years. Helped her out."

"Never helped me."

"Well, no one helped me either. I helped myself."

Dad goes to get up but Mum stops him.

"Don't, please. Your daughter is next door."

Mum quietly suggests there is time for John to catch the last train if they leave now. Dad's had a few but they decide he should be okay to drive. Mum will go with them. John doesn't say goodbye but I don't mind; I hide in the kitchen and pretend to be cleaning.

The burnt sofa cushion gets turned over and we have it another few years. Sometimes, I would turn it back to look at the hole, neat and round in the middle of the green floral pattern.

#

"So you never spoke to Uncle John after that night?" Dad's tone has changed and I start to sense the discussion going downhill. I love my father but he's become so cranky since losing Mum that most conversations descend into arguments. It is the reason I don't contact him as much as I should, guilty as that makes me feel.

"Not really. I did pay for a carer to go around and help him cook and clean, but she quit a couple of months back. Said he kept trying to kiss her."

"Oh, right. And you never replaced her?"

"No, to be honest I was a bit cross about the whole thing."

"He was probably just lonely."

Dad lets out a long, loud sigh down the phone. "Poor old John. He was a good kid really, but he made his choices in life."

"Do you wish you'd stayed in touch?"

"How was I supposed to? I don't think he even had a phone. Anyway, how did Ellen know?"

"She found out through Facebook."

"Facebook. I see. Bloody Facebook knows our business before we know it ourselves."

I decide to end the conversation as soon as possible. We quickly make plans for claiming John's body. After I hang up, I think for a long time about how a man, no matter how sad and lonely, could die in such circumstances.

I open Facebook on my phone and notice Ellen has just put up a message:

"RIP Uncle John."

There are already twenty-six comments offering condolences. "Thanks everyone. We're doing ok xxx", she's replied further down.

It prompts me to start scrolling through Ellen's profile, looking at the pictures of her kids at their ballet performances and Karate gradings. The captions read:

"My little star!"

Or

"So proud my heart could burst!"

She's a compulsive uploader of kid photos but there's not a lot else – the occasional picture of her dolled up on a 'Mums' night out', smiling and holding a glass of wine up to the camera. Hardly anything about her husband or other friends or interests. It's impossible to tell if she's really happy.

Then I go to cousin Bill's page. He is a fitness nut and it's all pictures of him training for the marathon and one of those annoying trackers which posts his running times every day or two. I've heard that he's divorced with a couple of kids but there is nothing on there to indicate this. I don't blame him.

Finally, I look at my own profile – the last pictures I have up are of our family holiday to Thailand, six months ago. My two daughters sitting on deck chairs smiling; me in a silly sunhat drinking a cocktail. One photo of my husband holding up a Chang beer, face red with the sunburn I warned him he'd get for not putting on sunscreen. We'd niggled at each other all day, ending in a bitter fight that night, but in that photo he looks like he's having a perfect time.

It's unlikely many of my 273 Facebook friends would realise if I had been dead for five days. And very unlikely they had noticed the recent absence of pictures of my husband and me together.

Once my children grow and move away, will I really be that different to John?

#

We organise a little memorial for Uncle John in the park behind my grandmother's old house. Our family, together for the first time in years, talks about the positives in John's life. How he had been a sweet child who had grown into a man of simple tastes, with a deep love of nature.

Afterwards, we make the same hollow promises to stay in touch.

Alex Cain is a writer and journalist who makes a living penning stories on everything from pharmaceuticals to planes. She is also working on The House with Eleven Windows, a series of historical fiction novels set in Finland and Russia.

Fishing

Chris Foster

Harold Butterfill looked at the thick, woolly clouds. They were as grey as his hair. His voice grumbled like distant thunder. "Reckon it might rain."

His son Henry glanced up before pulling out a smartphone and tapping it twice. "Eighty-five per cent chance of showers."

They both nodded, satisfied. Their tinny bobbed slowly from the leftover ripples of a passing boat. Henry put his phone back into the waterproof pocket of his jacket and stared vacantly across the river.

Harold studied the water's surface as his hands threaded a loop knot through the lure. He pulled it tight without a glance, felt how far it would stretch before it snapped. Often he misjudged and lost a prized catch. A slight disturbance near the rocks caught his attention. The *whip whiz* of his cast sent the lure hurtling into the spot. Before his lure hit the bottom a bite tugged on his line. "Got something."

Henry looked across. "Yep." Again unzipping his pocket, Henry made no effort to assist.

Harold wondered if it was deliberate. As he pulled the fish into the boat he heard a click come from Henry's phone. "You take the photo when I'm holding it, lad, not when it's thrashing across the floor."

Henry looked up in surprise. "You want it photographed?"

His son showed him the small screen. "It's only a Bream. They're common round these parts."

"Been fishin' while I was out, have you?"

Again that blank look as if he was talking in tongues.

"The app has all the info."

"And you knew it was a Bream?"

Henry shook his head as if to say *don't be daft*. "The app used the camera to recognise it."

A glum smile tugged at the corners of Harold's mouth. "Well, now you know." He released the fish, checked the lure was still secure and dropped it back into the water. They drifted. A breeze caused Harold to pull a crumpled beanie out of his tacklebox and clamp it down, all the way so even his eyebrows were hidden. With fishing rod balanced between his knees, he zipped his jacket to the top, mouth covered and only his nose to be seen.

"*Dhempura fzz dhomphhh.*"

Henry looked across lazily, wires protruding from his ears. He looked at Harold for a moment before unplugging one side. "Say something Dad?"

A grunt came from under the zipped up package Harold had become. A hand left his rod and hooked onto the top of his jacket, pulling it down enough to be heard. "I said the temperature is dropping."

Henry's hand traced the wire still attached to him, followed all the way down until it reached the phone again. A moment later he nodded. "Yeah, they reckon there might be a cool change this s'arvo. Eighty-seven per cent of a storm now. There's a cold front driving it, so you might be right."

"No kidding."

Silence separated the two once more. Harold lost himself in a memory, trying to remember what it was like when his father brought him to this river. It had seemed so magical. All he wanted was to spend time with his son. The ungrateful git. Still, at least

Henry had agreed to come. Harold had thought his son would put up more of a fight. Ever since the new computer had arrived it had been grafted to the young man's fingers.

This is the new world, Henry had told him when he picked him up from the airport earlier.

Rot, is what Harold had replied. He had nothing against tech as a tool. Once upon a time he had been an engineer. But when more time is spent with faceless strangers than meeting people in the real world, well, it's a problem.

"You found a girlfriend yet?" Harold said across the boat.

Henry gave him a smile. "Playing the field. Not ready to settle down yet."

"How you playing the field when you never go out?" Before his son could answer he waved him off. "An app. I get it. Your life reduced to four inches of flickering lights."

"Five inches. I upgraded."

Harold shook his head. "Why?"

"It was old."

"So am I."

"Don't tempt me."

They smiled at each other. It had been a while since Harold had seen Henry smile at him. Henry so looked like his mother at times like this, mischievous eyes filled with laughter. Harold shifted in his seat and put an arm around his son. "What's wrong with ya?" Harold chuckled, feeling some resistance to his touch. "Don't you know how to hug?" Henry's body slackened and gave into the motion. "That's better." Harold squeezed.

The tinny lurched and rocked with the sudden waves from a speeding boat's slipstream, so rough it almost toppled them overboard.

"*Yahooligan*." They said in unison.

Thunder rumbled and Harold saw flickering on the horizon. He started the small onboard motor and they glided across the water.

Henry for once spoke without being asked a question. "How did you know Mum was the one?"

Harold took his time to consider his response. This was one of those moments a father hoped for – his knowledge passed down to his own flesh and blood, providing some sort of equipment to handle survival in an often confusing world. But all he could think of was Diane when she was sixteen, her floral dress, flowing hair, the way she danced. And her eyes. Those eyes that had locked onto his and hadn't let go. The memory distracted him so much he barely turned in time before the tinny ran straight into a rocky point. "There was something about the way she moved," he said getting the boat under control. "Then when she looked at me, I was hooked. I couldn't look away." He looked sideways at Henry, who seemed a bit deflated. "You were wanting to hear something else?"

"Nah, not really. Just I don't go to clubs."

Harold laughed. "Loud and horrible son. This wasn't a club, it was a dance hall."

"Like, old school church stuff?"

"Country Women's Association more like, if you know what that is."

Henry went to pull his phone out but hesitated. He kept it in his hand, ready and waiting. "How'd you look her in the eye?"

Harold slowed the boat down. They'd followed the river back to its beginning, where freshwater joined salty brine and Harold ran his fishing shack. Boats don't have brakes and if he misjudged the speed he might end up parking up on a rock, beach or if really lucky the beach side hotel's pool.

Henry waited for his answer. He helped tie the tinny under the sheltering arm of the jetty.

Harold smiled, it was fine knot. Once they were out of the boat he continued, "Well. I used my eyes, guessed where hers would be, and lined them up."

The joke was lost on his son.

"Doesn't your mother ever talk about it? Us meeting and all?"

Henry shrugged.

"Wouldn't be the same anyway. She'd be seeing it from her perspective." Harold desperately tried to remember something else, anything, that his own father had said to him – some sort of vocal heirloom he could pass on. But he came up short. They hadn't had much time together before the war stole him, used him and sealed him up in a neat rectangular package upon return. Nothing to pass on but some engraved scrap metal.

"You should come see her Dad, her and Bailey."

They walked down the jetty, wood groaning under their feet. Ahead was the sand, the beach, paradise. Yet all he could think about was the tubes, the machinery pulsing, cylinders spinning with red liquid like a mechanical heart – Bailey, his little champion, still lying on a bed kept alive long past his time. Harold wanted to remember his youngest when he was healthy, running around causing all sorts of trouble. Instead his memory had been overwritten by the wasting figure in hospital. When the doctors had asked, Harold had thought it best to flip the switch and end his son's suffering. Except his wife had other ideas and the only thing he ended that day was his marriage. To this day, Diane stayed by Bailey's side.

"How are they?"

Henry shrugged, his shoulders slumped with the weight of his tacklebox and rod. "Alive."

Harold grunted. "I wouldn't call that alive."

Henry swung round to face him, fishing rod whipping across. Harold almost lost an eye.

"What would you rather?" Henry snapped. "Bailey in a box? At least Mum tries! She's there day in and day out. Holds his hand gentle-like, shows him she cares. She doesn't hide away in some backwater. It's not like it's that far even, a plane would take only an hour to get there." Henry strode away. "I should never have come here!" he yelled. "I'm headed to the airport! You can rot here with your stupid Bream, I don't care!"

They had reached the sand and people were turning to stare.

Harold dropped his gear and grabbed Henry by the arm, turned him on the spot and stared him in the eye. Henry couldn't hold the gaze. "Don't you *dare* make out I don't care. You know I love them both. But there's a difference between saving a life and prolonging an existence. Do you really think Bailey is happy? I would love nothing more than to have him open his eyes and smile once more. It ain't natural to have a child go before their parent. It hurts like nothing you've ever felt." Harold could feel the anger in Henry's arm, the bristling. But he held firm.

Henry squirmed, trying to tug his arm from Harold's grip. "Let me go!"

"Never! Look at me! Listen to what I'm saying. I'd catch that plane if I thought it would make a difference. I'd give any organ he needs. Because there would be a point to it. But it's been a year now, a full year. Maybe I'm wrong, maybe I'm horrible. But in the real world you don't get fifty lives. You get one. When something's ended it's..." He couldn't bring himself to finish the sentence. "Please son," he lowered his voice, "there's nothing I can do about your mum, it's over between us. And Bailey," he shook his head, tears welling, "it's hopeless. I'm sorry. If I could change that, I would, but I can't."

Henry looked up, stopped trying to free his arm.

They looked at each other through bleary eyes.

"I just... want things how they were." Harold's voice cracked. "Do you know what I mean?"

"I know Dad. Wipe and factory reset."

This time it was Harold who looked away. He pulled his son closer and they embraced again, falling into each other like they wanted the world to go away. A wolf whistle emitted from Henry's pocket. They separated and Harold saw his son wipe tears away before pulling his phone out. The screen shone for a moment before fading off again.

"You're not going to reply?"

"Nah. Just a girl."

"That could be my future daughter-in-law you're hanging up on."

Henry smiled, although it didn't reach his eyes. "Plenty of fish in the sea."

They both looked at the empty fish bucket and laughed.

"Should have kept the Bream. Beautiful, tasty fighters."

They picked up their things and headed towards Harold's tiny fishing shack. The clouds rumbled and it started to drizzle.

Chris Foster is an Australian poet, novelist and dream maker. He started writing in his teens when he won an international literary award and now has six books on Amazon (with more on the way). Hard to track down, Chris travels so often he finds it hard to call any one place home. Luckily he is able to draw upon these travels and craft them into unforgettable characters and settings for his readers to enjoy. A lover of fantasy, he writes novels ranging from the adventure stories for middle grade to dark fantasy dystopia for adults. His focus is on helping to create interesting stories for teens, as well as poetry that hugs the soul.

Generational Breakdown

Suzi Green

"'Oh bugger." I flicked some switches.

A jolt, and then, silence.

With the little momentum we had left, I pulled the car over. It was dark. Really dark. We had left the street lights behind and clouds were hiding the moon.

"Shit."

"What's happened? Where are we? Are we home?" Mum snapped, probably because she'd been woken from her motion-induced snooze.

"No. We're..." I looked around for something to help pinpoint our location, but there was nothing.

"Well, are we alright? Where are we? Why have we stopped?" There was a panic in her voice, but I shushed her, conscious of not waking Billy.

"We're still about an hour from home." I made sure my tone was calm and quiet. I'd taken the back road to have fun with the brand new car – we were on our way home from picking it up from the showroom.

"Are you ill? Is it Billy?" She turned to look at my nine year old asleep on the back seat. "Have we...?"

"Mum!" I hissed, starting to feel angry but trying not to increase the decibel level. "Would you please stop with the triple set of questions?"

"'Have we broken down?' Was the last one I was going to ask, Bec." Even though it was too dark to see her, I knew she was raising her eyebrows at me.

"Yes Mum, I believe we have." My best bedside-manner voice. I rubbed my forehead and breathed in that new car smell.

"Well dear, I knew something like this was going happen. I said it, didn't I?"

"No," I knew I shouldn't rise to her. Well, I always know afterward.

"If I didn't say it to you I said it to someone else. You can't trust this new technology." She kept going but I zoned out. My mother had always been pessimistic about things that contained a chip; unless, as my Dad would've said, it was of the vegetable kind. She hated the fact that my new V6 Zion had no key. Push to start, voice control – modern technology? Yes. Futuristic cyborg taking over the world? I don't think so.

"Zion, mend thyself." I commanded, secretly hoping it would activate a built-in self-medication function. I also thought the humour might help the situation, but not a peep from the car or a chortle from my mother.

I turned my attention to the on-board computer. The screen was black. I pressed a couple of buttons. Then I pressed all the buttons, including pressing two at a time. Sometimes that works in the case of overriding total electronic meltdown.

"Fucking hell!" Now I was having a meltdown.

"Oh for God's sake, mind your language."

Now that my vision was adjusting to the dark, I could see my mother glaring at me. "Mum. Language? Really?"

"Huh? Wha's going on?"

Shit. "Sorry Billy." I grimaced at another single-parent failure.

Mother threw one of her disapproving stares before she tried to reach round to comfort her grandson. "It's alright Billy. We've broken down. We're going to get rescued any minute."

Oh, now she becomes an optimist!

"Where are we?" Billy said. And Mum got him chatting to keep him calm. She was a fantastic grandparent and I really ought to be more patient with her, especially given what she'd been through recently.

Unbuckling my seatbelt, I twisted round to check on him, and suddenly there was brightness. He'd swiped his iPad. Why didn't I think of that? I checked my iPhone in its cradle on the dash. More light, although zero reception.

Leaving Mum to look after Billy, who I could already hear was quite happy playing a game on his iPad, I turned my attention back to the car. I knew my cam-belt from my carburettor; Dad had taught me a bit about cars when I was little. Except the Zion doesn't have a carburettor. In fact, I'm not sure any car built this millennium has a carburettor.

"Ever heard of fuel injection?" Billy would probably say.

I reached underneath the steering wheel in search of the hidden handle to release the bonnet, it was like being at work, trying to find the hypothalamus when you've drilled in at the frontal lobe. Click.

Shining the phone over the engine, all I could see was smooth black metal. I was searching for something to waggle and had a memory flashback to one night with my first car. A bunch of us from college had spent the day at the beach. Someone else had volunteered to be designated driver, so I got quite tipsy. Halfway home, we'd had catastrophic failure. After a two-hour wait, a guy arrived with a van full of tools, but just one tiny wire had come loose. He'd re-attached the wire, and we were on our way. Only a few minutes later, it happened again. But even in my slightly drunken state, I had paid enough attention and was able to successfully re-attach the cable to continue our journey home.

But the Zion wasn't like my old Ford; everything here was pristine. There weren't any visible wires, let alone loose ones.

Mum stuck her head out of the door and yelled, "Do you have any idea what you're doing?"

I peered round the open bonnet and glowered at her.

"Well, do you?"

I took a long breath. This might've fazed any normal person but I was used to working under stress.

"Just because you're a doctor and can mend people, it doesn't mean you can mend cars." Mum said.

I wasn't going to wait for the usual nag about my long hair getting in the way. "Okay, that's it!" I let the bonnet slam shut so the whole car shook violently. "I'm going to walk up the hill, see if I can get a signal to call the breakdown service." I was about to ask her if she wanted to come with me, but I needed her to stay with Billy, and I had to get some space. I shoved the car paperwork into my pocket; it contained the phone number of the complimentary breakdown service that came with the new car.

"You're going to leave us here?" Mum sounded more annoyed than scared.

"What the hell do you think I'm going to do? Strap you both on my back and hike us all the way home?" My voice went up a whole octave and several decibels. I tried to look apologetic, but there were too many emotions flying around. From the boot I pulled out the emergency pack that I'd switched over from my old, less reliable Honda. I extracted a bottle of water, a blanket and an energy bar.

"You bought supplies? You knew this was going to happen? You don't trust this technology either do you?" She jumped out the car and actually wagged a finger at me.

I had intended to tuck the blanket around her, not that it was cold, but to calm her down. Instead, I opened it out and tossed it at her, like I would've done when I was a stroppy teenager. "Your pessimistic influence!" I glared at her, daring her to say more.

She too never seemed to know when it was the time to shut-up. "This blasted thing. I've never really liked cars. You know that? I always used to say that to your dad. He liked anything with an engine for some reason: cars, trains, planes. Me? Not at all. Messy dirty engines. But your dad... your dad..." She pressed her hand over her mouth and let out a huge sob.

I turned my back on her. I didn't want her to see my watery eyes. "Mu...Mum. I'll just walk up hill, I won't go any further than where you can see me. You remember, when I was little, how you used to say: stay where I can see you?" I opened my eyes wide, hoping the night air would dry out my tear ducts. I looked away from her as I steered Mum back into the car, and placed the blanket tightly around her. Billy climbed through to the front seats, offering to help. "I'll see you both in a few minutes, alright?" Gently, I shut the door.

A few steps away from the car, I inhaled the clear air and looked up at the stars. You couldn't see them from the city, or from home, but here, where the light pollution had almost disappeared... Was Dad up there? Looking down on us, wondering what me and Mum were arguing about? Oh Dad, it's never going to be the same again is it?

"Look! Look! I've still got the Zion webpage open on my iPad." Billy stuck his head out the open door. Within seconds he was excitedly jumping up and down on the side of the road in his socks. "Watch... old Pixar..." Then he stopped jumping. "Zion website: You remember when we were looking at it in the showroom?"

As I stepped toward him, he thrust the iPad in my face. I examined the pdf image of the engine, gripping the iPad carefully so as not to lose the page. I swallowed the lump in my throat as I heard my father saying, 'now look, but don't touch'.

"You've got a picture? A picture of the engine? What do you think you're going to do with that?" Mum said.

I concentrated hard on the image. In my head I could see the car earlier today, still in the showroom. It was crammed in and the salesman was saying they'd have to move the other cars to get it out. I knew he was looking at me thinking I wouldn't be able to reverse it out on my own. Bloody stereotyping car salesman. And he'd said, 'we're going to move the cars but…'. But? What was the 'but'? My stomach tightened. There was something.

"I don't understand, why are you just staring at a computer? That's not really going to help is it? I thought you were going to call for help?"

In a daze, I walked around to the front of the car.

It wasn't a 'but', it was an 'and'. As the salesman was handing me the paperwork, he'd gesticulated to the guy who was removing the SOLD sign from the front windscreen: 'Don't forget to take *that* off.' And he'd pointed to something in the engine. While I was reading the small print, Dave the salesman had been telling Billy a story about 'the time they forgot to remove the plastic insulator, and after half an hour it melted and killed the electrics'.

That was it.

But what plastic insulator? Something to protect something from something while it was in the showroom. Oh God, what the hell was it? A sticker to point out the fuel injection? Perhaps it was a picture of a carburettor to entertain people who'd be looking for one? Maybe it was just a protective plastic cover so that people didn't put their grubby fingers on the shiny new engine? Think! It must be something to separate two electrical connections.

I recalled the story to Mum and Billy.

"Oh yeah, I remember him telling me that." Billy said.

"And do you remember where the bit of plastic was?"

Billy rubbed his chin and looked to the sky. God he was just like Dad. I glanced at Mum who was looking away, shaking her head. She must've had the same thought.

"How about we play spot the difference?" Billy suggested, "compare the picture of the engine to the one in the car?"

So with the lights from my mobile phone, and a wind-up torch from the emergency kit, the three of us scrutinised the engine. Initially, we just looked around, expecting it to be obvious. Then, I systematically scanned from left to right and top to bottom. Nothing.

I made another pass using my fingers to guide me, my sense of touch would identify the anomalies.

Eventually, I felt a jagged edge. "I think I've found it." But the plastic had melted on, and I tried to pick it off with my fingers. "What tools have you got in your handbag?"

"What do you mean? You think I'm carrying tools? In this little handbag?" Mum responded.

"Hairbrush? Nail kit? Eyeliner? Something with a solid pointy end." I suggested.

Mum rummaged through her handbag and passed a hairbrush. I prodded at the edge of the burnt-on plastic; too blunt.

"Oh, there's the little penknife your dad always had on his key ring. I carry it as a memento." Her voice trailed off and she turned away again.

The lump in my throat returned and I couldn't manage a reply.

Mum picked at the bit of string that secured the keepsake to the inside lining of the bag. She placed the miniature penknife firmly in my hand. Our eyes met for an instant and we both quickly looked away.

"Well done Mum," I said slowly, praising her for everything from the penknife to holding it together since the death of her husband.

"You too." She nodded, "You too. You too." And she patted Billy.

I started prying away the melted plastic. "Ow, f…". The knife slipped and jabbed against my skin. "Good job it's blunt." I tried to laugh.

"Well your father used it for everything you know. Never went anywhere without it." Mum managed a watery chuckle.

While I performed surgery with the penknife, Billy scrolled through his iPad.

"What have you got there?" Mum leaned over his shoulder.

Billy showed her a screen of little pictures that he'd taken during one of our final visits to the hospital. "Just looking at photos of Grandpa."

They pored over the pictures together, Mum commenting on Dad's favourite shirts, his broken glasses and his funny laugh.

"But Grandma, you can't hear his laugh from a photo."

"I can Billy, I hear it every day." She nodded slowly. And just as she was about to explain how she heard her husband's laugh in her head, Billy clicked on a video he'd taken of Dad opening presents at his eightieth birthday. It was only fifteen seconds, but it captured him perfectly, chuckling as he tore several layers off a pass-the-parcel that Billy had made.

"You are clever Billy. Can I get a copy of that?"

"I'll upload it onto the family Dropbox when we get home, you can download it from there." Billy replied.

She hugged him so hard. And Billy, not wanting to be the kid any longer, tried to shrug her off. Mum responded by grabbing him even tighter, and ruffling his hair, which made him wriggle even more. We all managed to laugh then.

"Okay, let's try it." I pushed the start button.

The engine spluttered for a few seconds, then died. "Damn it."

"Try it again dear." Suddenly Mum was the calm one.

I tried again, it sounded more promising, but died once more.

"Your dad always said, third time lucky." Another of Dad's little jokes, something to do with Mum being the third girl he'd ever kissed, or so he'd said.

I pressed the button again and finally, after some noises like metal in the microwave, the car relaxed into a steady drone.

"Vrooom!" yelled Billy.

"You did it!" shrieked Mum, mouth aghast.

"Don't sound so surprised. Besides, Billy was the one who found the image."

Billy beamed.

"And the video." Mum added, her mind still with Dad. "You know, we should be grateful for this technology."

I waited to hear her explanation.

"Well, in the old days, us girls were at a disadvantage because most of us didn't think we had the strength to work in the same jobs as the men, but now we know, it's just about strength of mind, and women bring that in bucket loads."

I couldn't help smiling. "We sure as hell do, Mum."

"I'll have to put that on my Facebook page: my daughter just fixed the car. Now, how do I do that again?"

Suzi Green is a consultant, chorister and comic, having previously concentrated on things that begin with the letter C. Now she is working on a novel, called 'Friday Night Friends', about four friends who have a lot of fun, a few fights and lots of… passion. Once it's finished, it'll be fantastic.

Work Out

Harriet Cunningham

"Happy Birthday, darling."

Jenn planted a warm but efficient kiss on her husband's lips, and a package on the mound of his middle.

Rick opened his eyes, blinked, and attempted a sleepy smile.

"Thank you."

"Careful. There's a cup of tea on the beside table."

"Lovely."

Jenn watched as he heaved himself up into a sitting position. She was excited, even if he wasn't. Someone had to be.

"Well? Aren't you going to open it?"

Rick retrieved the package, which had fallen off his belly as he moved. He carefully peeled back the sticky tape securing the paper then, hearing Jenn sigh, pulled off the wrapping with a decisive rip. Inside, another box. More packaging. Black and silver and shiny pictures.

"Wow."

"D'you like it?" Jenn's face, full of hope.

"Wow. I..." He turned the box over in his hands, holding it at arm's length as he tried to focus on the text. "Multi-function... biometrics... cardiovascular... Bluetooth... GPS..."

She couldn't wait any longer.

"It's a new watch!"

"Yes. But…" He looked at the box, then at his wife, then at the box again. "I've already got a watch."

"It's a sports watch," she said, undaunted. "It does everything. Heart monitor, movement sensor, inbuilt fitness tracking software – it even has a GPS."

"Wow."

"And it's waterproof so you can wear it when you go swimming."

"But…" He was going to say, "I don't go swimming." He didn't.

"So now you've got no excuses not to get back into shape." She kissed him again. "I asked Bruce – you know, Bruce from down the road, he's at the same gym – and he recommended this one. It's state of the art. You can upload your stats, and there's an online community where you track your progress. Bruce swears by it."

She paused, like a breathless salesman. "Do you like it?"

He extracted the fearsome engine from its packaging and strapped it to his wrist. Then he held out his arm, turning it this way and that, looking at it with experimental reverence. "I love it."

#

Winter sunlight flooded the little courtyard cafe where Jenn and her friend of a thousand years sat, still in runners and lycra, enjoying a post-workout coffee. Skimmed latte for Jenn, skinny cap for Saskia, please. Oh, and maybe a lemon friand, to share.

"That's the thing with men," Jenn told Sas. "They respond so well to technology. Data. Buttons to push. That's what they like. What they *need*."

Saskia gave her coffee a stir, then popped the teaspoon in her mouth and sucked it, thoughtfully. "Mmm," she said. "Before Max joined Macquarie he was getting quite well-padded. Y'know…" Saskia massaged her haunches meaningfully. "The love handles were a bit more than a handful. Then he got a Fitbit as part of his joining package and, well, it's been amazing. It started as an office competition and now it's an obsession. There's a little group of them who are training for the half-Iron Man at Port Macquarie."

Jenn smiled. "I can't see Rick doing a half-Iron Man anytime soon," she said.

"Now now, Jenn. You might be surprised. Pleasantly surprised." Saskia gave Jenn a schoolmarmish look. "Things can change, you know. People can change. Look at Max, for example."

"Mmm." Jenn reached for the cake.

#

"New watch?" Max was leaning over the low partition separating Rick's work station from the photocopying area.

"Yeah," said Rick, without looking up. "Birthday present."

"Oh. Happy Birthday."

"Last week."

"Right."

Rick waited for Max to go away, but he didn't. Instead, he walked round the edge of the useless battlement and hitched himself on the edge of Rick's desk. "Can I see?"

"Sure." Rick stretched out his arm and pulled back his sleeve to reveal the device he put on, under the approving glare of his wife, every morning.

"Wow. It's an XP4800. That's serious shit."

"Is it?" Rick ran his thumb round the complicated bezel. The myriad of buttons and rocker switches made his fingers feel fat and stupid. "I haven't really worked it all out yet. To be honest, I think it's a heavy hint from her indoors. She got me the gear to match…" He glanced down at the expensively branded backpack which sat under his desk. Inactive activewear.

"Right." Max smiled. "Well, I can see her point. We're none of us getting any younger. And your Jenn, she must really look after herself."

"I guess."

"You don't want her trading you in for a younger model." He winked. "Tell you what," said Max. "Why don't you come to the gym with me this lunchtime? We can work out. Then you can go home and show Jenn how hard you worked."

"But..."

"No buts."

#

Jenn frowned at her iPad.

The kitchen table was still covered in the shards of dinner. 'No jabscreens at the table' was the rule, but they often broke it. Sharing that funny youtube video, or showing each other an old friend on Facebook – all part of modern life, surely?

"Ooh." She gave an excited squeal. "Look. Look at that."

A line graph on a black background was zigzagging its way from left to right, and along the bottom of the screen a series of numbers appeared. Different colours, different units.

"Heart rate... Distance... Duration..." Jenn's lips moved as she traced her finger over the screen. "Rick, look! This is so cool. It's got an analysis of your workout. It's tracked how many steps you took. How far you went. You can even get it to map your route."

She pressed another button.

"Oh." A map of the CBD, and a line going nowhere, like a kid's frustrated scrawl. "Okay, so you just went to the office gym. That makes sense."

"Yeah. I told you. I went with Max."

"Well, great." Jenn sat back and put down the screen. "Good for you. Well done. Awesome." Her eyes flicked away self-consciously. "Sorry. I sound like one of those dreadful personal trainers."

Rick didn't disagree. But his wife's anxious look told him a response was needed. "I felt like a hamster on a wheel in the bottom of a very sweaty sock," he said.

Her face fell further.

"But it wasn't completely awful. It's lovely when you stop." Jenn smiled.

"Yes," she said. "And you get to give yourself rewards."

"Really?" Rick brightened.

"Sure," said Jenn, reaching for the bottle of wine. "I reckon that workout was worth another glass of red. Or…" She paused as she unscrewed the metal cap. "Or should we just pack up and go to bed?"

Rick smiled and held out his glass.

#

"Ready?"

Rick looked up from his computer. Max was there, gym bag already on his shoulder.

"Mate. Is it that time already?"

"Sure is. C'mon, Rick. You know you love it. No pain no gain."

"Yeah right." He sighed. "It's just… I'm not sure I can make it today."

"But I thought you were getting fit so you could shag that lovely wife of yours all night."

Max gave a dry, wry laugh at his wit. Rick didn't. "Look, I might just have to give it a miss today."

"But you've got the watch and everything! Jeez, what wouldn't I do to have a go with the XP4800. It's light years better than my silly Fitbit."

Rick didn't react.

"Besides," said Max, "Jenn will want to know. And you know what that means. No pain, no gain. Play hookey, no nookie."

Rick looked at Max. The smile on his colleague's face had evolved into a leer. It wasn't attractive. Not to him, at least.

"Sorry, Max. Not today."

"Not tonight either, then," said Max with a shrug. His eyes looked hungrily at the blinking machine. "Unless…" He paused.

"Unless…" Rick looked at the hi-tech manacle around his wrist. Then he looked back to Max.

"Unless what?"

#

"Have you updated your stats?" Jenn asked brightly across the rattle and clang of evening chores.

"Not yet," said Rick, from his study.

"Shall I?"

"Sure."

Rick was hunched over his laptop, his eyes and nose wrinkling as he tried to divine the right word, *le mot juste*, for this tricky little moment in the screenplay he was writing. The screenplay he'd been writing for five years now. The one which was, one day, going to be a Hollywood sensation. What would the feisty young heroine say to the creepy older sleazebag? Well, she wouldn't describe herself as 'feisty' for a start, he thought, back-spacing with irritation.

"Nice work, love."

"Huh?" Rick heard Jenn call through from the kitchen, but he'd already lost the thread.

"Nice work at the gym. Good session today."

"Oh, right. Yeah."

"Can I get you anything?"

"Mm?…" Rick continued to stare at his computer screen.

"A drink? A massage, maybe?" The soft weight of a hand on either shoulder.

Rick stiffened. He hadn't even heard her come into the room. He hated people looking over his shoulder when he was writing. Hated it. He reached forwards and shut his laptop.

"Sorry, love," said his wife. "Am I interrupting?"

#

"So this watch has got a GPS on it, so you can track where you've been running or swimming or whatever."

"Jenn, honey, really. Unless it's got 'Cartier' on the side I'm losing interest fast." Saskia scrolled down and sighed. "So get to the point."

Saskia looked up to meet her friend's eyes. Looked closer. Jenn was staring at the table. Not at a phone. Not at a magazine. Just the table.

"Sweetie. What is it?" She put her phone down and reached a hand out to Jenn's arm.

Jenn shifted in her chair. She tugged at the strap on her sports bra.

Saskia put on her best interested look. "Everything alright?"

Jenn didn't meet Saskia's eyes. Her lips were pressed together. Her nostrils flared once, twice, like a nervous twitch. She took a breath then spoke, in a rush, racing to get her idea out before the urge to bury it took over again.

"So, you see, when Rick turns on exercise mode on the watch I can track where he goes. I can even get a neat little video map thing-y. So if he goes for a run I know where he's been, how long, how far."

"Neat," said Saskia. "But not exactly primetime viewing."

"No," said Jenn. "Not really. In fact, until a week ago he didn't go anywhere, anyway. He just went to the gym. But the last few times the data's gone weird."

"Oh?" Saskia leant forward and took a sip of her coffee.

"He's on the move."

"What, running?"

"Maybe," said Jenn. "I guess. Except it doesn't really look like a run. More like a..."

"Yes?"

"Like a side trip." Jenn picked up her phone and scrolled across a couple of screens in search of the relevant app. Then she found the right screen. "There. Look."

Saskia squinted at the little display. A wiggly line running through the city. She recognised the start point as being the building where Rick and Max worked. The line, however, didn't go terribly far. Just two blocks in fact. Then it stopped. Then it went back to the office.

"So? He went for a run."

"A run for one block?"

"Or he went on an errand."

"But he stopped for forty-five minutes, then turned around and came back."

"Maybe he was, I don't know, getting his hair done." Saskia gave Jenn an indulgent smile. "Having his back waxed."

"Twice this week? And twice last week, for forty-five minutes to an hour, in a block which, as far as I can make out, is an apartment hotel?"

"Ah." Saskia looked thoughtful.

#

"Coming to the gym today, Rick?"

Max leant over the grey wall of the grey cubicle where Rick sat hunched over his work.

"Nah, mate," said Rick. "Gonna catch up on my email."

"Sure?" said Max. "Karen's coming too. She and I are hoping to work up a bit of a sweat."

Rick looked up. Max had that irritating grin on his face again. That boysie clubbie full-of-himself look.

"You wish," said Rick.

"I do more than wish, I assure you," said Max. "I'm sweat central, I'll have you know."

Rick sat back wearily. What was he implying?

"C'mon. Do you good. Get some more k's on your data set." He leant forward and lowered his voice. "The view's lovely, I tell you. Especially from behind."

"Fuck off, Max."

"Suit yourself. But Jenn's not going to be pleased when she sees your heart rate tracker for the day."

Rick sighed. He knew what Max wanted. "You owe me, Max."

"No mate. You owe me."

#

"So I've decided. I'm going to confront him with it."

Saskia leant in greedily. Sometimes life was even better than Netflix.

"I'm going to go in at lunchtime and see if I can catch him coming out of the gym. Follow him. See where he's actually going."

Saskia felt herself fighting the urge to wriggle with excitement. "Is that wise?" she said. "What if he sees you?"

"I'll say I was just dropping by for lunch. It is my birthday, after all."

"Right." Saskia sounded doubtful. "You *never* meet Rick for lunch. He'll see through it instantly. Wait…"

Saskia had picked up her phone. "I'm sure I can find a better plan. Hang on. I'll Google it." She stabbed purposefully at her screen. "Here we go," she said triumphantly. "'How to tell whether your husband is having an affair.'" She tapped, waited, then read silently for a few seconds. She scrolled down. A bit further.

"Interesting," she said, shifting her chair. "Listen to this, Jenn. It says…"

She looked up, but Jenn was already on her feet, and rummaging in her handbag. Out came a set of car keys.

"Sorry, Saskia. You were saying?"

Saskia opened her mouth to speak, but Jenn interrupted her.

"Actually, can it wait? Sorry, but it looks like he's already on the move. I have to go now if I'm going to catch him when he leaves the gym."

Saskia closed her mouth. Then she opened it again. "But..."

Jenn blew her a feverish kiss.

"Bye. Wish me luck."

#

Jenn saw the lights at Cowells Road turn orange from a hundred metres away. She accelerated.

"Green as grass," she said to herself as she slipped across the line. The Mazda purred in agreement as she dodged a truck clogging the lane ahead of her. If she hadn't been so utterly terrified of what she would find, this would almost be fun, she thought. Jenn Taylor. Digital sleuth. Hi-tech gumshoe. She allowed herself a quiet smile.

The traffic gods were smiling as Jenn wove her way into the CBD. York Street was uncharacteristically clear and, as she approached Rick's office block, she saw a people mover parked fifty metres ahead indicating right. A glory park. A good omen. A birthday gift I can actually use, for once.

It was only when she got out of the car and started walking towards the building that the real purpose of her mission came back to her in all its uncomfortable glory, writhing like a bag of snakes in her stomach. She swallowed. What would she do if she found Rick was indeed having an affair? What would she say? What would he say? Was it too late to turn back? Sweat prickled beneath her arms, across her shoulders.

#

"Hi."

Jenn jumped. There was a man standing in front of her. He was dressed in suit trousers and a white shirt, with no tie, and he had a gym bag over his shoulder. His hair was wet, combed straight back from his face, and his eyes were hidden by sunglasses.

She looked left and right. He was talking to her.

"Hi. Jenn. It's me. Max." The man pushed his sunglasses up onto his forehead, and she realised it was her friend's husband.

"Oh, Max. Sorry. I didn't recognise you for a minute there." Her hand went self-consciously to her face, her hair. The hair she'd blow-dried with such care an hour earlier. (After all, you want to look your best on your birthday. Or if you're spying on your husband. Or both.)

He smiled. A relaxed, ease-making smile.

"I thought it was you. I wasn't sure. I haven't seen you for ages." He stepped forward, put one hand on her arm and leant forward to kiss her cheek. "Why haven't we seen each other for so long?"

Jenn, flustered, received his kiss and made to offer the other cheek.

"Oh," said Max. "French style. OK."

Jenn could feel her face glowing.

"And to what do I owe this unexpected pleasure?" said Max.

"Um," said Jenn. Her mouth was still recovering from the badly-aimed cheek pecks. "It's… It's my birthday. I'm here to meet Rick."

"Your birthday?" Max beamed. "Happy Birthday! Yes, of course, Rick. Silly me. Rick. Now…" He looked awkwardly back up to the door to the gym. "Now where could Rick have got to?"

"Oh," said Jenn, leaping on the trail again. "Was he here? I assumed he was at the gym. He's been working out so much recently, I thought I'd catch him here. I mean, meet him here."

"Right." Max nodded. "Working out. Yes. That's right. Rick's been… Rick's ah…"

Jenn looked at Max, trying to read his expression, trying to hear the clues hidden in his guarded words. The vaguely hunted look coalesced rapidly into an apologetic smile.

"I'm so sorry, Jenn. Rick's gone. He's been and gone. He went early today – told me he'd got a meeting at one, so had to do his gym session early." Max's voice was gaining strength and authority.

"Yes. That's it. A meeting." He paused to meet Jenn's eyes. "Sorry. Did he not text you? What a stuff up."

Jenn looked down. She felt her lips twitch, involuntarily, her eyes itch. Then she felt frustration creep over her. She was mortified. Humiliated. Angry. She heard a loud sniff. It was her. This won't do, she thought.

"Hey."

She felt Max's hand on her arm again, softer this time. She raised her eyes and bumped straight into his.

"What a bugger, hey," he said, quietly, thoughtfully, taking in her confusion, beaming his confidence. Then, with an easy grin, "So it looks like *I'm* taking you to lunch for your birthday." He stood there, smiling, proud, like a child who's just had a brilliant idea. "What do you think? Shall we?"

Jenn swallowed. It was hard to disappoint such a gallant, boyish gesture, but she was still smarting with the shame. Mortified. Just mortified.

She blinked. He was still looking at her, eyes wide, hopeful.

She looked back at him. Mortified, humiliated, angry. And intrigued.

#

"You'll have a glass of wine, won't you," said Max, looking up from the wine list. "I mean, it is your birthday."

Jenn blushed. Again. She could murder a cold chardonnay.

"If you're having one."

"Oh, come on. You're the birthday girl. You deserve a little pick-me-up. I, of course, never drink at lunchtime, but just this once I will have a glass to keep you company." He winked. "It's only proper."

Jenn giggled. Max was being, well, rather fun. And after such a wretched start to her day she was ready for a bit of fun.

"So," said Max, after they had raised their glasses, and both taken a greedy gulp. "Tell me all about yourself. Tell me about the beautiful Jenn."

#

It felt like they'd talked non-stop – like she'd talked non-stop – for an hour. She must have stopped, because she'd eaten and she'd drunk. Max was, nevertheless, a magnificent listener. Magnificent Max. Magnetic Max. Jenn smiled to herself as she played with the words.

She looked at the man opposite her. He was paying the bill – "Of course, it's your birthday, and the pleasure's all mine" – and chatting affably with the waitress. She could see the waitress found him attractive. She was smiling. He was smiling. Did they know each other? Jenn realised she was frowning at the thought.

Then Max was putting his wallet in his pocket, standing up, waving to the waitress. Reaching out for her hand, no, grabbing her hand.

"Come on. Let's get out of here."

#

It was only when she felt the buzz of her mobile phone through the side of her bag that she remembered Rick. Remembered, then chose to forget. After all, the feel of Max's hand in the small of her back, of his knee pressing against hers as they sat, too close to each other, was a powerful amnesiac. Still, it was a choice, and she could have chosen to remember. Then she thought of the birthday present, the tell-tale watch, and that terrible feeling of betrayal. She made her choice.

\#

They didn't speak during the short walk across the road to the hotel. They barely touched, apart from Max's hand, guiding her with the lightest of pressure. Jenn was vaguely aware of an unreal ringing in her ears. Her skin was alive, acknowledging every passing electron. She heard their steps, amplified, across the polished floor of the hotel lobby, saw the tiny striations across the brushed steel walls of the lift. And when the doors opened Jenn thought she heard this hoarse sigh of relief. Was it her? Was it Max? No time to wonder. Nearly there. So nearly there. Don't stop now.

\#

The sex was quick and dirty and good. So good. No words, apart from a muttered 'fuck' as Max struggled to kick off his shoes, and a hissed 'Christ' as their bellies met, skin to skin. Just wave upon wave of good, really good, yes, there, yes, oh God yes. Then that gradual transition, from mindless sensation, to physical awareness – sweat sticky skin, a bony hip – to self-consciousness – me, Jenn, lying here under him, Max.

Oh shit.

\#

Max rolled over to lie next to Jenn. They were both still breathing heavily.

"Fuck," he said. "Fuck, you're good."

Jenn didn't speak. She was trying, in vain, to hold onto the pleasure, but it was draining away, like dishwater down the sink, too fast, leaving nothing but grot and grease.

"Fuck," said Max, again. He swung his legs off the bed. "It's three o'clock. I've got to go."

He looked back at Jenn. "I'm sorry. I've got a meeting. A *real* one."

Jenn raised her eyebrows. "Right."

"No, seriously," said Max. "But you stay here. Don't rush. Chill for a bit. Just pull the door to when you go." He was at the mirror, fiddling with his collar, eyeing her reflection as she melted back into reality. Then he reached out his arms and straightened his cuffs. A glimpse of black and silver on his wrist. His left wrist.

"What did you say the time was again?" said Jenn.

Max swivelled round and turned his wrist so she could see the digital display: 3:02. The numbers filling the generously lit panel on the chunky band encircling his slender arm. She knew that band. She'd seen it before.

"Ah," said Max, intercepting her look. He paused for a moment in his hasty toilette to meet Jenn's eyes. He saw the understanding steal across her face. "Ah," he said slowly. "Sprung."

Jenn couldn't speak. She was too busy processing the data. Cardio. GPS. Dates. Times. Forget the sleuthing. Forget where and when. It's who. I know who's been taking the watch to the gym. And, she thought with a sudden wave of nausea, I know it's not the first time he's been here, in this room. No. I know his every move.

I've been an idiot, she thought.

"Still," said Max, breaking the silence. "It was a magnificent birthday present." He bent down, took Jenn's chin in his hand, pulled her face to his and kissed her, wetly. "Happy Birthday to you."

Harriet Cunningham – aka @harryfiddler – is a freelance writer based in Sydney. In print she is best known as one of the Sydney Morning Herald's classical music critics. Harriet wrote her first novel aged seven. She wrote her second forty years later and is now working on a third. In the intervening years she moved from London to Edinburgh to Sydney, worked with performing arts companies in Australia and internationally, and most recently made headlines as the critic who got banned by Opera Australia. She still hangs out at the Sydney Opera House, still plays the violin, and still hasn't published any of those novels.

What Is A Disease

Gill Schierhout

"What I see are two contradictory trends. One is that, for some, maybe a lot of people in medical science, it's the genome. That's the thing. We've cracked the human genome. I've had deans at medical schools say, 'Oh this is such a wonderful time to be in medical science, now that we've got the human genome'. But the other trend is the increasing recognition of the importance of the environment in which people are born, grow, live, work age to their health and health inequities. So we've got these two trends going on at the same time. One reduces health to the biological imperative... And the other is looking up at society...."

Michael Marmot

I should not have been surprised by what happened to my parents because it is the way of the world we live in. Yet I was. After all this was my mother, my father, my own flesh and blood and it was not my mother's way to be defeated by anything. It was not my father's way either – he had his own way of holding his ground.

But people do change, I believe that we change, in some ways, at least. I used to be part of the health risk factor brigade – SNAP – Smoking, Nutrition, Alcohol, Physical Activity. I couldn't tell before, but now it's quite clear to me that there's a whole alphabet missing, and that I probably don't know the half of it. Naming these four letters to the exclusion of all else takes the focus away from the bigger picture. Unfortunately, the perfect round apple a day does not keep the doctor away.

Why do we put up with it? Why do any of us? We are so silent in our lives. We put up with so much.

3 July 2006: Instant message today from Mom. She is hoping that I will stop working long enough to talk to her on Skype. "You like statistics, there are 4,400,000 people online. I wonder when it is our turn?"

5 July 2006: Eventually had a chance to speak properly to Mom today. She is having a lung biopsy on Friday. I am going to fly to be with them, although (as expected), Mom says there is no need.

7 July 2006: Dad has deteriorated since I was last here (three months ago I think). A lot. Took about ten minutes to walk up the hospital corridor to the high care ward. There she was – my indestructible mother! Five different tubes connected her to this earth, three punctures to the skin. It was reassuring though to hear the machines beeping in time to her breathing and to see the low spikes of the graphs. Want to write this next bit now, so I don't forget in years to come: I held my mother's hand. Nothing happened. But when my father, sitting quietly beside her, reached out to touch Mom's arm, the green lines on the monitor attached to a wire clipped to her thumb spiked up right to the top of the screen. When Dad took his hand away, the lines on the monitor returned to the low half of the screen, spikes back to flat, or near as. When Mom eventually came around we pointed out this curiosity. We tested it again and again – he touched her, the lines spiked up, I touched her, no effect. We laughed together at this unexpected diversion. (Note to self, later, after own twenty years of marriage – perhaps the racing heart signalled anger with Dad, not passion – but then again, it shows the body felt something.) (Later still – what was my fixation with the charts all about? It's all there, in the body, whether attached to a machine or not. I think my mother knew that, my father too. It's just me, slow to catch on as usual).

9 July 2006: The results of Mom's lung biopsy came back today. Pulmonary fibrosis.

"Praise the Lord it's not cancer," she said.

I looked it up on the internet. Pulmonary fibrosis is actually worse than cancer. It's not treatable.

"We will fight it with everything we've got," the doctor said.

Someone is going to have to tell Mom and Dad that pulmonary fibrosis is not treatable, that most people with this disease suffer a great deal and eventually die of it, but I know I am not supposed to interfere.

12 July 2006: heard on the news today that ductal carcinoma in situ will soon be able to be 'flushed out' with something likened to 'draino.'

12 August 2006: Has taken a while for the news to sink in. And there is more. My mother does not just have pulmonary fibrosis – this gradually progressive lung condition for which there is no cure, not even 'draino' – she has also been diagnosed with Parkinson's Disease. That makes two – both of my parents have Parkinson's. What kind of bad luck is this for my mother to have two illnesses, not one. Parkinson's is terrible but people don't usually die from it. Here, my mother has a terminal illness and both my parents, a disabling one. Thinking for the first time how nice it would be to live closer. Is that possible? In the meantime, I've decided I will pull out all stops and go as often as I can, take the children to see them too. Went into the red booking tickets for us all for December holidays.

15 August 2006: Mom had a follow up visit with the Specialist today.

"Are you still smoking?" he asked. "You smoked of course."

I nearly exploded when she told me this but I tried to stay calm for her sake. Had I been there! Tonight I read that while smoking is a risk factor for pulmonary fibrosis, it may be protective for Parkinson's. Really!

? September 2006: I have decided that I don't like definitions of disease. These definitions that seem to revolve around large things going wrong in microscopically small places – definitions that pretend to explain, or at least we accept them as explanatory – when as far as I can see they mostly just describe. My parents live now very decidedly in the kingdom of the sick. I am just a visitor.

5 November 2006: Mom said Dad is getting worse. Just a matter of adjusting the medication, that's what the doctors said. I don't know the details. I don't ask. He doesn't talk much on the phone. Mom on the other hand, terrified of losing her speech, talks all the more, much more than she did before. Both still so much themselves in all of this.

December 2006: Schools broke up yesterday. We arrived on the overnight flight in time to take my parents out for lunch. The Harbour Restaurant was my treat. Just fish and chips, nothing fancy (without the fish please, said my youngest). Growing realisation that that may be the last time.

#

I barely had a chance to open the menu and see what I was in for, and my mother was already launching into a serious topic. She was determined to 'use the time together', not to waste it on triviality.

"They want to talk to you," she was saying.

"Who wants to talk to me?"

"The people at the University. Some study on genetic links in Parkinson's."

"So who in your family had Parkinson's?"

"No one," she said. "No one."

"And Dad?"

"No one, no, no one I know of."

Dad just sat, wiping crumbs from the table with his napkin, dusting, dusting, dusting, that table had never been so clean. He didn't say a word. [note to self: how quickly Dad's silence became the new normal. Not sure when that happened.]

"Auntie May thinks it's contagious," I said. "That's why she doesn't kiss you and Dad on the lips anymore".

"Did you tell her? Did you tell her that we don't know what causes it?"

To the East stretched the sea, and across the bay stood the closest reach of the Hottentots' Holland, its leeward slopes laden with ripening peaches, apricots, and vines dripping with grapes. If you knew to look for it, several times a year, spraying time, you would see the haze of the pesticides hanging over the valley and smell the sweet acrid smell.

The Harbour Restaurant that day was my treat. It was his dream, my father used to say, to live close to the sea, to walk out on the rocks in the evenings, looking for bait. But he would fall now, break a limb. I imagined him returning to the wild coastline of his childhood near Qolora River Mouth. He would be slow to get going. Then his face would set in its determined politeness, walking faster and faster off the edge of a cliff, unable to stop. I wondered, as my mother hovered beside him that day at the Harbour Restaurant, anchored as close to him as their place settings would allow at the table, whether or not she saw in him her own nemesis. He was set inside himself, an ancient troll watching us all, immobile in the face of a rock.

"Don't you think it's strange," Auntie May had said, "that both your parents have Parkinson's? Do you think it is contagious?"

But I hadn't been ready to see the strangeness of this thing at the time, to see the obvious. My mother was fifteen years younger than my dad, yet they developed this illness around the same time.

The children were hungry and beginning to squirm and fidget, and my mother, looking for something to distract them with, began to scratch around inside her handbag. Amongst the crumpled tissues and peppermints, she closed her fingers around her pepper spray. She brought it up to the surface of the table. The pepper spray had a white plastic nozzle, the kind you get on aerosol furniture polish. My children sat forward, entranced.

"I keep my pepper spray right beside my phone," she was telling the children. "So if someone tries to steal my phone, I can spray them with the pepper spray."

My parents live in a dangerous city. To digress: my mother has a spear hidden inside her walking stick. I kid you not, the tip of her walking stick swivels off to reveal the shiny tip of a spear. That afternoon in the restaurant I was suddenly afraid that my mother would press the nozzle and set off the pepper spray. And that is exactly what she did.

My father mustered a delicate cough. Within a few seconds the children began coughing and spluttering. Sarah started jumping up and down as the fumes irritated the bare skin of her legs. I went over to the sliding door of the Harbour Restaurant and pushed it open. The path from the door led straight to a precipitous pier beyond. My mother looked from me, to my father, to the children, and back again.

"Go outside." I said to the children. "Be careful. Stay away from the edge."

"But we're hungry. It's too cold."

"Just go outside."

The fumes eventually dissipated. No harm done.

You put up with this kind of thing here – living with spears on the end of your walking sticks and carrying pepper sprays in your handbag, and you live with the pesticides fogging up the hillside – and nobody says a word – it is just the way we live. And after all, we have good hospitals here and, thanks to private health insurance, the best medical care that money can buy.

#

February 2007: At the pulmonologist today. Mom was sent into a little room to breathe into a respirator. She knows the drill. After reading the print out, the doctor said he was pleased with her.

"What if she can't do it next time?" I said. "Will you be displeased with her then?" He is doing a good job of documenting the decline of my mother's lung capacity that doctor, I'll say that much. I'd be surprised if he doesn't get a journal article out of this.

"Not a journal article", he said when I pressed him, "more like a book."

August 2007: Took my parents to the neurologist today – two trips for the price of one. I wish – no family discount here. When it was my father's turn, the neurologist held up some scan to the light and pointed out all the fuzzy white bits where the grey matter ought to be. Said my father was an imbecile, more or less. A few thousand dollars for that piece of information.

April 2008: Yesterday Dad had pulled open the wrapping, and took out the sheepskin gloves I had picked up from the duty free in Sydney airport. He pushed his hands right into the gloves, knowing just what to do. This is my dad, I wanted to shout. I'm so proud of him, look at what he can do!

April 2008: About 7pm, Dad spoke. Professional interpretation using the best imaging technology available has long ago dismissed out of hand the possibility that my father could still speak. This evening, he asked me if my mother was happy.

May 2008: My mother at her monthly check up with the pulmonologist (the neurologist plays second fiddle, he says, as in her case the lungs trump Parkinson's). She stands like William Tell, the apple on his head, wondering if the arrow will split the apple, or miss. The standing still, the reaching for the pen, the scratch of the script against the page.

January 2009: Twang. Another vertebra cracked, and another. Side effect of the cortisone. Mom can barely walk anymore. She has a curious-looking back brace now. She ties it around herself, trying to hold her torso upright. My evidence search tells me that whilst ten to fifteen per cent of people with idiopathic pulmonary fibrosis improve a little with corticosteroids, twenty-six per cent develop serious, sometimes fatal complications from these drugs. No randomised controlled trial can provide us with a society in which there are no drug companies, or no value chain of modern western medicine. What would such a life of freedom look like?

February 2009: I suggested (trying out some humility) that Mr Reverend Pulmonologist reduce my mother's dose of cortisone. He says he has already tried that, and she was on the minimal dose possible. Walked out of there with a couple of referral letters. Referral for back surgery, and something to do with her heart. When we got home I read the letters, "Please see this unfortunate woman…' each began. My eye!!

July 2010: I sat with Dad while he ate. If I hadn't stopped him, he would have swallowed everything at the place setting, the paper napkin included. The levodopa has stopped working now. A hoarse kind of howling comes over him when he tries to swallow. Despite that, he still eats. After dinner he looked out of the window, staring at something. I pushed him in his wheelchair out into the gardens, following his gaze. He waved his hand royally in the direction he wished to go. We lingered a while and watched a blue butterfly amongst the white daisies. I will never forget how gently he reached out and stroked the dying heads of the flowers as we passed.

#

When my parents eventually died, they died within a year of one another, despite that my mother was fifteen years younger than my dad. I don't know how he knew it was time, but it was. By the end, all he wanted was that simple dignity of partaking of life as best he could. I had to fight the doctors to stop them force-feeding him with a tube.

My mother phoned to tell me, and then, "you don't have to come right away, I know you are busy." Of course I came right away. And when I was nearly there, she phoned again, "where are you? What is taking you so long?"

The year before my mother died there were two things she hung on to with equal ferocity – the bible given to her by my father on their engagement, and the pair of maroon epaulettes that she used to wear on the shoulders of her nurse's uniform signifying her rank. She always called the epaulettes maroon, not purple. By then she had been stripped of almost everything else. Her brain a little confused, she could not even be trusted to have a phone beside her bed without dialling strangers or others at random at all hours of the day or night. Right through the last months of her life, unable to do much else, in her rasping gasping voice, wracked by fibrotic lungs, she still told the staff what to do and they all called her Sister. Before her move to the Frail Care Centre, a bedsore had sprung up overnight on her nether regions. Mortified she had not told anyone and things had gone from bad to worse. You could make a circle with your fingers, wrap it around her upper arms and your fingers would touch – that's how thin her arms were. In the essence of her, she was anything but frail – she was so very much alive. After all, she made me promise to write this story.

Ziram, Maneb, Paraquat, they take on a sort of a dance in my brain, banned or severely restricted in eleven countries, including in the entire European Union (although Paraquat is still used in Australia, despite having been under review since 1977), and sprayed indiscriminately all over my mother's washing, the food they ate, the drinking water contaminated, there where they lived nearly across the road from the vineyards. Where are these other things too, in our definitions of disease, these things we need to speak up about, vote against, picket and boycott, and walk away from, reject out of hand, refuse to purchase, take a stand against –

at least or more these other letters of the alphabet – more than any cigarette or glass of wine?

Gill Schierhout has no business writing, having seldom held a job that did not require statistical software. In her spare time, on maternity leave, on afternoons off watching swimming carnivals and the like, and with the help of many candles she wrote a few short stories, published in various places around the world, and a novel, The Shape of Him (Random House UK). In between writing she has a professional life focused on health issues that affect disadvantaged populations in Africa and more recently, the Asia Pacific region.

A Poetical Science

Susan Steggall

> [I]n the second half of the twentieth century, and in the millennium beyond, science and art are intertwined in a tight double-helix such that it is impossible to separate technological advance from cultural impact, cultural process from technical device.
> Julian Meyrick, 'The Two Cultures', *Sydney Review of Books*, August 2016

It was earlier, in the first decades of the nineteenth century, when the technology of the industrial revolution began to make a significant impact on public and private life. Steam power in Britain for example was enabling the mass production of consumer goods. Travel from London to Edinburgh took less than a day rather than two weeks and news could travel the same distance in an instant. The urban population overtook the rural one and London was transformed into the world's first modern metropolis with all the attendant problems of noise, overcrowding and pollution. The sounds of industry rang out in cities and towns, drowning out the quieter rumblings of country life.

The 1840s heralded in the railway era. The train lines provided the perfect route for carrying wires for the telegraphic signals needed to coordinate an increasingly complex network that demanded ever faster and more efficient communication. Concerned about security, nineteenth-century citizens were quite rightly wary of the electric telegraph, presaging twenty-first-century concerns about the scourge of Internet hacking. No one in that earlier time though, could have envisaged the developments that would flow from the invention of telegraph, phonograph, telephone, radio and television – the all invading-pervading worldwide web of the twenty-first-century with its Pandora's box of marvels and mischiefs.

Technological innovation might progress at an exponential rate, yet in evolutionary terms *Homo sapiens* operate with the same physiological and anatomical configuration it did in the nineteenth century. Neuroscience might show just how 'plastic' the human brain is in its malleability to learn and recover from injury, but it would seem that the sites for emotional and moral responses to scientific innovation have not entirely adapted to what Meyrick calls 'the vast spangled empire of digital entertainment now available at the touch of a button'. More research is needed into the ways in which interactive technologies not only affect our values and our behaviour but also our mental and physical wellbeing.

Defined as a 'set of processes, methods, procedures, rules and operations applied or executed with the aim of obtaining a certain product' technology is far more than electronic gadgetry. In medicine, technology is today performing what would have been considered miracles two hundred years ago: the eradication of serious infectious diseases such as smallpox (the rise of Ebola and Zika notwithstanding), the development of pharmaceuticals to treat cardiovascular and other life-threatening conditions and advances in gene therapy with potential 'cures' for many forms of cancer and inherited disorders. As 3-D printing becomes increasingly sophisticated, 'printed' implants suitable for human use can potentially repair almost any part of the human body.

In February 2016 there was a report on ABC-TV about a man who had successfully undergone surgery to remove a hard-to-reach tumour in his neck and have it replaced by a titanium implant.

"To be able to get the printed implant that you know will fit perfectly because you've already done the operation on a model… was just a pure delight," neurosurgeon Dr Ralph Mobbs told ABC reporter, Tyler Koslow. " It was as if someone had switched on a light and said 'crikey, if this isn't the future, well then I don't know what is'… For me, the holy grail of medicine is the manufacturing of bones, joints and organs on-demand to restore function and save lives."

The technology driving the machines that will create these miraculous prosthetic replacements was foreshadowed almost two centuries ago. Through her understanding of mathematics as a 'poetical science' Augusta Ada, Countess of Lovelace, unleashed some technology that ultimately led to the development of machines that could manipulate numerical calculations independently – in short, computers. Using her imagination to think outside the square Ada transformed a dry discipline into an exciting challenge. She saw mathematical science, not merely as 'a vast body of abstract and immutable truths', but as 'possessing a yet deeper interest for the human race'.

Ada Lovelace is regarded as the first computer programmer because of her instructions (written in the 1840s) that told Charles Babbage's Analytical Engine what calculations to perform. This engine, she wrote, was far more than a mere 'calculating machine' in its ability to combine symbols of unlimited variety and extent. It also established a link between the physical manipulation of matter and the abstract mental processes of mathematics. Ada predicted the development of a new and powerful language in which to process analytical calculations, one that would lead to speedier, more accurate and practical applications 'for the purposes of mankind than the means hitherto in our possession have rendered possible'. She was less concerned about potential negative aspects of technological intrusion into human lives than the possibility of a world in which people would be freed of menial mental tasks.

With the benefit of hindsight, today we recognise that technology – whether valuable, useless or dangerous – should also be held to account according to the ethical principles that govern a civil society.

#

In 1959 physicist C.P. Snow delivered a public lecture entitled 'The Two Cultures and the Scientific Revolution' (it appeared in book form as 'The Two Cultures'). In 1962 literary critic F.R. Leavis denounced Snow's opinions, thus creating the 'two cultures' impasse: if science and technology save the world, it is culture and language that make it worth saving. According to Julian Meyrick science is now on top, and culture is what it is on top of, and the advent of social media has expanded our cultural choices to a degree unimaginable twenty-five years ago. C.P. Snow's comment that if we cannot know the future we must leverage what we know to imagine what we don't, holds especially true for Ada Lovelace.

Her instructions for the Analytical Engine include what would come to be recognised as the first algorithm intended to be carried out by a machine – a pioneering moment that would take human society into the information age in the second half of the twentieth century. In 1980 the US Department of Defense named the standard programming language for its military systems, 'Ada', in honour of her achievements. The Department even acknowledged the year she was born in its choice of military standard specification number: MIL-STD-1815. For the two hundredth anniversary of Ada's birth Oxford University designated 10 December 2015 'Ada Lovelace Day'. Robyn Williams also marked this date in his Science Show program, 'Reflecting on women in science – two hundred years since the birth of Ada Lovelace' (Radio National, 26 March 2016).

Her life spanned the era that began with the Battle of Waterloo in 1815 and ended with the Great Exhibition in 1852 – a period when social, intellectual and technological developments were opening up deep divisions in society: romance was splitting away from reason, instinct from intellect, art from science. Ada embodied all that the future technological revolution would offer: fantasy and scholarship, ambivalence and certainty, failure and success.

#

A window into Ada Lovelace's life and achievements unexpectedly opened for me at a performance of Tom Stoppard's 'Arcadia'. I had enjoyed the 1994 Sydney Theatre Company's production of the play and was looking forward to a similar experience. The occasion did not turn out quite as expected...

Act One was highly entertaining – a verbal jousting match of ideas and ideals even if, at times, some of the characters were hard to understand. In Act Two, perhaps because I was tired and it was getting late, much of the dialogue was seriously indistinct, especially one long scene between the tutor Septimus and the aristocratic Lady Croom.

In a play like 'Arcadia', in which Stoppard has honed the craft of writing to a high-art form, this lack of clarity became increasingly frustrating, almost to the point of distress. It was vital to follow not only the cut and thrust of the conversations but also the complex ideas being presented – Chaos Theory, Determinism and Newton's Second Law of Thermodynamics – as well as the interplay of human relationships and the foibles of contemporary 'publish or perish' academia. The capacity to shape one's own destiny in terms of the search for everlasting life, was also on the table.

As I walked from the theatre under a shower of rain and into a long wait for the Manly ferry, I thought about the science that had enabled many people to shape, at least in part, their own destiny. If technology can replace virtually every worn out organ with a brand new model, would this mean, barring accidents, that humans will live double their three-score-and-ten, or more?

In the light of my less than satisfactory auditory experience in the Drama Theatre, I became interested in the technology behind the 3-D printing of components in human ears, a process enabled by the algorithms Ada Lovelace helped develop, and which have allowed people to hear better in our decidedly aural contemporary world. On the ferry I looked around at my fellow passengers. Most were as firmly attached to their smartphones' earpieces as patients in intensive care to intravenous lifelines. Ears, and hearing, are everything to us modern humans.

The somewhat disconcerting image of a perfectly formed 3-D 'printed' ear floating in a Petrie dish made me think more about such fascinating machines and the algorithms that command them – step-by-step sets of operations that perform calculations, data processing and automated reasoning. The word 'algorithm' derives from the name of Mohammed ibn-Musa al-Khwarizmi, a Persian mathematician, astronomer, geographer and scholar at the royal court in Baghdad and who lived from about 780 to 850 AD. A partial formalisation of what would become the modern algorithm began with attempts to solve the 'decision problem' posed by David Hilbert in 1928 and subsequently resolved in Alan Turing's machines of 1936-37 and 1939.

A branch of science that would solve another problem – that of seemingly inexplicable and uncontrollable events – took a little longer to appear. James Gleick's book 'Chaos', first published in 1987, transformed Chaos Theory into a discipline that is now fundamental to our understanding of natural laws. Prior to this, scientists worked on the basis that the future of the universe would be perfectly predictable. Yet they often had to resort to approximations and dismiss phenomena that did not fit their paradigms as unimportant or peripheral. Chaos Theory overturned this compromise and was soon recognised as universal: from the movements of planets and stars, to the rhythms of nature itself and the vagaries of human behaviour.

It was Stoppard's reading of Chaos Theory that influenced his decision to explore the ideals of both romantic and classical temperaments in 'Arcadia' and have them acted out in two time periods: 1809 and the present day. In the early nineteenth century romanticism and its preoccupation with emotion, imagination and experimentation, was at odds with eighteenth-century classicism that advocated order, rationality and logic. It was the poet Byron who gave the world the original romantic hero – 'a moody, passionate, and remorse-torn but unrepentant wanderer' – so Stoppard made Byron an influential, albeit invisible, presence in his play. On the side of reason he placed the heroine of 'Arcadia', Thomasina Coverly, as a mathematically gifted thirteen-year-old, who is reputedly based on Byron's daughter Ada Lovelace.

On my ferry trip, I recreated the stage setting for 'Arcadia' in my mind – a grand salon framed by floor-to-ceiling glass-paned French doors and in its centre a long book-covered table. The furnishings that decorated the scene gave an impression of luxury and privilege. It was a mansion in which Ada and her titled mother might have lived. Beyond the doors there was a terrace that hinted at extensive grounds – a wealthy estate.

A girl walked onto my stage. I saw Augusta Ada herself instead of Stoppard's fictional Thomasina...

A pencil sketch of Ada, drawn when she was seventeen, depicts a girl with a round face and large reflective eyes, her dark hair fashionably dressed in cascading ringlets. A portrait painted in 1840, five years after her marriage, shows an elegant young woman splendidly attired in satin and lace, Spanish style. In a painting from 1852 Ada is an emaciated figure, her once lively hair now falling lankly either side of her thin pale face – clearly a woman ravaged by the cancer that was shortly to claim her life. These three portraits frame a life of great achievements and moments of despair, imagination and science, drama and intrigue in an age that was both 'eerily familiar and startlingly strange' in its mix of rapid technological change, outmoded medical practices, entrenched prejudice and a dawning social conscience.

Responsible for some strange and radical technology was mathematician, philosopher, inventor and mechanical engineer, Charles Babbage. Born in London in 1791, he showed an exceptional ability in mathematics from an early age and after completing his studies at Cambridge set out to reform that field of study in England, which at the time was far behind that of the Continent, particularly France where Newton was held in high esteem thanks to the work of Gabrielle Émilie Le Tonnelier de Breteuil, marquise du Châtelet (1706-1749). Her translation and commentary on Isaac Newton's 'Principia Mathematica', published posthumously in 1759, is still considered the standard French translation.

In the 1820s Babbage constructed a working model for a machine that aimed to produce numerical calculations free of human error. His Difference Engine consisted of a series of vertical shafts (the axes) on each of which a large number of disks were stacked by means of holes at their centres. The disks did not touch each other but could be independently turned around their axes due to an attached toothed gear wheel. Each wheel had ten teeth, corresponding to the ten divisions marked on the edges of the disks, one for each digit zero through nine. To twenty-first-century humans, accustomed to the most sophisticated digital technology cached behind easy-to-use interfaces, Babbage's 'thinking machine' would have been a fearsome engine indeed. Yet Babbage wanted to push the technology of the Difference Engine further and began work on a calculating machine – the Analytical Engine – that would be capable of multiplication and division as well as addition and subtraction.

It was a time when science was a hot-button topic for

professionals and amateurs alike. Panoramas – scenic paintings stuck to the interior of immense cylinders – combined science with spectacle, foreshadowing the invention of moving pictures. The National Gallery of Practical Science blended instruction with amusement and showed the latest in technological advances. Not to be outdone, Charles Babbage set up a demonstration of his Difference Engine (the Analytical Engine was still a work-in-progress) in a private house and invited the public to inspect it. The sight of this machine on 17 June 1833 was a revelation to Ada Lovelace who saw the 'great beauty' of the invention. It was Mary Somerville, the noted nineteenth century researcher and scientific author and Ada's friend and mentor, who introduced her to Babbage, thus setting her on the path to the professional future she craved.

Ada was the only legitimate child of George Gordon, Lord Byron, and his wife Anne Isabella (known as Annabella) Milbanke, Baroness Wentworth. Byron separated from his wife a month after Ada was born and left England forever four months later, dying in 1824 in the Greek War of Independence when his daughter was eight years old. Raised by her mother, Ada had a conventional girls' education: a little of everything, including foreign languages and art (watercolour painting but probably not sculpture, which was considered inappropriate for what Linda Nochlin called the 'mobile fancy of the feminine'). Ada was given extra instruction in mathematics and logic to counter any excess of that 'mobile fancy' or signs of the emotional instability manifest in her father's character. Annabella's agenda for her daughter was not entirely successful: Ada's intellectual ability, particularly in mathematics, was undeniable but her personality bordered on the eccentric. Her zest for life led to rash decisions and romantic attachments that had disastrous consequences not only for her own emotional wellbeing but also for that of her family. Like Germaine Greer, Ada was known for sending a tremor through many an occasion with the uninhibited expression of an extraordinary idea.

In July 1835 Ada married William, eighth Baron King. He was made Earl of Lovelace and Viscount Ockham in 1838. They had three children: Byron (born May 1836); Anne Isabella (born September 1837), and Ralph Gordon (born July 1839). Throughout her life Ada suffered from a variety of ailments usually diagnosed at the hysterical end of the medical spectrum in keeping with Victorian views of women's constitutions, and probably exacerbated by the laudanum prescribed by her doctors. She managed to continue her education and was privately schooled in mathematics and science by William Frend and William King. Her tutor in 1842 was the mathematician and logician Augustus De Morgan, University of London's first Professor of Mathematics, who was impressed by her lively and enquiring intellect. Ada often questioned the perceived separation between art and science, believing that intuition and imagination were critical to the effective application of mathematical concepts. She also viewed metaphysics and mesmerism as tools for exploring – in 'the laboratory of her mind' – 'the unseen worlds' around her, by which she meant phenomena such as electricity and electromagnetism.

Ada was exhilarated by the pace and impact of technological change and longed to be part of it. She rebelled against the impositions of her social class and gender and yearned for real and challenging outlets for her intellectual energies:

"There seems to be a vast mass of useless and irritating power of expression which longs to have full scope," she once wrote to her husband.

A focus for Ada's drive and curiosity arrived in the form of a paper, published in French in a Swiss journal following a scientific meeting in 1840 of Italy's foremost scientists who had gathered in Turin to discuss their nation's slow progress in applying the laws of mathematics. The organisers had invited Charles Babbage as guest of honour through the initiative of mathematician Giovanni Plana.

Babbage showed the plans and diagrams for his Analytical Engine to a group of eminent geometers and engineers including Plana and Captain Luigi Menabrea, a young mathematician and military engineer who would go on to become Prime Minister of the newly unified Italy. Menabrea was given the task of recording Babbage's ideas for his latest machine. The Analytical Engine incorporated an arithmetic logic unit in the form of conditional branching and loops and integrated memory, making it the first design for a general-purpose computer that could be described in modern terms as 'Turing-complete' and essentially the same as that which has dominated computer design in the electronic era. Today, the distinction between hardware and software helps us understand the idea that information is in some way separate from the machines that process and display it. In Babbage's time, machinery could only be understood in the language of cogs and ratchets. This made the Analytical Engine a tough proposition to grasp and required both a vivid imagination and some calm reflection to understand its workings.

Menabrea's paper attracted the attention of the publication 'Taylor's Scientific Memoirs', which published English translations of important articles from foreign journals. Physicist Charles Wheatstone proposed Ada Lovelace as the most appropriate person to translate it.[1] She readily accepted; it was surely a project that embraced her 'peculiar combination' of qualities and would give her standing as a 'professional person'. She began translating Menabrea's text towards the end of 1842 and completed it in 1843. Babbage suggested she add some explanatory notes. Women rarely

---

1   L F Menabrea, 'Sketch of The Analytical Engine Invented by Charles Babbage. With notes upon the Memoir by the Translator, Ada Augusta, Countess of Lovelace', 'Bibliothèque Universelle de Genève', No.82, October 1842; fourmilab.ch/babbage/sketch.html

wrote papers for scientific journals, and the few women who wrote about scientific subjects were usually making ideas discovered by men available to a mostly female lay readership. The notes Babbage proposed would be for scientific male readers. Ada had to decide whether this was the 'intellectual-moral mission' she had been awaiting. With a thorough grounding in algebra she felt herself well prepared for the job.

Ada famously observed that algebraic expressions were like "sprites and fairies", "deceptive, troublesome and tantalising" little creatures that could adopt any form they chose. The ephemerality and capriciousness of fairies were characteristics that embodied Ada's ambivalence towards science and the feeling that a part of her was too romantic for Babbage's solid, scientific world. Yet to grasp the true significance of the Analytical Engine required science combined with just such an imagination.

It soon became apparent that Ada's explanatory texts would be substantially longer than the paper they were to annotate. Labelled alphabetically from A to G, her 'Notes', would become the definitive (the only) detailed account of the Analytical Engine's design and applications. Note A, a discussion of the feature that distinguished the Analytical Engine from the Difference Engine, is a sophisticated analysis of the ideas about, and implications for, mechanical computation. It is the least mathematical and most metaphysical, and possibly the most important, note of the entire work.

In Note G, Ada describes in detail a protocol for the Analytical Engine to calculate an endless sequence of numbers (the Bernouilli Numbers) that stretches in a haphazard fashion towards infinity.[2]

---

2   The Bernoulli numbers were discovered around the same time by the Swiss mathematician Jakob Bernoulli, after whom they are named, and independently by Japanese mathematician Seke Kowa. Seki's discovery was posthumously published in 1712 in his work Katsuyo Sampo; Bernoulli's were also published posthumously, in his Ars Conjectandi of 1713 wikipedia.org/wiki/Bernoulli_number

In what would be considered the first algorithm ever specifically tailored for implementation on a computer, she used Babbage's data to break down the equation for calculating these numbers into a series of simpler formulae. By means of a table, she showed how each formula would be entered into the machine. It is this table that is used to justify the claim that Ada was the world's first computer programmer.

To explain the Engine's architecture, Ada drew on the analogy of a cotton mill, one part being a 'store' that held the numbers to be processed, the other a 'mill' in which to process them. Like the Difference Engine, the numbers were stored in columns of cogs but, in a bold technological innovation, Babbage had proposed a new method for controlling these cogs: punched cards of the kind Joseph-Marie Jacquard had invented to 'program' power-driven looms to create complex patterns in textiles. The adoption of a card system opened up a new technology for designing machines that could manipulate symbols rather than just numbers and brought the abstract realm of mathematics into the physical world of machinery in a way never before possible. In Ada's colourful but decidedly unmathematical language, the Analytical Engine would weave "algebraical patterns just as the Jacquard-loom weaves flowers and leaves", making her Notes not just a work of mathematics, but something of a more speculative, experimental nature. Calling mathematics a 'poetical science', and adding imagination to its study, Ada saw what they could achieve together that separately they could not.

At ease in the company of eminent men scientists, she was nevertheless conscious of the Victorian era's insistence on modesty for women in her decision to sign each of her Notes with her initials: 'A. A. L.'. She did not want to advertise her authorship but nor was she prepared to accept the pose of a shrinking violet that female authors were expected to adopt. She showed further evidence of her feisty personality when Babbage tried to insert a criticism of the government's handling of the development of his Engine as an unsigned preface, which would imply that Ada had written it. Ada had no objection to its publication but felt Babbage's text should be clearly distinguished from her work. Babbage asked Ada to withdraw her manuscript from Taylor's. She refused to do so: she was not 'another clockwork Silver Lady' for Babbage to pirouette before his public. Her engagement had been unconditional and could not be made subject to terms dreamed up in retrospect.

To avoid a stalemate the Menabrea translation and notes were published as scheduled in 'Taylor's Scientific Memoirs'. Babbage's statement appeared anonymously in the 'Philosophical Magazine'. Ada's work was well received. De Morgan sent her a letter saying how good he thought it was. Friends were impressed. William was proud. Ada was pleased with the power of her writing: "It is especially unlike a woman's style surely; but neither can I compare it with any man's exactly."

The full version of the Difference Engine and all subsequent designs, including those for the Analytical Engine, remained on the drawing board so Ada's code was never tested. It was thought that this was because the machines demanded a level of engineering sophistication not available at the time. The Analytical Engine for example, required tens of thousands of parts machined to the finest tolerances, to be intricately assembled in a frame the size of a small locomotive and probably requiring about as much steam power to drive its enormous bulk. In 1991 to mark the bicentenary of Babbage's birth, the Science Museum in London used the materials and tools that would have been available in the mid-nineteenth century to build a complete model of Difference Engine No.2. The resulting mechanism worked, proving that the reasons for Babbage's failure to start the computer revolution were not due to engineering but to the limitations of that early-modern socio-economic climate.

#

Whether technological developments are free or closed behind patents and paywalls, thanks to the pioneering efforts of Ada and her Notes, and Babbage and his engines, we have today algorithms that enable computerised technology to enhance human lives. Among these are the 3-D printers that create perfectly replicated human organs, for example ears. Biocompatible material manufactured by cells from the patient's body is another innovation. Such advances in the field of tissue engineering are pushing these techniques from the realm of science fiction into everyday medical practice – not so much fearsome as functional.

The most dramatic technological development of the last decade is something of a double-edged sword: the smartphone revolution and its dominance in daily life, worldwide. On the one hand these 'thinking' machines have changed the way human beings communicate with each other, and allowed those same human beings to hold the knowledge bank of the world in a single device. On the other hand, they have become a contemporary obsession. Surveys in the US and Europe indicate between 1.5% – 8% prevalence of excessive Internet use in the general population, although these statistics fail to differentiate between different kinds of usages. Some researchers maintain that Internet addiction is not a true addiction, but may be the product of other existing disorders such as depression and anxiety, or a 'phase of life problem' – marital, academic or professional – or sleep deprivation.

Excessive Internet usage can be considered problematic when it becomes compulsive, interferes with the normal activities of daily living, or when the playing of violent video games causes a shift in behavioural tendencies towards aggressiveness.

Yet pro-social video games can encourage empathy; computer-based brain-training can improve working memory function and may help slow rates of cognitive decline. More research is needed to understand better how the Internet is currently used for informal and formal learning by all age groups, and how it might best be used in the future. As technology evolves, so of course will we, and a vital part of this process will always be creative dissection of technology's influence on society by writers such as Augusta Ada, Countess of Lovelace, and writers such as those included in this anthology.

As I realised on my ferry trip home that night, the script of Stoppard's 'Arcadia' cleverly juxtaposes the irrational with the reasonable, often leaving its contemporary characters floundering. Writing within the framework of the 'two cultures' debate, Julian Meyrick sets out an interesting dilemma: if physicist C.P. Snow saw, in the ignorance of his classics-trained leaders, an inability to comprehend the industrial processes of the twentieth century; then perhaps we can see today, in our technology-obsessed ones, an incapacity to grasp the cultural processes of the twenty-first?

Time will tell. But in the meantime, scientists and writers will continue to think and discuss, analyse and observe. Language, whether poetic or mathematical, is our means of ordering, classifying and manipulating the world. It is through language that our lives become comprehensible and meaningful. It is how we bring into existence the community in which we live.[3] 'Language is the 'freightway' of ideas' (Meyrick). Thus writers who can imagine the future, rather than scientists and their experiments, are often better equipped to encompass the problems that occur when technologies take on levels of sophistication beyond those of their users and the potential dangers of unrestrained innovation, as well as the freedom from menial mental tasks that Ada Lovelace envisaged. Whatever the future holds, the arts and the sciences must work together to repair the fissure that began to open up over two centuries ago. Our past has depended on it, and so will our future.

---

3   Dale Spender, Man Made Language, 2nd edition, Pandora Press (HarperCollins Publishers), 1990, pp 1-3.

#

Although that night's performance of 'Arcadia' did not quite live up to my expectations in terms of theatrical experience, it did allow me a glimpse into the pioneer days of some amazing technology, and an understanding of how humankind learns to interacts with technology. As my ferry pulled into Manly Wharf, a siren blared out through the streets of the village. Not the 'screaming trains' of Ada's nineteenth century, but the sounds of a modern vehicle – an ambulance, fire engine or police car. It was all in the ears!

Susan Steggall's publications include: 'Alpine Beach: a Family Adventure' (1999), its French translation 'Sydney-en-Chablais: Aventure Savoyarde d'une Famille Australienne '(2002); novels, 'Forget Me Not' (2006) and 'It Happened Tomorrow '(2013), plus articles, exhibition and book reviews. Susan has edited anthologies for the Society of Women Writers NSW Inc, and was editor of ISAA Review 2010–2015. She is President of the Society of Women Writers NSW Inc (2016-2017). Her biography, 'A Most Generous Scholar: Joan Kerr, Art and Architectural Historian' (LHR Press) was a winner in the Non-Fiction section of the SWW Biennial Book Awards 2013. Susan has provided the following references for those who might be interested in pursuing the themes of her piece in further detail:

FURTHER READING

Background and biographical information for the early Victorian era in which Ada Lovelace and Charles Babbage lived has been taken principally from the following publications:
– Dorothy Stein, Ada. 'A Life and a Legacy', MIT Press, Cambridge Massachusetts, London MIT Press Series in the History of Computing), 1985

- Benjamin Woolley, 'A Completely Professional Person', in 'The Bride of science: romance, reason and Byron's daughter', Macmillan, Basingstoke, 1999

Discussion on the effects of digital technology on human society:
- Paul Howard-Jones, 'The impact of digital technologies on human wellbeing', 'A State of the Art Review': nominettrust.org.uk
- Liana Pop, 'Philosophy and Technology', https://www.bu.edu/wcp/Papers/Tech/TechPop.htm
- Julian Meyrick, 'The Two Cultures', Sydney Review of Books, August 2016. Meyrick is referring to the mid-20th-century debate between physicist C. P. Snow and literary critic F. R. Leavis.

Information about algorithms:
- wikipedia.org/wiki/Algorithm

Notes written by Ada Lovelace:
- L F Menabrea, 'Sketch of The Analytical Engine Invented by Charles Babbage. With notes upon the Memoir by the Translator, Ada Augusta, Countess of Lovelace', Bibliothèque Universelle de Genève, No.82, October 1842; fourmilab.ch/babbage/sketch.html

Reviews of 'Arcadia':
- Colin Golvan, review of 'Arcadia' (Sydney Theatre Company), 'Australian Book Review', No.379, March 2016, p.42.
- Diane Stubbing, 'There's a play in that: the ideas behind 'Arcadia'', program for the performance of 'Arcadia' at Sydney's Drama Theatre, February-April 2016, p.15

Acknowledgements

This anthology would not have happened without the sterling efforts of many people – a group too numerous to mention by name.

The fantastic authors of the Northern Beaches Writers' Group are the spine and viscera of this collection. Their creativity, professionalism and dedication were all essential to the creation of this work.

We'd also like to thank our team of editors and helpers, Alex Cain, Amy Spurling, Harriet Cunningham, Kylie Pfeiffer, Susan Steggall, Tony McFadden, and Zoya Nojin.

Chris Lake & Zena Shapter

Also by the
NORTHERN BEACHES WRITERS' GROUP

northernbeacheswritersgroup.com

www.ingramcontent.com/pod-product-compliance
Lightning Source LLC
Chambersburg PA
CBHW020610300426
44113CB00007B/581